Those Who Remain

CONTEMPORARY AMERICAN INDIAN STUDIES

J. Anthony Paredes, *Series Editor*

Those Who Remain

A Photographer's Memoir of South Carolina Indians

GENE J. CREDIFORD

THE UNIVERSITY OF ALABAMA PRESS
Tuscaloosa

The University of Alabama Press
Tuscaloosa, Alabama 35487-0380

Manufactured in the United States of America

Typeface: Bembo

∞

The paper on which this book is printed meets the minimum requirements of American National Standard for Information Sciences-Permanence of Paper for Printed Library Materials, ANSI Z39.48-1984.

Library of Congress Cataloging-in-Publication Data

Crediford, Gene J.

Those who remain : a photographer's memoir of South Carolina Indians / Gene J. Crediford.

p. cm. — (Contemporary American Indian studies)

Includes bibliographical references and index.

ISBN 978-0-8173-1639-6 (cloth : alk. paper) — ISBN 978-0-8173-5518-0 (pbk. : alk. paper) — ISBN 978-0-8173-8120-2 (electronic) 1. Indians of North America—South Carolina—Portraits. 2. Indians of North America—South Carolina—Interviews. 3. Indians of North America—South Carolina—Ethnic identity. I. Title.

E78.S6C74 2009

975.7'00497—dc22

2008035771

Contents

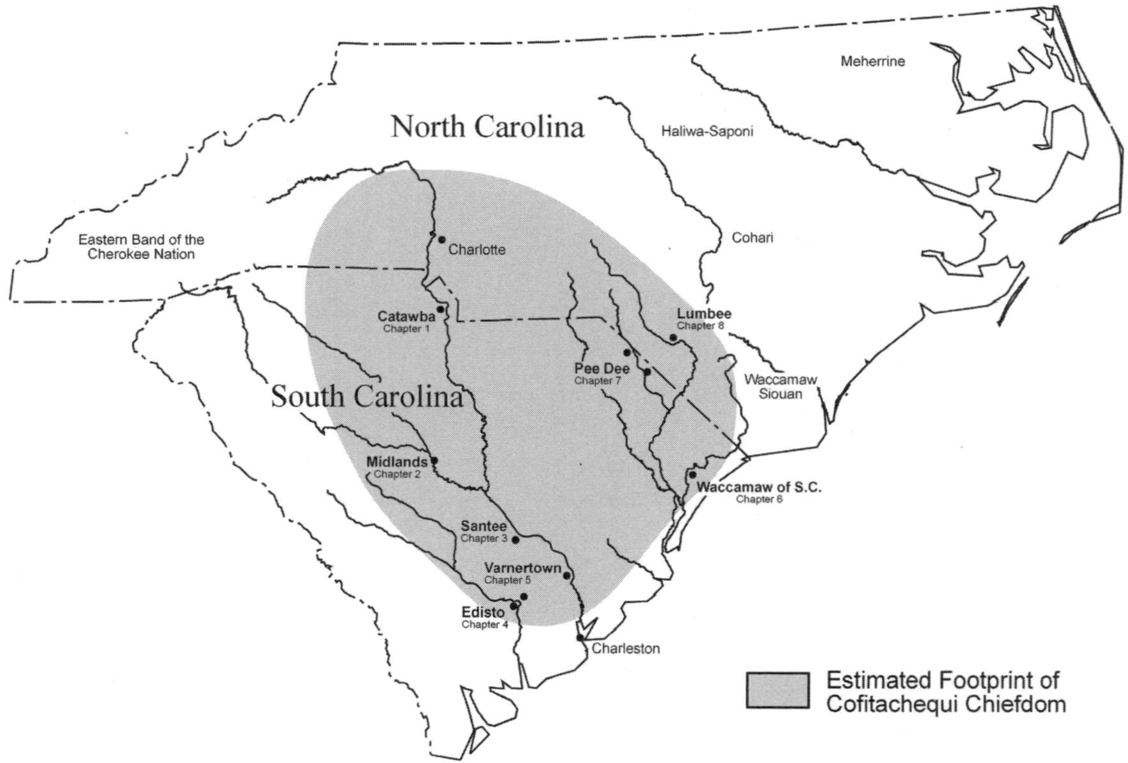

Contemporary American Indian tribes within the limits of the Cofitachequi chiefdom

Illustrations

Preface

Professor Gene Crediford attempts through the combined processes of interviews and photography to deal with the very sensitive issue of Indian identity that North and South Carolina Native Americans face. All too often authors have written books about Native Americans and have interjected their opinions about them and their communities as if the author/photographer were the established authority, and therefore in these books the authors' views have been projected to reflect the authors' opinions by either posing Native people in a manner to editorialize their view or by only presenting interviews that support their opinions. This type of irresponsible journalism and invasion into the tribal community is inexcusable and extremely condescending! However, Professor Crediford, through his photography and interviews with Native Americans, deals fairly with the tough issue of Indian identity and other issues. His approach is refreshing in that he does not attempt to "portray" Indian People. He presents the material and photographs without staging a desired editorialized outcome.

As director of the Catawba Cultural Preservation Project and Tribal Historic Preservation Officer, I am often appalled by the tactics of so-called and self-appointed historians who want to capitalize on the public's desire to know more about Native people by publishing materials that they have written for "Native people, about Native people, on behalf of Native people, and without Native people." As an enrolled member of the Catawba Indian Nation, I am very suspicious when authors approach me about a project involving publishing an article, book, or video about the Catawba Indian Nation. However, Professor Crediford has shown his integrity by asking us at the Catawba Cultural Preservation Project for editorial comments and proofing of the section of his book that deals with the Catawbas. Obviously, speaking as a Native person, I feel that this was a good faith effort, showing respect and a desire to not put into print any more erroneous information about Native Americans than has already been published.

Professor Crediford's photography is pure and refreshing. He allows his photography to speak for itself without staging the subject and without asking the subjects to be something that they are not. His photographs have the unique quality of showing people as they are and not dressed as the photographer thought they should be. One of the programs that our Cultural Center offers is an After School and Summer Immersion Program for children. When children see photos in which tribal members whom they know are only asked to dress like the author/photographer wants them to be viewed by non-Indian readers, this negatively affects their self-esteem. The message that the children pick up is that they are not good enough being themselves but in order to gain approval from the outside world, they must look like the outside world wants them to even if this is inaccurate. Since the lack of self-esteem is such a big issue with Native American children, we try very hard to make sure that their Elders are not portrayed in a demeaning and false manner.

Indian identity is not a major issue for me because my parents raised me to be proud of my Indian heritage. They have instilled in me the thought process of being secure in who I am and where I have come from. Although the federal government recognizes for federal Tribes that they should have sole authority in determining who holds membership in their own Tribe, this decision is not the case for state- and non-state-recognized Native-descent people. The requirements for becoming a federally recognized Tribe are quite stringent. This often pits federally recognized Tribes against non-federally recognized groups. There are many reasons for this tension. Numerous federal Tribes feel that if there were not stringent requirements for being recognized as a federal Tribe many individuals would lay claim to being a Native American without any legitimacy. There have been some groups, even in South Carolina, that have allowed people to pay a fee to join their group without having to prove their heritage. If groups such as these were afforded federal recognition they would be entitled to services that should be going to legitimately recognized federal Tribes. However, sometimes the rigid requirements that have been set up for groups to be federally recognized have real problems. Such is the case for one of the family members of our Nation. In the Catawba Indian Nation, there are two blood brothers who are proof of the pitfalls of an imposed system. Because one brother was not in the area when a census was taken, whereas the other was, one brother is recognized by the federal government and the other is not. How absurd! What I feel is the irony of the whole debate is that this entire system of who is or is not considered by the federal government to be a federal Tribe is a system that was not created by the Indians themselves.

Other issues of Indian identity that are equally disturbing to me are those that non-Indian people impose on Native Americans during the course of conversations such as "You don't look Indian." Tribes are extremely diverse. There isn't a Hollywood version cookie-cutter template of what an Indian looks like. The issue of being an Indian is very complex. Looks are just one component. Other components are familial descent, cultural values and practices unique to one's Tribe, and a system of community and government that is unique to that Tribe. One should also understand that European contact has affected Tribes quite differently. The Tribes east of the Mississippi obviously have had their culture impacted by European contact longer than Western Tribes. However, the changes that a Tribal community has evolved through make them no less Native American than Western Tribes.

Perhaps the issue of diversity among Tribes can best be related through an old Cherokee Indian legend titled "How Grandfather Made Snake." To summarize this legend, Grandfather was creating a creature one day and was momentarily interrupted. In the absence of Grandfather, the creature crawled away since Grandfather had not yet made legs for the creature to walk on. When the creature encountered man, man was afraid of the creature and beat it because of its looks. The creature had several other skirmishes with man and woman in which he was beaten only to be left wounded and able only to crawl away and hide under a rock at night, crying, his eyes frozen open due to the cold night and with his tail having picked up beads while escaping from woman beading by the fire. Snake was left to contemplate why man or woman did not welcome him. Expressing one of the parables of the story, Grandfather told Snake that he was picked on by man and woman because he was so different from them. One of the parables of the story was that "Different just means different. It does not mean better or worse, it just means different." Perhaps when the human race realizes this concept, there will not be the need for "proving one's identity."

Wenonah G. Haire, DMD

Acknowledgments

How is it really possible to use my barely adequate words to do credit to all those who have helped put this document together? Perhaps, as a photographer, I could take more portraits and put together a montage, an assembly of photographic images to include all those who have labored for me, for the possibilities of this work. This montage would at the least entail my immediate family: my wife, the grammarian; my younger daughter, Susan, for her help and encouragement; and my older daughter, Cassie (with some help from her husband, Jason), who somehow has taken my often-chaotic ideas, my fragmentary knowledge of how computers work, and my tendency toward wordiness and has somehow carved out this piece of sculpture.

Then there is Mary Caldwell Kane at the Ringwood (New Jersey) Public Library, whom I must label as Mary the Magician. Mary reached out to other libraries, to countless colleges, and to the very ends of the Internet for answers to my requests. Thanks also to Cara Edelbach, who has mastered all those word-processing electrons. I wish to commend the excellent work of Kathy Cummins, the copy editor assigned to the manuscript by The University of Alabama Press, who is a marvel of eye-brain-knowledge coordination. I cannot forget my debt to Christina Lee of Eagle Camera, whose skills for scanning and organizing photographic images far exceed anything I am remotely capable of.

And I must praise all of the contributions from the Carolina Indians who have allowed me to do their portraits and who over these twenty-five years have encouraged me to believe that the journey has been worthwhile. In particular I wish to thank four Indians who not only have kept me up on current developments but also have read and critiqued those chapters pertinent to their tribes. They are Beckee Garris and Wenonah Haire of the

Catawbas, Will Goins of ECSIUT (Eastern Cherokee, Southern Iroquois and United Tribes), and Harold "Buster" Hatcher of the Waccamaw of South Carolina.

Finally, many thanks to Wes Taukchiray for sharing his knowledge and experiences and for critiquing certain chapters of this book.

Those Who Remain

Introduction

The great chain of mountains, once spelled "Apalatian," that runs on a slant from north to south along the eastern United States is the watershed for nearly half the nation. The Appalachians were the water source and the spirit source of pre-Columbian North and South Carolina.

In the near center of this land, in North Carolina, lies the Catawba River, called the Guatari by the Spanish because it was on the road to the village of Guatari. Uncertainly at first the river heads east, and then, still in present-day North Carolina, abruptly makes a southward turn from which it varies little on its course through the Piedmont regions of North and South Carolina. The Piedmont, the feet of the mountains, is irregular, with its hills mixed with many wide agricultural valleys between hardwood and pine forests, a land ideal for villages, hunting, fishing, beans, and corn.

The Catawba River becomes the Wateree River at Landsford Shoals and then, in concert with the geography of the Piedmont, drops dangerously down huge boulders and rocky outcroppings at Great Falls. In pre-Columbian times, Atlantic salmon came this far upriver to leap the falls and spawn. This area marks the beginning of the end of the Piedmont.

The river, however, continues on its way, etching a path southward through flatter territory called the sandhills. The landscape is one of varicolored sand mixed with fertile land interspersed with swamps, a land of less rain but many more pine trees, the loblolly land.

Not far from Pinewood, South Carolina, the Wateree is joined by the Congaree River, which has, sluggishly, made its way south from the state capital, Columbia. Then the river forms a lake, called Lake Marion, where it splits into two rivers. One branch, now called the Santee, urges itself toward the ocean in a most direct, easterly way. The other branch heads more southerly to form another lake near Moncks Corner and becomes a river again, the Cooper, which helps form the harbor of Charleston.

From the mountains of North Carolina to the seacoast of South Carolina, the rivers were trade routes and the fertile arteries of survival for numerous precontact, civilized Native American tribes. Historians have pieced together a picture of tribes with spiritual and religious lives and complex social and governmental systems. They built large villages, some of which had monumental mounds and earthworks; they enjoyed artistic achievements. They maintained a flourishing economy based upon agriculture and trade and complemented by time-honored fishing, hunting, and gathering techniques.[1]

In 1540 the Spanish conquistador Hernando de Soto came through this region. In what is now central South Carolina he encountered, and took hostage, a woman in leadership of a vast chiefdom called Cofitachequi.[2] This land encompassed even more than the area described above, stretching as it did, some sources say, northwestward into the mountains of South Carolina, into portions of the high hills of North Carolina, and into the eastward sandhills of South and North Carolina.

At the time of de Soto's violent march through this province, the "Lady Cofitachequi" told him that her territory extended to the village of Guaxale in the Appalachian Mountains.[3]

Then in 1566 and again in 1567 another Spanish explorer, Juan Pardo, came through the province. He was greeted, at first, by fourteen chieftains (who had under their control lesser chiefs), including those of the Sampa (lower Santee River area), the Pee Dee—perhaps the Vehidi—(middle reaches of the Pee Dee River), and the Yssa (the Catawba villages on the Catawba River).

Continuing on his way, Pardo met with chiefs from eight more villages in diverse geographic areas. Farther on he came to the village of Otari, where he met with three more chieftains. All of the chieftains are believed to have been part of Cofitachequi, which had a total population of well over eighteen thousand prior to 1567.[4]

This confederation of tribes with a central authority reflects the ability of American Indians in this region to practice advanced political and social methods. What apparently helped the province organize its confederation was a common language. Many of the tribes spoke languages belonging to the Siouan family. This group of languages is distantly related to the Siouan languages spoken from the Plains to portions of the eastern Piedmont.[5] It is worth noting that the last speaker of the Catawba language was Chief Sam Blue, who died in 1959. It is also worth noting that his granddaughter Beckee Garris is instrumental in a Catawba effort to reclaim their language.

The wingspan of the Cofitachequi spread over much of central, southeastern, and eastern South Carolina. It also extended over large parts of southern North Carolina. The precise extent of this region is uncertain since authorities disagree as to its limits. However, the "footprint" of the Province of the Cofitachequi is the footprint of this narrative and book. There are nine chapters, seven of which reflect tribes in South Carolina—the main domain of the Cofitachequi—and two chapters with interviews and photographs of North Carolina American Indians. Many of these Indians probably had roots in the precontact Cofitachequi, although the migration of American Indians from other parts of North America is a fact.

At this point it is important for the reader to understand how it is that of all the many Indian communities and tribes in the Carolinas I chose the eight that are in this book. My photography and research started in 1983 when my wife was hired to help write grants and do secretarial work for the Council of Native Americans of South Carolina. This not-for-profit organization was based in Columbia and directed by Grace Lowry, a Lumbee Indian living in South Carolina. In fact, Grace, a few years previous to 1983, started this organization (commonly referred to as CNA) with the purpose of organizing Indian communities and Indian associations so they might have a unified voice in their efforts to gain formal state recognition. CNA was also active in gaining grants and other sources of income to help member groups in their efforts to bring better services to the communities, such as adult education, health care, and more public visibility.

Through (in part) Grace's grace, I began to travel to various communities to meet with and photograph many of the people interviewed in this book. At that time CNA's membership was composed of the Santees, Edistos, both branches of the Pee Dee, and a Piedmont urban association. Although the Catawba Indian Nation was not a member at this time, it later joined. These groups and attendant communities became the core of my research. The second director of CNA was Murphy Woods, also a Lumbee Indian. However, CNA lost its momentum and was dissolved in 1993. During these early trips to the various communities I met Wes Taukchiray, who was doing genealogical and historical work for some of the above groups as well as for some families of the Varnertown Indians. In addition, Wes had worked for many years for the Lumbee Indians primarily doing research in their efforts to regain federal recognition. It was also through Wes that I became acquainted with Buster Hatcher, who had just retired from the military and had become chief of the Waccamaws of South Carolina.

The members of these groups are identified as being Indian in this book primarily based upon their direct ties to local Indian communities, rural or in very small towns. This identity comes not only from the people themselves but also from non-Indians who live nearby to the communities. However, this cannot be, I maintain, the sole criterion to define who is and who is not an American Indian in the Carolinas. In this regard I am convinced that urban groups of Indians should have a voice in this narrative. Hence I have included in Chapter 2 interviews with three people who have left their immediate roots to join others in an urban group. I believe their perspectives are vitally important.

Although there are other recognized tribes and groups within the Cofitachequi footprint, time and space do not allow a complete rendering. My apologies to all the members of these groups that are not included.

Centuries after de Soto, this story is told with the photographs and words of those who remain, a book written to bear witness to those who have survived five hundred years of foreign diseases,[6] colonization, enslavement, and a variable purgatory of prejudices and neglect. Since there are few "pure bloods" left in the region,[7] and since most American Indians today in the Southeast have, biologically speaking, a mixture of Native American ancestry with European and/or African ancestry, the ordeal of "proving" one's Indianness persists into the twenty-first century. The issue of Indian identity is often raised.

This issue is one of the main topics of the interviews. Having a tribal card is a proof of being Indian, hence the importance of being affiliated with a federally recognized or state-recognized tribe. Sometimes by simply "looking Indian" individuals can prove their Indianness. Better yet, if one can cite family, military, legal, church, school, or medical records, such as birth certificates or affidavits of Indian descent, then one's Indianness is accepted by others.

Viewed in one light, an affidavit is legal proof of Indianness. But in another light, the system of affidavits is a commentary on the antebellum South, which required written testimony by a white official that the individual was, in the opinion of the signee, not a "person of color" but an Indian. Possessing such an affidavit was an identity card, a passport in one's own land, and a means of avoiding enslavement.

But even those American Indians having such an affidavit were not accorded full rights of citizenship until the twentieth century. Wes Taukchiray found a number of present-day Indians who can trace their ancestry to holders of such documents, including the former chief of the Edisto Indians, Eddie Martin. Chief Martin's ancestor's affidavit is quoted, in total, in *Indians of the Southeastern United States in the Late Twentieth Century.*[8]

This necessity of "proving" one's ethnic identity is one of the most bitter bones that American Indians of the Southeast must chew upon, every day. Throughout the twenty-five years of my interviews and research, many Indians have asked why individuals from other ethnic groups do not face a similar, persistent questioning of their identity. "Why is it that we Indians are the only ethnic group in America that is not allowed to evolve?" I have been asked. "They just look at you in a funny way when you say you are Indian," another person told me, adding, "It's like they don't believe there are any Indians left; like you're lying."[9]

I recall with clarity an incident at a South Carolina visitors' center over fifteen years ago. There was a display case of Catawba pottery; I pretended ignorance about the pottery and asked a question or two of the attendant at the center. The attendant stated that there were no "real" Indians left in South Carolina. I wanted to tell her that just recently I had photographed Sara and Foxx Ayers, Nola Campbell, Evelyn George, Georgia Harris, and Samuel and Helen Beck, all of whom were alive at the time and had pots in the display, all of whom were born on the reservation, and all of whom could easily "prove" their Indian lineage back over a hundred years. But I said nothing. Why was I silent in the face of such obvious prejudice? Perhaps this book is a way of making up for my silence on that day.

Consequently, the major purpose of this book is to reveal, through my photographs (the outsider point of view) and the interviews (the insider point of view), a definition of contemporary Indian identity in the Carolinas. In this regard, photographic images that are printed in this book and on the accompanying CD are used to form a connection, a tension with the words of the interviewees. A good example of this relationship between image and word is the case of Sara Harris Ayers, a Catawba Indian. My photograph of her shows Sara in the foreground surrounded by her pottery. In the background is a replication of an early contact Catawba village found at the Shiele Museum in Gastonia, North Carolina. This image reveals, among other facts, that she is a very hardworking, productive potter in the Catawba tradition.

More information about Sara comes from a 1985 interview, a portion of which appears below. She and her husband, Foxx Ayers, appeared on a South Carolina Educational Television show called *Carolina Journal.* In this interview by Salley Jeter, with myself present, Ms. Jeter turned to Sara and asked:

Q: What does it mean to be an Indian today?

Sara: To me what it means is honoring my parents . . . they taught me to be proud that I was an Indian. Although at times we were not accepted . . . but my parents told me not to let it bother me . . . just be thankful that you are an Indian.

1. Sara Harris Ayers, Catawba potter, 1986

Q: [to Foxx] How was the Indian perceived or received in the state?
Foxx: For one thing, if I might say this, we weren't allowed to ride the school buses [that would take] us to high school . . . so if you had no way to get to school . . . then that was the way it was . . . until after the war [WWII] . . . then things changed.
Q: [to Sara] You have brought some beautiful pottery with you Mrs. Ayers . . . tell us about it.
Sara: I learned to do this pottery from my older sisters as I was growing up [Sara was born in 1919] . . . I was four or five years old and now my little granddaughter Amy is eight years old . . . she made this swan.
Q: Well, you have had a shining moment. I understand that one of your pieces of pottery now belongs to Queen Elizabeth!
Sara: Yes, I got a call from the University [McKissick Museum] and they got one of my large pieces to give to the Queen of England.

2. Foxx Ayers, Catawba, at Archaeology Day, 1993

Q: [to Foxx] What has been your business?

Foxx: I'm a house painter and I dig clay for my wife . . . and I also make small pieces . . . and help with scraping and firing her pieces . . . and I'm on the Catawba Tribal Committee.

Q: How important is it to continue teaching the heritage to your grandchildren?

Foxx: Very important . . . otherwise . . . you lose your identity.

Q: Do you feel there is still a long way to go for society in its perception of Indians?

Foxx: No, ma'am, I don't think so . . . not anymore . . . We're treated very good and we have come forward in the last forty years.

Q: [to me] We have about twenty-five seconds left. What was your hope for the project [a documentary of the assertion of Indian identity in the Carolinas]?

Crediford: Oh dear . . . my hope . . . my hope is to think that my photographs will move people to accept . . . and to realize the existence of this third very important ethnic group . . . and to accord them the same respect that the rest of us get.

So ended this television interview.

But what did the visitors' center attendant really mean that day by using the term "real" Indians? Perhaps she had in mind the stereotypic image often portrayed by Hollywood or the photographers of western America. Did she mean that any Indian who is not a full blood must not be a "real" Indian?

Aside from these speculations, the fact remains there are a significant population of American Indians and a number of recognized tribes in the Carolinas. In North Carolina there are seven state-recognized tribes, with the Lumbees being the largest. Additionally, there is of course the well-known Eastern Band of the Cherokee, which enjoys the formal state and federal recognition all the others aspire to obtain. Please refer to the appendix for a distillation of federal and state standards for formal recognition.

In North Carolina, as with South Carolina, there has been a dramatic increase in the numbers of people asserting their Indian identity on the U.S. census. In 1970, there were forty-four thousand reported American Indians in North Carolina. In 1980, the census reported over sixty-five thousand Indians in North Carolina. By the 1990 census there were slightly over eighty thousand who identified themselves as American Indians. In the 2000 census this figure had increased to almost a hundred thousand, a 227-percent increase since 1970.

As with North Carolina, South Carolina has seen a considerable increase in Indian numbers found in the census. In the 1970 census there were only 2,291 American Indians reported in South Carolina. In the 1980 census there were 5,665 people who identified themselves as American Indian. In the 1990 census the figure had risen to 8,246. According to the most recent census (2000) the figure had climbed to 14,718, which represents almost a doubling and a half of the population in those twenty years. It must be noted here that these data are based upon self-reporting. Hence interpretation of the above increases must be viewed in that light.

Although Indians make up but 1.2 percent of the North Carolina population, in some counties they have considerable power. In Robeson County they make up, easily, one-third of the population and can, it has been demonstrated, align themselves with African Americans, who also make up about one-third of the county population.

In South Carolina, however, it is a different situation. Indians are but a third of 1 percent of the total population. Nevertheless, the desire to achieve recognition at both the state and federal level is as strong in South Carolina as to the north.

One more issue needs to be examined in this introduction. When the viewer is looking at a photograph of an American Indian by a non-Indian, it is important to understand something of the history of this particular photographic undertaking. Why? Because over the past one hundred and fifty years a large number of very questionable practices have been utilized.

One of the earliest photographers of Indian people was John K. Hillars, a German native, who was a photographer on Major John Wesley Powell's second Colorado River expedition of 1871–1873. Hillars, with the very active help of Powell, used Plains tribal costuming on members of mountain and California tribes. One such photo shows a Ute Indian woman in a heavy buckskin garment. With her is Powell himself in a fringed buckskin outfit wearing a headband with a large feather sticking up. Is he trying to pass himself off as a Native? In some cases this staging even resulted in a subgenre, called by some "Indian Cheesecake." In 1872, Hillars did a full-length portrait of a Paiute woman dressed in nonauthentic buckskin with one breast exposed.[10]

Why did Hillars and Powell do these kinds of photography? In part, they sold their photographs (many for the stereoscope) to feed a huge public starving for views of the great West, authentic or not.

But Hillars was not alone in misrepresenting his subjects. A whole host of photographers dressed up their Indian subjects in inappropriate tribal dress and regalia and in so doing showed a disrespect for their subjects in the name of aesthetics. Delancey Gill, Christian Barthelmes, Major Moorhouse, and the gifted Civil War photographer Alexander Gardner used inappropriate costumes to help their enterprise of recording the then-prevailing stereotype of Native Americans.

After the War Between the States and until the turn of the century, perhaps the most interesting photographer was William Soule, who drew upon posing schemes derived from European traditions. He set up a sofa in his studio on which he placed bearskins (or the like) or blankets of Indian type. He had his subjects stretch out with their upper bodies supported by the high ridge of the hidden sofa. At times he would have his subjects support their heads with a hand, arm, or elbow propped on the ridge of the sofa. Sometimes he would pose an Indian woman without clothing on the upper half of her body, reclining on a woven blanket with her arm supporting her head. In "Studio Portrait of Wichita Woman" (1870), the subject is wearing only a cloth skirt and a bone necklace about her neck. The geometric composition reminds one of Goya's *Naked Maja* (1800) or Ingres' *Odalisque* (1814) or the sculpture by Antonio Canova, *Pauline Borghese as Venus* (1805–1808). It is difficult to ascertain whether Soule was a student of these artworks. Perhaps propping up his Indian subjects was simply his way of keeping them still during the course of the exposure or a means to give a more three-dimensional view. Or was it a form of worldly wise cheesecake?

Photographers continued to play with the truth into the twentieth century. Perhaps the most well-known photographer of Native Americans was

Edward Curtis. The images in his book *The North American Indian* are in many ways as powerful today as they were one hundred years ago. However, in his effort to create a vision of what was "Native" before contact, he resorted to elaborate staging, phony costumes, soft focus, even phony props, and in some cases phony Indians.[11] In one well-documented case in 1904 he dressed up three men as Navajos—two of them were the European-American brothers Charles and Sam Day. In the photograph they dress and dance in imitation of Navajo sacred ritual. Curtis, who was not allowed to photograph the authentic events, would observe the sacred ceremonies and then stage them, photographing them as though real.

Laura Gilpin, a respected photographer of Indian people, sometimes would go even further than Curtis. Through her persuasive persistence while visiting the Navajo at times from 1920 to 1950, she was able to somehow gain permission to photograph actual sacred ceremonies, which even to this day would be considered a sacrilege and grounds for the rapid ejection of the offender from the ceremonial grounds. In her book *The Enduring Navajo,* Gilpin, like Curtis, sometimes used inappropriate props. She was known to use the same blanket again and again. And in some cases the use of its woven pattern would not conform to normal Navajo ways.[12]

One photographer whose motives do not seem suspect, I believe, was Ansel Adams. Better known for his monumental landscapes and his astonishing understanding of photographic techniques, Adams was also a gifted portrait photographer. One example of his strong photographs of Native Americans is entitled "Navajo Woman and Infant, Canyon de Chelly, Arizona" (a copy of which is contained on the CD).

This portrait with a Madonna-and-child motif reveals upon close examination a respect for the subject, not the often-prevailing view of American Indians as objects for exploitation or sentimentality. A portrait from the waist level and up, the photo shows the mother holding her child on her left hip as her right arm comes diagonally down in a protective movement. The mother is looking down into the camera lens, in Adams' monumental style, causing the viewer to look up to the mother and child.

Perhaps more revealing of the respect felt for the mother is the look on her face. She is looking serious. She looks neither angry nor depressed nor hopeless;[13] neither does she appear "to be" what an exploitive photographer might want her "to be." In fact, this Navajo mother looks self-possessed, confident, willing to have her portrait made, but shortly after the occasion ready to go on to her duties in life.

Regardless, in total, the lighting and composition complement the overall atmosphere of the photograph. The photographer presents his subject with a dignity reinforced by a visually compelling style. Finally, unlike a typical Curtis portrait, however bewitching, Adams' portrait conveys emotions without sentimentality. It conveys esteem, not condescension from an "outsider."

Not until the 1920s did any Native Americans take up the camera to give the insider's view. To the best of my knowledge a Kiowa Indian by the name of Henry Poolaw was the first Native American photographer.[14] All previous images, both still and motion picture, were by European-Americans and, painfully, much of their work has been a detriment to Native people.

So it comes down to this question: Have my photographs (taken by a person of European ancestry) done justice to my subjects? Is there some truth to be found here? Or have I merely continued the pattern of reestablishing stereotypes? I certainly hope the latter is not the case, because my intent has been to make photographs reflecting the individuality of the person.

Another issue raised by some critics of photography, especially during the past twenty years, is that a photograph is inherently untrustworthy, a piece of fiction, even a lie. I am reminded of the opening words of the Australian film *Picnic at Hanging Rock:* "What we see and what we seem is but a dream / A dream within a dream."

These lines connect the film to the mythic belief of the Australian aborigines in the Dream Time, a period of earth and human creation, which for them mysteriously still exists today. Perhaps making photographs is an act of myth making.

Yet in the face of these uncertainties, my photographs are offered as more than fictional truth and as not harmful to the subjects themselves. In the words of Martin Scorsese, "I try to be true to the emotions which make us up as humans." Hence, this book is a realization that it is quite impossible to have my photographs, alone, accurately reveal the assertion of Indian identity in the Carolinas. This book requires the voices of those people who identify themselves as American Indian.

Perhaps this book is but a dream within a dream. Yet no one can deny that after all these years there still are viable Indian communities in North and South Carolina, there still is an Indian identity alive and asserting itself, and there still is a dream here of recognition, of equality, of a better life.

1

The Catawbas

It is September of 1984 in the Piedmont of South Carolina near the Catawba River just after the river has crossed the North Carolina border. Primed with the names of a few Catawba potters—but no phone numbers—I find myself in a tiny town with the name of Catawba.

I am possessed with the idea that in order to begin to understand the Catawba identity I should start with the people who make the pottery for which the Catawbas are well known. The Catawbas have for centuries been working with their hands to fashion a wide variety of pottery forms much in the same manner as did their precontact relatives. Having lost their language, their native religion—at least in considerable measure—and their original means of subsistence, pottery making remains. Surely this would be a sturdy link from the present to the past, I am convinced.

But the town of Catawba is not where the reservation is located, I discover. This town, perhaps ten miles from the Catawba River, lies along the Norfolk South Railroad amongst pine trees and a spreading suburbanization from Rock Hill—a city of some forty-five thousand people, ten miles to the north. Here in this town I find a convenience store with a pay phone and a telephone book. Connecting the names on my list with phone numbers, I make some unsuccessful calls to three potters: busy line, no answer, negative response. Then I try the number of a potter named Nola Campbell.

"Why sure, honey!" Nola says, "You just come right over and we can have a talk. What was your name again? Cradford . . . Creedyford . . . Crediford? Never heard of that name before . . . just come over."

She gives me directions to the reservation located six or seven miles east from the town of Catawba. And sure enough I find Reservation Road and then her home, a white wood-frame house, which I find out later is just off the reservation proper. There is a large yard and in the back I see what looks like a semicovered barbeque pit.

I introduce myself to Nola and she in turn introduces me to her husband—a white man—who shortly disappears. Nola tells me that her first husband was a Catawba. She is a cheerful, outgoing person with obvious self-confidence. It is also obvious that she is used to meeting and engaging with people.

Q: Thank you for inviting me into your home. Could we talk awhile and then I would like to take your picture . . . perhaps while [you are] working on your pottery?

Nola: Oh shoot, who would want a picture of me! It would break the camera [laughs].

Q: Well, I guess I'll take that chance [both laugh]. For the record, could you tell me when you were born?

Nola: Oh . . . I sure hate to talk about things like that but I guess, for you [with a grin] I will; it was in 1918. Now don't try to figure out how many years that makes me, okay!

Q: Could you tell me your first husband's last name?

Nola: Harris . . . so my name is Nola Harris Campbell . . . actually it is Nola Harris Harris Campbell because my maiden name is Harris.

Q: How did you get started in pottery?

Nola: Well, I grew up with pottery making. My mother made pottery and I used to watch her.

Q: What was your mother's name?

Nola: Maggie Harris. And I watched others make pottery . . . and then I began to work with Georgia Harris . . . do you know Georgia? Wonderful potter . . . wonderful person!

Q: I know the name, vaguely. Does she live nearby?

Nola: Oh no, dearie, she lives over near Dave Lyle.

Q: Dave Lyle?

Nola: Dave Lyle Boulevard . . . over near Rock Hill . . . about eight miles away from here . . . you don't know much . . . about things around here, do you! Well, Georgia sure taught me a lot . . . she isn't that much older than me . . . but she learned early. She was a way head of me . . . at first she taught me to make little things . . . then later I made bigger . . . pots. I learned the way . . . the right way to do things from her. Now when I teach I go by the way she taught me.

Q: So she had a big influence on you?

Nola: Well sure . . . and she did other things for me. When I was still making little things she would take them along when she went out to sell her pots. And she was able to sell some of mine . . . and we would take some of that money and buy cloth and she would make dresses for me and show me how . . . Georgia is the best.

Q: Someone told me that you've gone different places to demonstrate pottery making . . . at museums and places like that?

Nola: Oh sure, I've done lots of that . . . you see it is good for us potters . . . and the tribe . . . to go off and show how pots are made . . . why did you ask?

Q: Well, I wonder if I could get you to make a pot for the camera?

Nola: You mean to take pictures of me making a pot from start to finish? You've got to understand that you can't make a pot in one day, don't you [seemingly amazed at my ignorance]!

Q: Well, I guess I understand that. Just go as far as you can. Okay?

With this plea, Nola Campbell—an award-winning master potter who has produced the full range of traditional Catawba pottery for most of her long life and is known for her large vessels and grand demonstration style[1]—agrees to my request. She gets up and goes to her kitchen and then points to a table in a dining area. I begin to set up my equipment. The light is coming in the windows and it is good light. She has two lumps of damp-looking clay in her hands. The lumps are separately wrapped in damp cloth, which she removes. The two pieces of clay look somewhat different from each other.

Nola explains, "See . . . we use two different kinds of clay . . . this one is called pipe clay 'cause it is only good for small things like pipes. But when you mix it with other clay . . . this is pan clay . . . then the two together are really good for pots . . . even big pots."

As she talks she begins to knead the two together. I am taking photographs. The camera is on a tripod because I must use a slow shutter speed. Even though the window light quality is good—it has a soft, enveloping feel—it is low in strength. Nola is really working hard now and not always stopping for the camera to record what is happening. I know some frames will be blurred.

Her hands, her hands of 65 years, are large and strong and quite beautiful in their texture, in their dexterity. Suddenly an intense feeling comes over me: I feel honored to be able to witness what is taking place before me, through the prism of the camera and through the prism of time. She is forming the pot in a way Native American potters have always formed their pots. It is a great moment to be alive.

Nola continues to explain:

> See . . . after I've worked the two pieces of clay into one I take some and flatten it into a round base . . . like this. Then I take most of the rest and roll it out on this board into a long rope . . . you see . . . now I take the rope and begin to coil it . . . starting on this round part . . . and just build up the coil, to make the pot . . . so that everything is equal . . . now . . . you can still see the coils, right? So now I get my favorite corn cob and begin to rub the cob along the outside of the coils . . . like this . . . What this does is smooth out the clay and the coils disappear . . . Now if I were to finish the pot I would let it dry some . . . maybe put a damp cloth over it and let it sit for awhile.
>
> Then I would want to begin the real smoothing . . . I use stones, spoons, even my deer antler, knives. It takes days and days to get the pot right. Even before I would fire it I would make sure it is really dry . . . I put it in my kitchen oven to begin to get it dry . . . Someday I'll show you how I set up a fire outside in that pit out there . . . would you like that?

Without waiting for an answer, Nola then asks me if I am finished with taking pictures. When I nod yes, she brings up her fist—there is a pause—and she suddenly brings down her fist, smashing the damp pot into a formless lump of sodden clay. There is a big smile on her face. I am so frozen by this unexpected event that I neglect to get a photograph of the new pile of shapeless matter. Then I realize the reason for her action—this pot was made for demonstration only.

So this was my first encounter with Nola. We kept in contact over the years and I was able to take more photographs: once with her using her various tools to scrape and smooth her pottery. On another occasion she showed me her firing technique and she also introduced me to Earl Robbins and his wife Viola, who is also Nola's sister, and to Nola's daughter Della Campbell Oxendine, who is an excellent potter and, of course, a student of Nola.

Besides teaching her family and relatives, Nola taught advanced courses in pottery making since the 1970s to other tribe members who have, of course, benefited from her reputation as an accomplished potter. Nola died in 2001. But before she did we exchanged letters and after her death I received a letter from one of her daughters, Rita Bogan: "I'm sorry to write and let you know that my mother has passed away last Dec. 17, 2001 . . . She was 83. She was born here on the Res. She was a master potter. She was the best. In my eyes she still is. Coming soon will be one year. Oh, Mother had 10 children, seven are still living."

So ends my story of Nola Harris Campbell. She has a special place in my memories of the Catawbas. She was the first to open her door and her spirit to me. For me she was the Great Earth Mother personified. In her work as a potter, teacher, and public demonstrator of the southeastern Indian pottery tradition of which she was very proud, she contributed to the survival of the Catawba Indian identity.

However, Nola was not alone in the post–World War II era as a representative of the Catawba pottery tradition. There were Georgia Harris, Sara Harris Ayers, Mildred Blue, Catherine Canty, and Arzada Sanders—all now deceased. And also Helen Beck, Evelyn George, Florence Wade, and Earl Robbins—to name a few of this productive generation—have passed on the tradition through their pottery making and teaching. Some of their portraits are contained in this book.

Catawba pottery making, and pottery making in southeastern North America in general, can be traced back many centuries. Yet all sources appear to agree that the actual techniques of constructing various ceramic objects have been very similar from precontact times to the present, Nola Campbell's techniques being representative.[2]

Precontact ceramics fulfilled numerous functions, including the spiritual and the practical. Although today pipes and bowls are still very much used by American Indians for ceremonial—that is, spiritual—functions, a very important function served by Catawba pottery is as a source of much-needed income.

Further, Catawba pottery is an important element in maintaining Indian traditions and identity. Equally important to this Indian identity has been the continuous tribal ownership of land and a recorded family genealogy that is most often connected to the land. Also of great importance to an enduring Catawba identity has been religion, especially in the past 125 years.

On Reservation Road near Nola Campbell's home there is a crossroads. A left turn at this junction would lead you to the reservation proper. However, in 1984, I continued straight and came to a construction site on the right. This was the foundation for a new Mormon church, completed a year later.

But how did the Catawba Indians, some two thousand miles from Utah, come to be members of the Mormon Church? Records indicate that in the 1880s the once-mighty Catawba Nation had been reduced by invasion, disease, war, and alcoholism to about fifty-five to sixty members living on a small reservation of five square miles.

These remnants had, however, adapted to post–Civil War white society.

Most spoke English, conformed to conventional Western religion, and accepted the white/black division of society.[3] Yet they were regarded by white society as "people of color" and as such were treated as second-class people, as people who were not even citizens in their own land.[4]

In addition to alcoholism, prostitution was common. Crimes of all kinds against or between Indians were largely ignored by the white justice system.[5] The Catawba tribe was on the cusp of complete disintegration.

Then in 1883 two missionaries of the Mormon Church successfully baptized five Catawba converts. However, local non-Indians reacted to the Mormon success and a vigilante committee horsewhipped the Mormon elders, who managed to escape. Yet other elders returned, some of whom were tarred and feathered, and finally their church became established.

What, then, was the strength of the Mormon teachings for some American Indians? First of all, Catawbas spoke English, making conversation much easier. By comparison, during that era, Mormon missionaries were not successful in converting Cherokees who still spoke their native language. Also, the Mormon belief that Native Americans were one of the lost tribes of Israel had great potency. After all, Native Americans had witnessed firsthand their own diaspora.

Mormonism offered new hope to the disintegrating Catawba tribe if its principles of behavior were adopted. Some of these principles of behavior were to work hard, abstain from stimulants such as coffee and tea, abstain from smoking and swearing, and abstain from alcohol and prostitution. Over the years there was conflict between Catawba converts to Mormonism and Catawba nonconverts, some of whom were involved in the alcohol and prostitution trades.[6]

There is a further reason that Mormon teachings took hold. These teachings were centered upon a male-dominated hierarchy that gave to Catawba men a role most had lost. Even as early as the 1780s women were more productive than men. Women made pottery, baskets, and mats for sale and raised gardens and crops in addition to filling the roles of bearing and rearing children.[7]

Further, Mormon teachings did not discourage intermarriage between Indians and whites. Given that era, when all traditional rules of tribal endogamy were useless (a situation that continues even up to the present), this openness to intermarriage helped prevent excessive inbreeding.

So, returning to 1984, across the road from the Mormon church construction site and on a slight rise is a red brick house surrounded by large oak trees. This is the home of Samuel and Helen Beck. A month has passed since my initial interview with Nola Campbell. I have returned to the reservation area to talk this day with the Becks. Samuel has agreed, in a phone call, to an interview and to take me onto the reservation to meet people. In exchange I am to photograph the new church in its various stages of construction.

Q: Could you tell me of your interest in the church and its construction?

Samuel: Well, it's because I am a Mormon and an elder in the church . . . and I've taken on the job of being a kind of overseer of the construction . . . I don't mean that I actually help with the work . . . but I know something about things like that. I'm an electrician.

Q: Could you tell me more of your background?

Samuel: I was born on the reservation . . . the house is still there . . . I'll take you there, but not today. Oh, yes, I'm also the secretary/treasurer of the tribe.

Q: Did you go to an Indian school?

Samuel: Oh sure . . . of course . . . that's the white building across the road . . . it was the Catawba grade school. Only six grades . . . then I went to school at Leslie . . . It's a small town about three miles away.

Q: How did you get there?

Samuel: Well, the buses wouldn't come onto the reservation so we had to get there the best way we could . . . sometimes we would ride with parents who worked that way . . . or walk.

Q: I guess this was in the segregation era . . . at Leslie was it a school for whites or blacks?

Samuel: Oh, it was for white kids. [pause] We wouldn't go to school with blacks. You know some of us Catawbas had "white" marked on our birth certificates.

Q: But did you face discrimination at the Leslie school?

Samuel: Oh, it wasn't much bad . . . then I went into the Army and after that I took up a trade . . . like I told you.

Q: I guess I am confused. You told me that the buses wouldn't come on the reservation, but then [I hear] that the school is to be moved onto the reservation. Could you clear this up for me?

Samuel: When the school was a school and when I went there it was on the reservation . . . but you see some time ago the tribe voted to go along with a settlement we made with the government that was, let's see . . . in 1959 . . . but the final date wasn't 'til three years later. You see, the land this house is on was once part of

	the reservation . . . just like the school and the land it is on . . . like a lot of people's land near here . . . The tribe went along with the government so that some families could have land of their own . . . Each family member could get five acres or $250. Some people built their own house like we did . . . Others, well, they just wasted their money or sold their land [with disgust in his voice for those who had squandered their birthright]. So that is what made the reservation smaller.[8]
Q:	Thanks for clearing that up. About how many people now live on the reservation itself?
Samuel:	Well . . . I don't exactly know . . . people come and go. I think there are about forty trailers and houses . . . Look, let's go over to where the church is going up.

Which is what we do that day and three more times over a period of a year. Two months after our initial conversation, related above, I return to Samuel and Helen's house. The church has grown quickly to have exterior walls that are now supporting the wooden ribs of the high roof.

Q:	Samuel, the church is beginning to really take shape. Tell me, how much will it cost?
Samuel:	It will cost around one million dollars.
Q:	Will the members of the tribe [who] are Mormons pay for it?
Samuel:	[Looking at me as if I understand so little of life] Oh no . . . of course not . . . we are poor people . . . The Mormon Church in Utah is paying for it.

Then Samuel is looking up at the roof ribs. There is a blue sky overhead and I make a wide shot of this scene: the raw, light-toned wooden ribs, the blue sky behind, Samuel Beck with his brimmed brown hat angling upwards.

Afterwards we return to his home. Helen Canty Beck, born in 1920, is a small, light-skinned woman and an accomplished potter. I once was told by an outsider that she had other, younger potters do the initial stages of construction under her supervision. She, however, did all the finishing work. This system, if true, reminds me of a similar process of production found among some European master artists and artisans. I ask Helen and Samuel if I could take their portraits with some of her pottery.

We are using a long table and some of it is filled with her pottery. I see a framed portrait of a young man and ask who it is. Helen tells me that it is

Sammy, their older son, and I ask if we could put the portrait on the table with her pottery in order to include it in the photo.

Helen appears to me to be a quiet, shy background person to her husband's foreground personality. And to my eye her pottery has a strong adherence to traditional styles. In this regard there is a minimal use of decorative elements and a high degree of smoothness of the walls, both interior and exterior. It is as if she seeks perfection in her pottery, and in so seeking, seeks it in herself. It is as if her ego is embedded into her pottery, her work. She did not begin to sign her work until around 1976.

In April of 1985, I return to the Beck's and again take photographs of the church. Samuel, who is getting about with the aid of crutches, shows me around.

Q: Samuel, what has happened?

Samuel: Oh, I had a little accident . . . now don't take any pictures of me with these crutches. If you want to take pictures of me tell me and I will hide the crutches . . . okay?

Q: Yes, of course . . . I wonder when we can go on the actual reservation.

Samuel: Yes, okay, I've already taken care of that. I've called some people so they are expecting us . . . when we finish here . . . we'll go to the house I was born in.

So Samuel Beck and I drive onto the reservation—there are no gates, no signs as to the actual boundary line—to a small wood-frame house that appears empty. He stands a long time, leaning on his crutches, staring at the house. It is obvious that memories of his childhood wash over him.

Q: Could you tell me what you're thinking?

Samuel: Oh . . . I was just thinking about . . . well, about how hard we had it there . . . in that little house . . . but we had some good times . . . [his voice trails off].

Then he sets the crutches down and goes up to the house and stands by it, and then he leans on the house. I take pictures, but there seems to be no energy or interest to go inside. And then we get back to the car and begin a tour of the reservation with visits to three different potters: the aged Arzada Brown Sanders (born in 1896), her daughter Catherine Sanders Canty (born in 1917), and Evelyn Brown George (born in 1914). All allow me to do their portraits even as they work on their arts. As Samuel and I approach the car to leave the reservation I notice the sun is slanting down through the trees. There are big red oaks and scrub oaks and tall pine trees everywhere. There are wild flowers bursting and I can hear birds and I can smell the sweet air. On the reservation on this southern April day, I feel fortunate to be a witness to an ongoing American Indian identity.

Some months later, after the Beck interviews, the new Catawba Mormon church was ready for its first service. Samuel Beck's year of supervision had come to a close. That same year, 1985, I came to believe that the Catawba conversion to the Mormon Church was a contributing element in saving the Catawbas from extinction as an Indian nation.

But a further contribution to their salvation has been an openness to marriage with American Indians from other tribes, a tradition that goes back for hundreds of years. To help illustrate this I will interview three Catawbas from two different families.

First is the Peggy Harris family, to whom I was introduced in 1985 by Wes Taukchiray, a genealogist of Indian people. Peggy and her family have gathered together for me to do a family portrait. We are outside their home, which is painted a distinctive blue. It sits on a slight hill just off the reservation proper. With Peggy are her mother, Edna Wheelock Brown (born in 1911), and four of Peggy's children—the fifth could not come. Of her five children, four are married to whites. Only Kelly, a school counselor and teacher, is married to an Indian, a Pima woman from Arizona. They met in college at Brigham Young University and have two children.

Absent from the group is Peggy's husband, W. Alfred Harris, who is inside the house. I am told that he is camera shy. But years later I am told that he regretted not being in the photograph. At the time, he had grave doubts that his family circle would ever be given the photographs, revealing his distrust of outsiders.

The genealogy of this Harris family is revealing as to the varied influences upon modern Catawba identity. In 1880, a white woman living on the reservation gave birth to a child of a Catawba man. However, soon after the birth the woman disappeared from the reservation, leaving behind her female child. A widowed woman, Rhoda Harris, who herself was an orphan, took in the foundling and named her Rosie Harris. Rosie grew up on the reservation and learned pottery skills. She began serious work around 1900 and maintained a pottery trade until her death.[9]

During this era an Oneida Indian named Archie Wheelock came to the reservation from Pennsylvania, where he attended, or was forced into, the Carlisle Indian School.[10] Rosie and Archie married and had two daughters: Doris Wheelock Blue, who became a master potter, and Edna Wheelock

Brown (her second husband's name), who also became a potter. Edna was first married to a white man by the name of Thatcher and their child was Peggy Thatcher. Peggy married W. Alfred Harris, who Wes Taukchiray tells me was "a stomp down Catawba."

In 1985, Peggy and I get very little chance to hold an interview except she tells me that the land her home is on was once on the reservation. We promise to talk some time in the future.

Eighteen years go by between our initial meeting and 2003. I am again in the living room of her blue house. With Peggy is her daughter Doris Kay. The house is still neat and tidy and in good repair. But much has changed.

Q: Thanks for taking your time to talk with me. I was here almost twenty years ago. Could you tell me what has changed?

Peggy: Oh, well, I live alone now . . . my husband has passed and so did my mother . . . and all my children have moved off [she looks at Doris Kay]. None live around here anymore. And, I still work at Wal-Mart . . . to keep busy.

Q: What do you do there?

Peggy: I'm a greeter . . . now . . . been there . . . well almost twenty years now . . . it keeps me busy . . . I can't stand living alone here all the time . . . it sure is nice to have Doris here to pay me a visit every so often.

Q: How are your other children doing?

Peggy: Well, let's see . . . Kelly . . . he has three children now and he's a schoolteacher. They moved up to Greenville . . . they used to live in Lancaster [25 miles from the reservation]. And Darylon and Kenneth and Vickie are all married . . . to whites . . . and have children. Ah . . . I've got . . . nineteen grandchildren and two great-grandchildren. [pause] You know, the Catawbas are always marrying white folks . . . Soon there won't be any Catawbas left! [She tells me this with sadness, with an air of finality.]

Q: Doris, could you tell me what has happened to you in the past eighteen years?

Doris Kay: Well [sighs], I'll try . . . let's see, first of all I'm here because I try to get here for a few days two or three times a year . . . to be with Mama. You see, a long time ago, my husband and I and our two children moved from the reservation . . . I remember it pretty clearly . . . it was in July of 1975. We moved to Greenville [over one hundred miles away]. I was sad about

3. Peggy Harris and daughter Doris Kay Harris Medlock, Catawbas, 2003

it . . . you see, I was born here . . . my parents lived here . . . so were both my grandmothers . . . all nearby . . . both Mama and Dad were out working—which was a lot—so my grandmothers looked after me when I was growing up . . . especially Grandma Brown. She was my second mother . . . I missed her a lot when we had to move [there is a look of sadness on her face].

Q: Why did you have to move?

Doris Kay: Well, my husband . . . he's white . . . said he wanted to be near his parents. But he had a good job here [at a wood pulp mill ten miles away] . . . We had lived here seven years of being married . . . I thought we were all happy here [there is puzzlement and, then, bitterness in her voice] . . . but then one day—

out of nowhere—he told me he was going to quit his job here . . . but he didn't have a job up there! And it took him a while to find one . . . and when he found a job it wasn't nearly as good as the one he had here! [Her voice takes on a note of resignation] But we had to move . . . and I cried a lot . . . I missed my mama.

Q: Let's see, you had lived counting the seven years married a total of twenty-nine years on the reservation. It must have been hard to adjust.

Doris Kay: It sure was . . . it was the first time I had to live in a white world . . . [then, with anguish in her voice] I felt like a foreigner in a foreign land!

Q: Do your children identify with being Indian?

Doris Kay: Well . . . I think they are proud that I'm an Indian . . . and I think my daughter likes maybe the thought of being Indian . . . and I think my son likes maybe the thought of being Indian . . . I guess. And, well, years ago Grandma Brown showed them her pottery and taught them some of the ways. And I got them a book on the Catawbas . . . [her voice trails off].

Q: Do your children belong to the tribe?

Doris Kay: Yes, they are both on the roll . . . they both have their tribal cards [proudly].

Q [to Peggy]: With all your outside work, do you find time for making pottery?

Peggy: Oh . . . not much anymore. I learned from my mother, but don't do anything anymore . . . To make pottery you have to have lots of patience . . . guess I don't have that anymore. When I was active I learned that some pots need to be fired as much as three times . . . I just don't want to do that anymore.

With the end of our conversation we begin a photo session. The light in Peggy's living room is on the dim side. This seems to contribute to the air of melancholy in the room. We open the blinds to let in some light that splashes across Doris' face—the camera sees this. Then we go to the outdoor porch. Mother and daughter have very serious looks to their faces. Although the sun is shining on the porch, the two women are in the shadows. I take my final portraits. Three months later Peggy died of a heart attack. She was 76 years of age.

This journal needs now to go back in time to 1985 for another interview. It is with Hadden Johnson, a Catawba whose family has had, like the Peggy

Harris family, genetic influence from other Indian sources. Hadden is very "Indian-looking," in the Hollywood sense of Indian identity.

His house sits on land near the reservation and, unlike Samuel Beck's or that of Peggy Harris, is in some disrepair. He invites me to sit down outside in a lawn chair. As he takes another chair, his daughter comes from the house and climbs on his back as she wraps her arms around his neck. She appears to be five or six years old and is lighter in skin tone than her father. It is a wonderful contrast and I take their portrait.

Q: Could you straighten me out—are we on the reservation or just off?

Hadden: This house is just off . . . there ain't any line except in everyone's head . . . I guess [his face reflects, it seems, a very slight ironic smile].

Q: But this house was once on the reservation?

Hadden: Yeah . . . it's the kind of house you find here.

Q: Could you tell me something of your background?

Hadden: Background? What do you mean by that?

Q: Well . . . let's see . . . are you a Mormon?

Hadden: Me! Are you kidding . . . I wouldn't ever be one . . . they try to tell you how to live your life too much . . . they try to run everything their way [getting heated] . . . they think whatever they do has to be the only right way . . . I can hardly take some of them!

Q: But are you religious in any way?

Hadden: Me! No . . . not very . . . ask me about something else!

Q: How many children do you have?

Hadden: I've got this girl [who is going back into the house] and two boys. Yeah, and if you want to know, my wife . . . she is white . . . for me, I'm Catawba and Cherokee . . . my daddy was Cherokee.

Q: Could you tell me more about your parents?

Hadden: [After a pause and a hard stare] My daddy's name was Isaac Johnson but he went by Ike . . . you know, like Ike Eisenhower. He was born in Birdtown . . . Birdtown is on the big Cherokee reservation . . . not Snowbird . . . but on the big one . . . the Qualla.

Q: And your mother, was she Catawba?

Hadden: Sure was [proudly]. She was a strong woman . . . she used to carry me on her back . . . I remember that . . . she used to walk all over looking for work . . . [pause] my daddy . . . well, we were dirt poor.

Q: What was your mother's name?

Hadden: Martha . . . Martha Harris Johnson . . . her daddy was Ben Harris . . . ever heard of him? . . . He was a Catawba full blood . . . and he spoke it too . . . he could speak the Catawba language . . . one of the last!

Q: [I could see some random splashes of white paint on his face and clothes] I guess that you are fixing up your house?

Hadden: Yeah . . . but if you are asking what I'm doing for a living, then I do a lot of different things . . . you know that song that goes "doin' a living as best I can." That's me.

Twenty years have gone by since that session and I have lost track of Hadden. I do know that he no longer lives by the reservation. And I am told that Hadden has sided with a dissident faction that is challenging the authority of the established tribal administration—the same tribal leadership, led by Chief Gilbert Blue, that filed a 1980 lawsuit and changed the history of the Catawba Tribe.

In 1840, the Catawba Tribe signed away 144,000 acres of land in a treaty that was seen 140 years later as being illegal.[11] Facing countless expensive lawsuits by the many landowners enrolled in the suit, the state of South Carolina agreed to a settlement in 1993. The tribe agreed to dismiss its land claim and in return obtained a reinstatement of its federal recognition status, lost during the Eisenhower administration. In addition, the tribe was to receive over a five-year span some fifty million dollars to be used for health care, housing, and a per capita distribution the size of which depended upon the final number of members on a new roll. The tribe also received permission to enlarge, within limits, the size of the reservation. Further, the tribe received permission to start gaming establishments with a limit of two in South Carolina, presumed to be the only such gaming in this conservative state.[12]

During crucial negotiations leading to the 1993 agreement, a division existed between the "cash crowd" and the "land crowd." The land group wanted more funds from the settlement dedicated to the buying back of tribal land than did the cash faction. To illustrate this particular division, I need to report from a television documentary made at the time of the settlement.

Catawba Mike Wade had just come from a tribal meeting regarding the settlement when he appeared on camera. Mike expressed, in these words, the division and his position: "The cash Catawbas don't live on the reservation.

They don't want anything to do with the reservation. All they wanted was money. They don't want to be an Indian. 'Just give me some money,' [they say]. That's not being an Indian. The land is the Indian. Not the money."[13]

However, the settlement failed to give to the tribe all the privileges enjoyed by other federally recognized tribes. According to a letter published in *The State* newspaper in 1994, one year after the settlement, the governor blocked a young Catawba from obtaining college aid under an Indian fellowship program: "Shame on Governor Campbell . . . The ink isn't even dry on the settlement with the Catawbas, and the Governor's Office is already breaking its promises."[14]

By 2002 the government of South Carolina had approved a licensed state lottery and began obstructing the establishment of the second bingo game provided for in the settlement. A Catawba Indian told me that this action by the state government proves you can't trust the government and is another slap in the face of the Catawbas and another instance of the government going back on another promise. She then told me that she was ashamed of herself for having believed in the government at the time when the settlement specifically called for the right of the Catawbas to have two gaming sites.

Overall, though, the settlement has been a spur to the tribe and a considerable influence upon the efforts of other Carolina tribes seeking state and national recognition. Enrollment in the tribe has grown dramatically. In 1961 there were 631 enrollees and by 1996 there were 2,500. Many Catawbas who had moved away are returning and being active in tribal affairs. (See the appendix for membership requirements.)

At the time of the settlement, the reservation contained 631 acres and now, I am told, it is around 800 acres. The Catawba Cultural Preservation Project (CCPP), organized in 1988, had by 1996 over a dozen employees as well as many volunteers. Among its many activities are lessons in pottery making, beadwork, and basketry. Efforts to revive the language have been started to go with the teaching of Catawba history. The CCPP also reaches out to local schools, museums, and civic organizations to teach outsiders interested in Indian history and traditions. The CCPP is housed in what was once the Indian school for the first six grades. In 1989, this old school building was physically moved from its location next to the Mormon church to the center of the reservation next to the Community Center building. With this move the old school building was completely renovated and is now referred to as the Cultural Center.

Funding for the Cultural Center comes from various sources. According to Dr. Wenonah George Haire, who is by profession a dentist, as well as being the executive director of CCPP, a tribal historic preservation officer, and a Catawba board member, "the activities at the Cultural Center are funded in great measure by the frugal efforts of its staff and board. Grants, donations, programs, craft classes, lectures, demonstrations, archaeology, exhibits, craft store sales, and a $70,000 note from the tribe that has almost been completely paid back to the tribe are how the CCPP has survived." She goes on to explain that the center has benefited some from bingo gaming.

Buffeted from without, the Catawba tribal government has also had to face internal dissension in recent years. In 1998, sixteen dissenting tribal members filed a federal lawsuit against the seven principal leaders of the tribe, claiming mismanagement of the tribe and its funds. The suit was later dismissed.

One of the dissenters was Sammy Beck, the older son of Samuel and Helen Beck. In May of 2004, I meet with Sammy in his home on the reservation proper. He invites me into his living room, which extends to the dining room. He walks, with a limp, over to a sofa situated in the middle of the room, facing another sofa, where I take a seat. He looks to be in his forties but a reliable source tells me he is in his late fifties. He is thicker, stronger, and somewhat taller than his late father. He appears to be something of a dynamo. Joining him on the sofa are two small dogs that look to be pugs. One is more aggressive as he keeps getting onto Sammy's lap and, playfully it seems, nipping at Sammy's hands.

Q: I've talked with your father a few times and took his picture also. And I took your photo at the 1990 Catawba Festival. You were dressed in a buckskin shirt and pants and boots and . . .

Sammy: Well, that couldn't have been me 'cause I've never dressed that way . . . I go to the festival every year, but that wasn't me . . . I bet that was my brother Rod!

Q: Oh, really? But I sent this picture to Tom Blumer [author of books on Catawba pottery] hoping he would give it to you . . . or as the case is . . . to your brother. But recently I got back from you a signed release.

Sammy: Well, yes I did sign a release but I didn't get any photo . . . because you never took one of me!

Q: This is the first time I've ever gotten a release before I've even made a photograph!

We laugh at this. Then his cell phone rings and he gets up and starts to walk around the living room, into the dining area, down a hallway in a heated discussion. He then, after signing off, returns to his sofa. He grimaces as he sits down. The dogs bounce around him.

4. Sammy Beck, Catawba, on the reservation, 2004

Sammy: Sorry, but almost all my time is taken up with tribal matters . . . and I also look after my grandson . . . I take him to kindergarten and pick him up.

Q: Tom Blumer tells me you were in a bad accident.

Sammy: Yeah, I sure was . . . I got kind of crushed some in a truck accident . . . it's my hip . . . can't work at my old job . . . I'm on disability. But I keep busy!

Q: What kind of work were you doing?

Sammy: Oh . . . I was installing insulation . . . the kind you find in air-conditioning ducts . . . mostly industrial places . . . Before that I was an electrician . . . I began to learn that from my dad. And I spent four years in the Navy when I was an electrician.

Q: Thanks for filling me in. Sorry to hear about your accident. I wonder—I know you are busy with tribal matters—but I wanted to be sure and get a few photographs done and . . .

Sammy: Oh sure, we can do that . . . but first I want to tell you some things that are going on. You know about the Catawba high-stakes bingo casino we have, don't you . . . did you know we don't really run it? It was hired out to a white corporation . . . called New River Management . . . and they make most of the money . . . and they don't hire any Indians that I know of. [Note: some Catawbas do work at the game.] Here, let me get you this . . .

Sammy suddenly gets up from his sofa. The two dogs scatter, but he quickly returns with a printout, which he gives to me. It is a bingo financial report.

Sammy: See . . . look! The gross income for the past two and a half years has been nearly eighty-eight million dollars and look how little the tribe got—just one million dollars . . . and where has that money gone! A lot of bad financial things have been going on . . . and we don't know exactly about them 'cause a small group runs everything . . . and keeps the rest of us in the dark . . . and our constitution is clear. It calls—for a long time now—to have an election but that small group keeps us from having an election. It makes us angry.

Suddenly the phone rings again; the dogs jump around as Sammy gets up and paces about the house while on the phone. The dog that had been climbing all over Sammy comes over to my sofa, jumps up, and tries to climb all over me. Then as I try to pet him he begins to really nip and gnaw on my hand. Sammy finishes his phone call, and then we go outside for a photo session. I am glad the dogs stay in the house.

We go to his front yard where there is a tall, thick pine tree. Sammy Beck stands near the tree and leans out his right hand to support himself. Then in a flash I recall his parents, outside of their home, standing together under a huge oak tree. It was in the autumn of 1986. Now, eighteen years later, and as with his parents, I take his portrait. His very slight smile reminds me of his father.

We part in good company, I believe. I watch him walk up the outside stairs of his house. He seems to be wincing from his injury that forced an early retirement. Yet, with obvious determination, he has new purposes in life: to look after his grandson and to look after his tribe the best way he sees possible.

On that same day in late May of 2004, I drive out the Avenue of the Nations on its new extension, to its very end. There, sitting on a bluff facing eastward, is the new tribal office called the Long House. If it were not for all the trees to the east, one could probably see—below and in the distance—the Catawba River. The Long House is a substantial stone-and-brick structure with seating in the main hall for perhaps 350 people. Also there are meeting rooms, a day-care center, a health-care room, and an exhibit room for pottery and other objects. The Long House also contains the tribal offices.

The reservation looks much the same as it did in 1985, although there seem to be a few more white-painted, wood-frame houses and trailers. If anything, the older houses appear to be in better repair.

I am looking for Beckee Garris, who works for the Tribal Historic Preservation Office. I locate her not at the renovated former Indian school but in a building behind it, deeper in the woods, the archaeology building.

During the Catawba Festival of 1991 I took a photograph of her dancing to the drums; there was a sunny, even ecstatic, look on her face. Today I want to interview her because of her work for the center and to do a follow-up photograph. I have been trying to do a follow-up photograph with some American Indians as a means of revealing what time does to people. Time individualizes us until we turn to dust.

On this day I find her sorting through various pieces of Catawba pottery for shipment to a museum that is sponsoring a large exhibit. She is holding a large cooking pot. It has a distinctive rounded base with very smooth walls. Its colors are brown and black in a variegated "free" pattern created by the firing process.

Q: Whose beautiful pot is that?

Beckee: Earl Robbins made this. Its original purpose was for cooking . . . see, the cook would slowly spin it around with the base near the coals of the fire. People would have had maybe corn and beans in with water and would hold it like this [she demonstrates the technique that Indians used when pottery had a functional purpose].

Q: I wonder if I could talk you into going outside with this pot. The light out there is much better for photography.

5. Beckee Garris, Catawba, with Earl Robbins' pot, 2004

Beckee agrees to this request and because she is so busy, as is the man working with her, I do not try to interview her then. Instead, she gives me her mailing address for me to send her photographs and a questionnaire. She also gives me her e-mail address in anticipation of additional questions. Here is the result of this interview process:

Q: When were you born and where? And the names of your parents, please?

Beckee: I was born on May 28, 1947, on the reservation, as was my mother. My father was born in New Philly, Ohio. My mother's name was Marie Sanders and my father's was Grant Simmers.

Q: As you grew up did you have any memorable experiences (good or bad) associated with being a Catawba Indian?

Beckee: I had to walk to school through the fourth grade. It was the reservation school. But buses would not come onto the reservation to take you to public school until the mid-1960s. My mother's generation could go to public schools but had to furnish their own transportation.

For those who went to public school they had to ride with a parent to where the parent worked—wait in the car until time to walk to school. This meant some had up to fifteen-hour days since they had to walk back to where the parent worked and wait in the car until they got off work (summer and winter).

I personally never had anyone to insult me. But [I] know of my cousin who had to fight some girls almost every day she went to school. War whoops were common walking down school halls.

I saw my first movie (inside a theater) because the owner let the whole class in for free. I was in the 4th grade at the time . . . I saw *Sayonara!*[15]

Q: I see you wear a cross; which religion do you belong to?

Beckee: Mormon and yes we are Christians. I had a woman tell me this Saturday that Mormons were not Christians!

Q: Do you know any Indian, Catawba or otherwise, who practices any traditional religious or ceremonial ways?

Beckee: Some Catawbas do the sweat lodge, smudging ceremony, talking circle, pipe ceremony—I can do most of these, but don't very often.

Q: I am not familiar with the talking circle; could you tell me about it?

Beckee: The talking circle is where a group of people sit in a circle. Anything that is discussed in this circle doesn't leave the circle. The only person who can speak is the person holding a special feather for this type ceremony (usually an eagle feather). You cannot interrupt the speaker until they stop talking and say they will answer questions.

Q: What is your position with the tribe?

Beckee: I work for the THPO (Tribal Historic Preservation Office). I help with programs performing for schools, visitors, tour groups, drumming, singing, dancing, pottery classes, and we are beginning to teach language.

Q: Tell me more about the language class.

Beckee: The Head Start program here on the Res has started teaching the Catawba (and non-Catawba) three- and four-year-olds colors, animals, and other phrases for the last three years. Claudia Priest is our linguist, non-Catawba, who has compiled a Catawba dictionary for her master's thesis. She is Canadian.

Q: Wes Taukchiray tells me that Sam Blue was the last speaker of the Catawba language. Did you know him?

Beckee: Grandpa Sam Blue is my maternal grandmother's (Vera Blue Sanders) dad. When I was very young he used to speak some to me but I was too young to pay attention. I regret that! Grandpa Blue had twenty-four children but not all lived through infancy . . . He was married twice . . . My grandma Vera had eleven. My mom (Marie Sanders Simmers) had nine. And I have three . . . My son is a soldier in Iraq.

Q: Thanks for telling me more about your family. I can see now your interest in the language. Do you do any pottery making? If so, whom did you learn from?

Beckee: I do make some pottery. I started about the time you took my picture [1991], but have only gotten serious in the last four years. Nola Campbell showed me how to make a turtle.

Q: Nola was my favorite potter; who has been yours?

Beckee: Evelyn George, Florence Wade, Caroleen Sanders, Keith Brown.

Q: In your letter, you said that "time has not smiled upon me with kindness"; have you had a serious illness?

Beckee: No, I have not had any major illnesses. But have had major sorrows in my life, but who hasn't? My mother died from domestic abuse, had a brother die from alcohol-related illness, and I have divorced. At times my job is very stressful and at others a joy. As in your line of work I know you know all about the good, the bad, and the ugly.

The storied Catawba Tribe has survived to face three crucial events in the twenty-first century. In December of 2004, the Catawba Indian Nation's administrative building and Cultural Center were closed, sending seventy-some employees home temporarily unemployed. There was a dispute between the tribe and the U.S. Bureau of Indian Affairs that appeared to revolve around some accounting irregularities, which caused the BIA to suspend financial support until any irregularities could be accounted for. Nevertheless some employees continued to work, but unpaid.

A second major shock to the tribe was the bankruptcy of its bingo game, which had been a source of income to the tribe since the 1993 settlement. This dissolution of the bingo business, located in Rock Hill, was caused by a number of factors. First and foremost, contend tribal leaders, was the institution of a state lottery in 2002. Attendance dwindled from a high of a thousand on a weekend night in the 1990s to two hundred fifty to three hundred people after the lottery was started. "Profits were cut in half, effectively killing the tribe's only revenue stream," stated a newspaper report.[16]

Contributing to the bingo hall's demise was a law passed by the state of South Carolina that banned video poker machines, resulting in about a 40-percent reduction in revenues. From the very beginning the state was taxing 10 percent of the gross income from bingo. However, after the state lottery started, South Carolina passed a special "Catawba Tax," which required that the tribe collect eighteen dollars from each patron who entered the bingo hall. "That killed what little we were bringing in and it closed us down," Beckee Garris told me.[17]

Consequently income from bingo stopped by the end of 2007. The tribe attempted to start other gaming halls in other parts of South Carolina but all efforts have been vetoed by the governor. According to Beckee Garris, "He says it is against his religion to gamble. But the state voted to allow the lottery, which is classified as Class 3 gaming which is what casinos are classified as. Yet we still get treated like the plague and 4th class citizens . . . but my thoughts are, if they were getting 10 percent taxes on the gross of one bingo hall and they got more back in taxes the very first year than they ever paid us to settle our land suit, what idiot thought banning us in another part of the state was a good thing for the state?"[18]

A third shock has been the resignation in March of 2007 of their long-term chief. Gilbert Blue was best known for his leadership that led to the 1993 settlement. According to U.S. Representative John Spratt (Democrat, South Carolina), Chief Blue "brought the Catawba tribe back to life and gave it a new footing . . . Gilbert kept his hand to the plow."[19] Apparently Chief Blue could no longer take both internal and external dissension, conflict, and discord.

Yet by the end of 2007 the Catawba Tribe seems to have achieved a new equilibrium. A new chief has been elected, Donald Rodgers, with an assistant chief, Gene Blue. A new secretary/treasurer has also been elected as well as four people to the Tribal Executive Committee, two of which are women. It would appear to me—as an outsider—that this election has resulted in a balance between the different factions of the tribe.

Additional good news has come to the tribe. BIA money has been restored, although none for the Cultural Center salaries. Yet this center has been very effective in gaining financial support from outside sources, including friends of the tribe who are non-Catawbas. Beckee Garris reports, "All the years of sweat, tears, toil and prayers are finally paying off."[20]

A recurring theme among some Indian groups in the Carolinas is the desire to assert, to express sometimes at the very personal level, their right to be counted as an Indian. In so doing Beckee Garris has written this poem:

> Funny You Don't Look It
> by Beckee Garris, Catawba
> © July 29, 2004
> Funny you don't look it
> Is what you said to me
> When you ask me if I'm an Indian
> As if I'm just pretending to be
>
> I don't look like the TV Indians
> Or the Tribes you meet out west
> Since I'm not a "full blood"
> You think that makes me less than the rest
>
> Yes, I have a white father
> And a Catawba mother
> What is in my heart
> Makes me embrace the latter
> Without denying the other
>
> Sorry if I'm not who you expected
> Or exactly what you thought you'd see
> BECAUSE FUNNY—I DO LOOK IT!
>
> For that proud Catawba reflected
> In the mirror
> IS ME![21]

In July of 2004, Beckee sent this e-mail:

> The Catawba Indian Nation/Cultural Center has just been the host tribe for the Native American Boy and Girl Scouts (close to 300) convention. And we have been extremely busy with them. We held a mini-

> Pow-Wow, pottery demonstration, Catawba History lesson, flint knapping, language classes, etc. . . .
>
> Also they were surprised by our women's drum group at the Cultural Center. And some even want to go back and form their own drum groups. In some tribes it is a major taboo for women to drum period!
>
> Since we don't have data on whether it was or wasn't taboo for Catawba women to drum, we just did it! As it turned out, it was a good thing since none of the [Catawba] men drummers showed up to drum at the mini-Pow-Wow we had at the Center. Some of them [Catawba men] do refuse to drum with the women. But I (personally) think that is because of them hearing it from other tribes they meet on the Pow-Wow circles, not because of any traditional set rules the Catawba Nation had in the past. So it is now a modern tradition for Catawba women to drum.
>
> But the exciting thing was that I quoted my poem to them. People had tears in their eyes and one group gave me an ovation! . . . I changed about a third of my poem the night before they arrived. It never crossed my mind I would be sharing my poem with them. It just felt right to do so. I was and wasn't surprised at how many of them had almost the same words said to them as well.

Beckee Garris seems to say that tribal identity is complex because it is a combination of family and tribal history, a mix of old and new religious beliefs, and a maintenance of strong cultural tradition including the study of language. Nola Campbell believed that the tradition of pottery making is the wellspring of Catawba identity because of its uninterrupted process from precontact times to the present. Mike Wade says, "The land is the Indian." Sammy Beck thinks that a responsive tribal government is the key. A Catawba medicine man might respond that a belief in traditional native spirituality is a major contributor to a persistent, strong Indian identity.

In the next chapter we will travel to the central part of South Carolina to look at two Indian groups that have had neither land nor a continuous tribal leadership since the colonial era. How, then, do they define their Indianness?

2

The Midlands

Seventy-five miles south of the Catawba reservation is the capital of South Carolina—Columbia—which, in its own way, is a reservation. Better said, it is the home of three reservations, none Indian. First is the military reservation of Fort Jackson that literally is a reserve and perhaps the largest center in the country for the training of infantry soldiers. I know this well, as I spent two months of 1955 there in "tent city."

A second kind of reservation is the state government, whose political forces have become increasingly the reserve of the conservative movement. In 1955 when I was stationed at the fort, Columbia was a highly segregated city. Today, official segregation no longer exists due, in great part, to the strength of the civil rights movement. Yet segregation of the de facto variety appears to still exist, in some ways, in the state capital.

The third reserve, and perhaps this stretches the metaphor too far, is the University of South Carolina, which in the past twenty years has been trying to encourage minorities to enroll—with limited success for American Indians. However, the enrollment for other minorities had, until recent years, been slowly increasing. In 1994, total minority enrollment, including American Indian, was at 22.4 percent. By 2000, this total had risen to 24.4 percent. But four years later the figure dropped to 21 percent.[1] The major cause of this decrease appears to be a state government that continues to reduce its monetary support for the state's flagship university. In consequence, tuition has to be increased, which, in turn, reduces minority enrollment.

The existence of the military, governmental, and educational institutions makes Columbia recession proof. Or so said a medical doctor to me when I first came to teach at the university. Columbia, also, is at the confluence of three rivers. There is an old saying that an important city is known by its rivers. For Columbia these rivers are the Broad and Saluda, whose roots are in the eastern slopes of the Appalachians. In Columbia they join forces to form the Congaree River. At this point, on the west side of the river, the artillery of Sherman in 1865 announced its thunderous presence by sending cannonballs across the river aimed at the state legislature building. To this day there are pockmarks visible on the west wall, constant reminders to some of that fateful era.

The Congaree works its way southeastward and forms a large swamp fifteen miles south of the city and then reforms into a river that shortly slides (the land is flat now) into the Wateree (née Catawba) River.

This general geographic region is sometimes called the sandhills for the reason that the soil is sandy and the topography is now one of gently rolling hills and wide flat plains, being south of the fall line. The Congarees were the primary tribe here and came to official colonial attention in 1692 when a delegation of them, with their allies the Waxhaws and Esawas, visited Charleston officials.[2]

In 1716, the Congarees were recognized by colonial powers as potential trade partners. However, by the 1720s, disease and "several slaughters and blood sheddings lessened their numbers."[3] The Santees and Congarees combined had, by then, but 125 people. At that time the Waccamaws—from the Winyaw region—still had some six hundred members.

Any brief description of the Native American presence in the Midlands would not be complete without a discussion of the Cherokees. In the sixteenth century, and at least from A.D. 1000 to 1450, the Cherokee Nation occupied the southern Appalachian Summit, which covered areas of western North Carolina, parts of eastern Tennessee, a small part of northeastern Georgia, and the upper reaches of northwestern South Carolina, primarily in what is now called Oconee County. By the eighteenth century, the Cherokees had expanded into more areas of northwestern South Carolina and into northern Georgia and northwestern Alabama, and they claimed portions of Virginia and West Virginia and most of Kentucky as hunting grounds and buffer zones.[4]

During the colonial period the Cherokees became involved, in addition to the occupation of hunting grounds, in trade, especially with the settlers. In fact, the famous Cherokee Path that ran from Columbia to Charleston and from Columbia to the Cherokee heartland has present-day markers that establish a limited presence of the Cherokees in the Midlands. However, this presence became diminished by the end of the 1700s due to the loss of their territories from warfare with the ever-expanding settlers.[5]

Yet census records supplied to me by Will Moreau Goins, who holds a doctoral degree in American Indian Studies and is the leader of the Eastern

Cherokee, Southern Iroquois and United Tribes of South Carolina (ECSIUT), indicate that numerous South Carolinians living in the Midlands, as well as the upstate, have Cherokee roots. His Indian group draws members from Oconee, Greenville, Newberry, Pickens, and Anderson counties as well as from the Midlands, where the headquarters is located, in Columbia. ECSIUT membership criteria are based upon proof of a "direct lineal ancestor with documentation of Native American (ethnic) status of classification in historic documents."[6]

In 1992, an article in *The State* newspaper, provocatively titled "Indigenous Chic: American Indian Numbers Grow with Changes," reported that 2,425 people in South Carolina call themselves Cherokees. This article did not give a geographic location to go with these data but it could be assumed that some can trace their roots to Oconee County (called the "Lower Towns") and others have migrated into South Carolina from the "Middle Towns" (extreme western North Carolina), "Overhill Towns" (east Tennessee, northeast Georgia), or "Valley Towns" (North Carolina–Tennessee border). However, it also must be noted that a certain percentage of people who have unknown Indian roots often refer to themselves as Cherokees (which many people think is the same as saying "Indian").[7]

What is clear is that the Cherokee heartland was never a part of the original Cofitachequi territory, although, in all probability, the present-day state capital was a hunting and trade area. Yet in the past one hundred years the Cherokees have played a role of influence upon the tribes of the old Cofitachequi areas. One such influence, I believe, is the desire for resurrection of the native language, especially with the Catawbas.[8]

In 1994, I visited the Snowbird reservation in North Carolina and, at the Trail of Tears gift shop, spoke with Nicely Rattler, an elderly lady who spoke English and Cherokee. She told me that she now travels about thirty-five miles from her home near Robbinsville (Graham County) to the Qualla (the main reserve in Swain County), where she teaches Cherokee children the native language.

She went on to tell me that she experienced, as a school-age child, language repression at an infamous boarding school for Indian children. There she was punished, as was any other child, with verbal abuse, isolation, or whippings anytime she was caught speaking her native language. Yet her language skills have persisted and now—sixty-five years later—she proudly is making use of her native tongue. She also informed me that she is not the only Cherokee adult who has kept the language—it is used daily by some Snowbird Cherokees.[9]

The Snowbird band makes up but one of three Cherokee areas in western

North Carolina. The other two reserves, the Qualla (Swain County) and the Tomotla (Cherokee County), are separated by the Snowbird (Graham County). This geographic distance also reflects, to some measure, a division amongst Cherokees in regard to "blood percentage."

There are the "full bloods," who must have at least a three-fourths degree, sometimes referred to as maximal-degree or maximal-blood Cherokees and at times as "real Indians." The minimal-degree Cherokees must have at least one-sixteenth degree (at one time it was one-thirty-second and pejoratively referred to as "white Indian"). These standards are set by the tribe itself using a system that attempts to define Indianness genetically rather than socially. Sharlotte Nealy in her book on the Snowbird Cherokees says that racial factionalism goes back to a geographic correspondence in the nineteenth century when most minimal Cherokees lived south in the lower hill country while most full bloods lived to the north in the mountains.[10]

Further, the geographic areas are sometimes associated with this "blood" consciousness. On the Qualla there is a mix of people associated with the maximal and minimal categories. But the Snowbird Indians are closest to being all maximal whereas the Tomotla Indians are predominately minimal-degree Cherokees. How this "blood" division affects internal relations is unknown to me. Yet these divisions do not appear to affect negatively the basic sense of Indian identity by tribal members. Over my twenty years of teaching in South Carolina I have had two students who were Cherokees of the minimal-degree status. Both were very assertive of their heritage.

One student was very active in Cherokee ceremonies and crafts. Although he lived in South Carolina, where he worked for the state government and attended the university, he traveled regularly to the Qualla reservation to take part in dances, powwows, and rituals, some of which were ceremonies kept secret from non-Indians. Only those six thousand Cherokees on the rolls may attend the secret ceremonies (although perhaps other American Indians may be permitted). I once asked my student if I could be an observer or do photography. He clearly informed me that being a non-Indian, I could not.

Eastern Cherokees, even considering their internal divisions, appear to be very united. They maintain a democratic political structure and a newspaper (*Cherokee One Feather*), and they hold festivals as a means of unifying the entire tribe and encouraging tourism. Tribal members have become fairly prosperous, not because of tourism but because of profits from the video poker operations of their casino, located on the Qualla reservation. This Harrah's Casino is reported to attract 3.3 million visitors and pay out $48 million in salaries each year.[11] All that the Cherokees have accomplished is what many Carolina Indians seem to want to accomplish.

Returning now to the South Carolina Midlands, I need to go back to the newspaper article cited earlier, "Indigenous Chic," which was based upon the 1990 U.S. census. That article reported that there are a thousand American Indians living in the Columbia metro area (out of a population of over a hundred thousand in the 1990s). From my own experience these Indians come from the Catawba, Lumbee, or Waccamaw tribes as well as from many other parts of the country, in addition to those with Indian roots directly in the large geographic area called the Midlands.

Unlike the tribes covered in the other chapters of this book, the Midlands Indians did not have a tribal structure until recent times. By the 1960s and 1970s the Santees, Edistos, and Pee Dees were re-forming based upon local traditional communities. Within the Midlands, certainly, there was an Indian consciousness centered around family structures, but again no central organizing force. Hence all these factors indicate that if an Indian group were to form it would probably be seen as an urban group.

In addition to ECSIUT, another Midlands organization came into existence in the 1990s. In 1995, the Midlands Intertribal Empowerment Group (MIEG) was created and brought itself into public view with its first powwow. Since that time it has held yearly powwows, usually in May at the state fairgrounds in Columbia. Like all powwows it attracts participants and spectators from all over the Southeast. Photographs I have taken at these powwows appear in this book, and two of my favorite images are from these powwows. The first is a wide-angle view of a family, with an infant in the foreground, drummers in middle space, and dancers in deeper space. The other image is of Curtis Boone, who is holding up his shirt to show the puncture marks from a recent gallbladder surgery. His arms are stretched out so as to give an impression, along with the torso, of a cruciform.

I had known Curtis Boone for a number of years prior to the time of this photograph, as he managed a store in Columbia that sold cameras and other equipment. He at first was active in MIEG but since then became a member of the statewide organization already mentioned, ECSIUT.

Boone is quoted in a *Columbia Free Times* article as saying, "There's not a lot of American Indians living in Columbia, but those who are are very politicized and divided." He goes on to say that he would like to see more attention paid to Indians living in poor, rural areas: "We've been pushed to the outer communities of South Carolina and we've suffered for that."[12]

Boone's new organization is led by William Moreau Goins, PhD, whose Indian roots come from South Carolina and Robeson County, North Carolina. Goins' vision for his group appears to be different from that of other Indian associations with which I have made contact. In a formal letter to me

6. Will Goins, ECSIUT, with members Elsie Goins and Dorothy Taylor, 1999

in 1999, when I donated a portfolio of photographs to his organization, he wrote that ECSIUT is organized to "preserve, present, protect and document Cherokee history and other Native American Indian tribes' cultures and individuals, material culture, historic buildings, and folkways in South Carolina."[13]

Beyond the tribal goals, ECSIUT aims "to provide an intertribal forum for the Native American people throughout the State of South Carolina to caucus, to discuss educational, health, spiritual, and economic development needs of their respective communities and . . . to foster a spirit of unified voice among the Native American communities."[14]

In other words, in filling the void created by the demise of the Council of Native Americans, Will Goins appears to view his group as a statewide organizing center for Indian programs, publications, and political support, hence the "United Tribes" part of the tribal name.

In fact, his group has been successful on a number of fronts. He created Phoenix Publishers and produced in 1998 a book entitled *South Carolina Indians Today* and in 2002 *The People Speak,* which is composed of poems, stories, nonfiction, and interviews by Indian people living in the Carolinas. He helped organize, in its early stages, the Native American Prison Project (now led by the Catawbas as the Native American Prison Program). He has helped organize for over seven years the Native American Film Festival held each year in Columbia.

In 2000 ECSIUT had, as reported by Maria Jackson in *The Holly Hill Observer* newspaper, a statewide outreach project at various Indian communities "to foster an accurate count of Native American people which has been lacking in previous censuses."[15]

Further, Dr. Goins assisted a historic Indian community, informally called the Varnertown Indians, in their documentation for state recognition as an Indian group, which they achieved in 2005, becoming formally known as the Wassamasaw (Chapter 5). In addition to the Wassamasaw, Dr. Goins' ECSIUT organization received formal recognition also as an Indian group.[16] For a more detailed definition of a recognized "tribe" as compared to a "group," see the appendix.

More recently, in 2007, Dr. Goins was instrumental in the production of a 152-page guide, available at universities and libraries, to American Indian sites in South Carolina. This guide is based upon work done by state archaeologists, a team from Clemson University, and the South Carolina Native American Heritage Council.[17]

The leader of ECSIUT, Will Moreau Goins is a complicated and determined person. He, like so many people in the Southeast with American Indian heritage, still faces a certain level of skepticism on the part of some non-Indians as to his right to claim Indian heritage. This theme is a recurring one in this book. In particular there is a conviction held by some that there are no "real" Indians left. A corollary to this conviction is that a person must "prove" (as in a court of law) their tribal inheritance. Behind all these shadowy convictions, I think, is the issue of ethnocentrism.

With the historic ebb and flow of genetic tides in the southeastern part of the republic, there are, to the best of my knowledge, few if any "pure bloods" left, that is, those whose ancestry is 100 percent Native American. Hence, for a culture that continues to view race as a major determinant of identity, there is an almost unspoken, informal standard by which people can be judged to be Indian. This standard mold appears to have three factors.

First, if a person can furnish a birth certificate, church or school record, census evidence, or a Civil War–era affidavit of Indian descent, or if a person can prove descent from a relative on an established, official tribal roll, then this satisfies legal requirements.

Second, if a person was born and reared in a known Indian community of an established tribe, then their assertion of Indianness is usually taken for granted regardless of Indian "percentage."

Third, if a person has certain classic physical features—which of course are filtered through contemporary perception of what constitutes "Indian features"—then that person's claim is seldom in question. So, for this three-sided prism, there is one that is legal, another historical and social, and a third physical. Perhaps the ideal is to be able to claim all of these.

But why does the burden of proof of one's own identity have to fall upon the shoulders of each individual? There is no easy answer to this question. In a country that extols the belief that we Americans are free to define ourselves at all levels, there are counterpoint forces aimed at limiting such freedom. And these counterbalancing opinions may come both from within the Indian community and from non-Indians.

I personally know of one non-Indian who has done extensive research for and about numerous Indian communities in the Southeast. This person, Wes Taukchiray, holds to the opinion that the primary definition of an Indian is one born into or with direct lineage to a community associated with a particular tribe.[18] His standard is a much more narrow one than the standards set forth above. He seems to concede that if a person "looks" Indian then he or she is but nevertheless must "prove" tribal connection in order to fully claim that identity. In other words, it would seem that if someone is Indian, but has lost exact tribal ties over the centuries, that person is in perpetual Indian limbo. His position on this volatile matter has caused some grief amongst some American Indians, especially some urban Indians, who consider his position much too narrow.

Specifically, Taukchiray has challenged the Indian identity of Will Goins, the head of ECSIUT. In regard to this volatile issue and for other matters related to this book, I submitted in 2004 a set of questions to Dr. Goins (please note that the questions here and all questions in the book are aimed at revealing individual, subjective views that are not necessarily my own opinions).

Q: Would it bother you if I report[ed] your exchange with Wes Taukchiray?

Dr. Goins: You do not have my authority or permission to use any portion of the correspondence sent to Wes White [Taukchiray]. Wes White is somewhat of a self-made anthropologist who has delved into genealogy. More importantly, and the purpose of my comments . . . Wes White does not know anything about [my] genealogy or ancestry. Furthermore, he knows nothing about whom I am enrolled with and who I am not. Not to mention who I am eligible to be enrolled with. In addition, he knows nothing about what Indian community I was raised in [and] what cultural heritage has been passed on to me by my ancestors.

I respect the collection of work that Wes White did in the 1970s that is housed in the South Carolina Archives and History Center, but that work does not make him an expert on every individual person's genealogy and history.

His comments [in their communication] clearly denote intonation of racism and arrogance over information that he knows nothing about . . . His comments do not take into consideration my grandfather being born in the Indian community of Prospect, North Carolina (Robeson County) and raised in the community with the Cumberland County Indian Association of Fayetteville . . . I have never denied my ancestral ties and parental heritage in Robeson County . . . ask any Lumbee, Tuscarora or person in that community. They all know me . . . including my cousin Chief Jimmy Goins of the Lumbee Indian Tribe! His comments do not take into consideration the Eastern Cherokee heritage and culture passed down to me by generations on my mother's side. Obviously, I was not hatched.

Here is an example that will remove my personal insult and bias, while continuing to try to explain to you how wrong Wes White is . . . People can be Eastern Band Cherokee Descendants and not be able to be on the enrollment because of blood quantum requirements.

One member of ECSIUT is Robert D. Chastain. Born in July 1951, in Anderson SC . . . He presently holds a CDIB (Certificate of Indian Birth), which is distributed by the Bureau of Indian Affairs . . . He is 5/16 Cherokee with bloodlines both on his mother's side as well as his father's side. His ancestors are on [five] rolls. He has relatives still living both on the Qualla Boundary as well as relatives living in the Nation at Tallequah, OK. Yet he was only able to get a CDIB, because of the enrollment requirements of the Eastern Band Cherokee Indians of North Carolina.

Each nation has its own criteria of determining who is enrolled and who isn't since 1972 with the federal policy of "Indian self-determination." Cherokees have intermingled their blood with non-Indians for centuries . . . Acknowledging my multi-tribal heritage seems to be the problem here. Not being purely from one tribe seems to call into question Native ancestry. Well since miscegenation laws were enacted, Natives have had to marry other Native Americans. It is a shame that my work, compassion, effort, and honesty is called controversial or provocative as opposed to real and that my refusal to have any part of me ignored, cancelled, or blotted out is not applauded and respected like the civil rights of great Americans of the past like Martin Luther King that asked for acceptance and respect for his people.

Q: The major purpose of the book is to reveal a definition of contemporary American Indian identity in the Carolinas. Is there anything you can add to help bring out this thesis?

Dr. Goins: The recording of blood quantum is both a product of white racism and of white social science theories of a racist nature, and also a product of a plan wherein Native nations are expected to vanish when the white blood quantum reaches a certain level (above three-fourths, for example).

Yes, I (Will Moreau Goins) am Multi-tribal and have "White Blood" too, does that make me "White"? How many times have you mentioned in passing that you are Cherokee to find your conversation interrupted by intrusive questions about percentage? It would be rude to ask someone how Hispanic they are, but we accept that people can ask us how Cherokee we are. How Cherokee you are is more determined by how you live, how active you are in the tribe, how you grew up, and what you know of Cherokee history, culture, and language.

Q: Does your tribe (ECSIUT) have a roll? About how many belong?

Dr. Goins: Yes, we do have a roll for Cherokees of South Carolina tribal members and also a membership listing for supporting members and Natives who are enrolled with their respective tribal community. Our total membership is approximately 450 members. This is ever changing, for our membership is still open.

Q: I would like to ask you a personal question: What is it like, at this time, to be an Indian? What are the good things? And the bad?

Dr. Goins: I am not sure what you are asking here! . . . What is it like to be White? And what is good and what is bad about being White?

To answer Will Goins' last question, pointed as it is, I submit that this book is my realization that, being a non-Indian, it is quite impossible to have only my photographs accurately reveal the assertion of Indian identity in the Carolinas. Hence is the need for the insiders' opinions through interviews such as the one with Dr. Goins.

Which leads to other interviews. In the greater Columbia area, there are many who have Indian heritage and who support Will Goins in his efforts. Some were not born in an identifiable Indian community or tribe, yet are demonstrably Indian. One of these is a young man who has chosen to keep his name to himself in this interview. He has straight black hair, brown eyes, and medium-brown skin tone.

Q: Could you tell me when and where you were born?

Mr. B: I was born in 1970 in Lexington County [west of Columbia].

Q: Could you talk about your Indian heritage?

Mr. B: Well, both my father and mother are Indian.

Q: Do they belong to a tribe or were they raised in an Indian community?

Mr. B: Oh no, there are no Indian communities now in Lexington County! Not for a long time anyways.

Q: Are they proud of their Indian heritage?

Mr. B: My father is proud of being Indian . . . but my mother is not real proud of it . . . she never talks about it . . . she kind of hides her Indian background.

Q: How come the difference?

Mr. B: Well, you see, my father grew up in poverty . . . his parents were tenant farmers . . . maybe that had something to do with it . . . and he looks real Indian.

Q: And your mother?

Mr. B: Well . . . she is lighter in looks . . . and she came from a family that wasn't so poor . . . they owned their own land. They were small farmers. But both families can trace their Indian roots back to the war . . . the Civil War. Oh, yeah . . . my father now is not so poor . . . he has his own small business.

Q: Where did you go to high school?

Mr. B: I went to Lexington High.

Q: How did you like it there?

Mr. B: Ah . . . well . . . you know . . . whites run everything there.

Q: Could you tell [me] more about that? What do you remember the most?

Mr. B: What I remember most? . . . It was the way the cafeteria was laid out . . . there at the high school . . . it was mostly white and in the cafeteria there would be eight to ten tables of white kids and maybe two tables of blacks.

Q: How did you fit in?

Mr. B: I usually would sit at the end of the table of blacks closest to a table of whites or at the end of the table of whites closest to the blacks.

Q: How did the Asians fit in?

Mr. B: [laughs] Oh, they would always sit with the whites . . . they were always made honorary whites.

In 2003, at a powwow, I spoke again with this man.

Q: How are things going?

Mr. B: Oh, okay . . . see, I'm carrying my own camera now.

Q: Tell me, what is going on at MIEG [Midlands Intertribal Empowerment Group]?

Mr. B: Oh, the usual things . . . lots of inside fighting . . . I don't get too involved lately . . . I am so busy . . . oh by the way . . . I had a story published . . . it's in an anthology of Native American writers.

Q: Excellent, that must be very rewarding! Could you tell me why you are no longer active in MIEG?

Mr. B: Oh well, if you want to know [pause] . . . We got some white Indians who are . . . a pain! . . . Sometimes they say kind of stupid things. Maybe all this has to do with color tone and . . . oh, favoritism.

Q: In what way? What is a "white" Indian?

Mr. B: Well, if you want to get . . . to really get into that, then you ought to talk with [he gives me a name]. She's here today . . . I'll introduce you . . . She'll tell you anything you want.

Q: Yes, I would like to talk with her. But what did you mean by "color tone?" And "favoritism"?

Mr. B: [pause] Okay, here goes: A person's skin color is . . . well, joined up with whether or not that person is favored by others . . . All right, here's what I think. Now . . . with African Americans the person with the lightest skin tone is the person most favored by outsiders . . . You see it is on a line, a continuous line from light to medium to dark . . . with dark-skinned people being the least favored, at least by outsiders. But with Indians it is different . . . it is all the opposite—at least within those who are really Native American.

Q: How's that work?

Mr. B: It's because . . . the most favored are people with the darker skin tone as long as the features . . . your face . . . your hair reflect being Indian.

Q: All this is extremely interesting, but how does that connect with MIEG?

Mr. B: Well, I think I've said enough . . . let me go find [name omitted] and you can ask her.

As he goes to find the person in question I go over to watch the main attraction of any powwow, the drumming and dancing. MIEG's first powwow was held indoors at the National Guard Armory in November of 1996. More than thirty tribes came to that first Columbia Powwow, and the festival's theme was "honoring our elders." "The elders are the ones we have to look to for the teaching of the culture," said Yolanda Martinez about this theme. Martinez is an Apache singer and drum maker born in New Mexico and living now in Asheville, North Carolina. Interest in American Indian culture is "probably at its height here right now," said the 1996 powwow's master of ceremonies, Woody Richardson, a Lakota Sioux.[19]

From my experience of attending powwows over the past twenty years, these reports of a 1996 powwow reflect the diversity of tribal connections of the participants. A powwow held in central South Carolina is, most often, a regional powwow and even, in a certain sense, a national one. It is through powwows and the dancing and the drumming that a Pan-Indian culture and identity is spread.

According to Charlotte Heth in *Native American Dance: Ceremonies and Social Traditions,* "American Indian dance exists everywhere in America and in every venue, from the most traditional and private spaces to those most public and accessible. Thousands of dancers perform every day in out-of-the-way places—not to satisfy paying audience or patrons, but to assure the continuation of ancient lifeways, to honor deities and each other, to associate with friends and kin, and to affirm their Indian identities."[20]

The music at powwows begins with the drums, which reflect, I have been told, the sounds and rhythm of the heartbeat of a pregnant mother. Hence, the heartbeat is a way of passing on the drumbeat to the unborn and to the future.[21] The dances and dancers in this era of Pan-Indian adaptations are much more varied than the casual eye detects. To name eight, there is first the men's tradition in which the dancers are distinguished by a large single bustle worn on the back and in which they dance low to the ground with lots of upper body movement.

Then there is the women's traditional dance with the wearing, often, of beaded buckskin in which the dancer keeps time to the music by bobbing with a slow forward movement. The style calls for a reserved, dignified carriage.

The men's fancy dance calls for intricate footwork with lots of spins and body movements, and the dancer usually wears two bustles, often brightly colored.

With the women's fancy shawl style, the dancers use footwork, ribbons, and spins as a representation of butterflies. Other styles are the men's grass dance and straight dance, the women's jingle dress dance, and the Cherokee stomp dance.[22]

On this day at the May 2003 powwow, I return to the place where the young man and I had been talking earlier. He comes up to me and volunteers: "I am taking pictures . . . that's my job today . . . to get some shots for our website. Last year you gave me some of your shots, which we used. I'm going to help out that way . . . here she comes." He introduces me to an Indian woman. She is wearing a T-shirt that has, in all capitals, the letters *AIM*. She has dark hair pulled tightly around her head into a bun. She appears to be very somber and, perhaps, very stiff. She has chosen to have me not use her name.

Q: I am told that you can tell me more about how being an Indian and skin tone are connected.

Miss P: I don't know what all that he has told you, but the wannabees [want-to-be Indians] here in South Carolina are the ones I don't care for.

Q: Why is that?

Miss P: Why? Because . . . now I'm talking about white people who steal our ceremonies, our religion. Some even claim to be medicine persons! And some Indians sell out to these wannabees . . . some Indians say "I'm not white enough to be an Indian here" . . . We call them the "nausea people."

Q: "Nausea people?" I don't follow you.

Miss P: These are wannabees who have just recently started up a tribe and the way you pronounce the name of their new tribe . . . Well, it sounds like the word *nausea*.[23] You see, wannabees are not honoring what real Indians have gone through. I know an Indian who has an expression for them: "They don't know anything about walking about brown." And it doesn't end there . . . these white Indians always have an air of superiority . . . their whole way of dealing with things takes on the character of the oppressor!

Q: How's that work?

Miss P: Well, it's like what has happened in the past to blacks . . . white wannabees act better than Indians and some Indians can, and do sometimes, think that they are inferior to the wannabees . . . they [Indians] internalize what is the view of the oppressor . . . and this leads to low self-esteem. And there is another side effect. Here in South Carolina what we should have . . . and that would be natural . . . is . . . an alliance between African Americans and real Indians . . . especially in urban centers. But since there is no alliance, then Indians have little say-so in the things that are important to them!

Q: But why is there no alliance here?

Miss P: Because the white wannabees work to prevent it! It's a form of racism.

Q: Are all whites involved?

Miss P: No, of course not. A non-Indian can be a supporter . . . that's someone who is not paternalistic. Someone who doesn't try to get involved with inside matters, to take sides.

We then have a brief photo session. However, the light seems harsh and I get the feeling that I am not making any good photographs, so we end the session.

After our interview I begin a conversation with another person, a man with solid Indian credentials who is knowledgeable of the background concerning the woman just interviewed. He tells me that her Indian roots spring from her mother's side. The family was counted in the 1920 census (from a county about forty miles northwest of Columbia) as Cherokee Indian. Her father is non-Indian. This same source tells me also that she spent a number of years in South Dakota at the Pine Ridge reservation, where she was introduced to the American Indian Movement.

I am reminded of a conversation I had in the mid-1980s with an Indian from North Carolina. He told me that, in his opinion, the Indians of South Carolina were very passive as compared to those in North Carolina. This no longer seems the case to me now into the twenty-first century. The woman interviewed above seems to reflect this more assertive change and in her comments makes a number of good points. I sympathize with her protest, yet I wonder just what constitutes, in her mind, a litmus test for being a "real Indian."

In the 1970s when the Council of Native Americans became active with a primary purpose of having its members—three community-located tribes and one urban association—achieve state recognition, only the Catawbas had such status. Now, more than thirty-five years later, there are many tribes/groups in South Carolina, some of which are splinter groups from the more-established tribes, still striving for state recognition.

But what are the rewards for all the hard work of tracing genealogy, doing interviews, filling out forms? According to *The State* newspaper writer Joey Holleman in the article "Native Americans Claim Birthright," this recognition does not mean much financially for the tribes: "They don't get any state funds. But they now legally can label their work as Native American art and can apply for some grants targeted for Native Americans . . . [see appendix for information on the Arts and Crafts Act of 1990] Spiritually, it means everything."[24]

The writer continues with a quote from Dr. Goins: "'It is the most significant thing South Carolina has done for Native American Indian people in 300 years,' said Dr. Will Moreau Goins, chief executive officer of the Eastern Cherokee, Southern Iroquois and United Tribes of S.C. 'For the first time, this state is going to embrace their people who happen to be Indian.'"[25]

In a separate article Sherry Moss Cowan, a member of ECSIUT, states: "[Recognition] lifts a burden off you. You're not in the closet anymore. To be state-recognized lets people know I'm Indian, and no monetary value can replace its spiritual value."[26]

So striving for formal recognition certainly has value. In the next chapter an Indian community near Holly Hill, the Santees, will be examined. The Santees joined the Council of Native Americans in the late 1970s but did not apply for state recognition until 2004. This and other topics will be explored in the coming chapter.

3

The Santees

Seventy-five miles south of Columbia along the eastern shore of Lake Marion—once the Santee River before being dammed—is the Santee National Wildlife Refuge. Within this park is a prehistoric mound called the Santee Indian Burial Mound. However, in all likelihood it was a temple mound built during the Mississippian period. These kinds of mounds were not often used for burial, as were the early Woodland's Hopewell mounds found in the Ohio region. By contrast, a temple mound was built as an effort to establish a sacred domain elevated high above adjacent villages and used primarily for religious ceremonies and as a display of political power. Yet signs of a limited burial use of this mound have been discovered.[1]

When used by the original Americans the Santee Mound surely stood high to the villagers living along the river. Of course now with the dam having raised the water level it appears less monumental. Currently, strong wooden steps lead up one side of the mound—as high as a three-story building—in a zigzag rhythm to the flat top. This top occupies roughly one hundred by seventy-five feet. Although rarely used by Native Americans for defensive purposes, the British during the Revolutionary War maintained a fort there until overrun by the rebellious Americans.

Now, over 175 years later, it sits in quiet repose except in warm weather when tourists crawl about and park staff roll lawnmowers, by a system of ropes and pulleys, up and down its steep slopes.

Today a four-lane bridge carries traffic across the lake from the park side. Along the west side of this lake is the town of Santee. South of this town some eight miles along the lake is the smaller town of Eutawville and, then, four miles west from this town is the White Oak Indian Community, home of the contemporary Santee Indians.

The land here is flat and the soil sandy and thin looking. There is, however, some large-scale farming in this general region. This land must be fairly dry, as it is irrigated with long-armed sprinklers that are geared by machinery as they crawl about the landscape—sort of giant, mechanical daddy longlegs.

Skirting the Indian community and the town of Holly Hill, which is three miles away from White Oak, is the long arm—and occasional fingers—of Four Holes Swamp. This swamp stretches about sixty miles from its source near the Congaree River, moving sluggishly until it empties into the Edisto River. All along the sides of the swamp, and also because of occasional low-lying ponds, the land is too poor for much farming or home building.

Here, near the ponds and swamplands, is where aboriginal people found refuge from the colonial storms. War, disease, loss of land, and enslavement were the storms. Remnant groups were faced with limited choices: escape to the Catawba Nation, become enslaved, or find marginal land and become as obscure as possible as second-class citizens while the storm lasted, which it did for centuries.

Leland Ferguson, an anthropologist of Native and African Americans, states the situation clearly:

> Understanding the contemporary Indians of South Carolina requires some consideration . . . of a colony . . . founded upon principles of racial inequality. Settled by planters from the West Indies, South Carolina was, from the beginning, a colony designed to draw labor from a substratum of slaves. The colonists began enslaving the aborigines through a variety of processes; and by the time of an official census of slaves in 1708, one third of the slave population of the colony was Indian.
>
> In 1712, an act was passed in South Carolina stating that every Negro, Mulatto, Mestizo or Indian residing in South Carolina was a slave unless they had been declared free or they could "prove they ought not to be sold as slaves." The burden of proof was on the Indians.[2]

Dr. Ferguson writes from some personal experience, as well. He was born and reared in North Carolina, where his grandmother, who was of Indian ancestry, passed on to him her experiences living in a segregated society.

In this cited publication Ferguson states that in nineteenth-century South Carolina, most whites were unwilling to accept Indians—whatever their bloodline—as Indians. Instead, Indians were considered to be "mulattos" and had to go through considerable legal hurdles to prove otherwise.

Given these difficult times, few aboriginal Santee Indians were able to survive to the present. Certainly, to survive, they would be obliged to give up their tribal language, culture, dress, and any other obvious aspects of Indian identity.

According to one historian of Indian people, the present-day Santee Indians (the name the White Oak Community gives to their tribe) are in part descendants of a large band of Pee Dee Indians who had been living in the Pee Dee River region, which is near the North Carolina border. These Pee Dees, and a few Cheraw Indians, acquired between 1737 and 1742 a tiny one-hundred-acre reservation on the western side of Four Holes Swamp. This reserve—called Indian Fields Swamp to this day—was too small for their survival. They, therefore, migrated to the eastern side of Four Holes to the area associated with the White Oak Community. Official records showed their presence there until 1753.[3]

Although there is a gap in the official records for one hundred years, the federal census of 1850, as well as those from then on, reflects the existence of Indians living in this area.[4] Especially evident are certain names associated with being Indian and living in and around White Oak and Eutawville, which in that era was part of the north end of the parish of St. James Goose Creek. Now this physical area is a part of Orangeburg County.

Names identified as being Indian are Crummie, Pratt, Russel, and Sweat in the White Oak Community.[5] Then, in the twentieth century the surname of Scott became associated with being Indian in the community.

In the 1930 federal census there were 134 American Indians identified in Orangeburg County, from the White Oak–Eutawville area, most likely. By 1982, the population in the White Oak area was listed at 286.[6] However, the 1990 census reflected a decrease in Indians in this area. There were 214 counted. This last fact also reflects a concern by White Oak leaders, who have reported to me that the population is decreasing. And why? Evidence indicates that young people have increasingly migrated out to find better job opportunities.

In regard to local job opportunities, there has been a shadow over the Indian community. In 1983, there were three cement factories, a wood-products corporation, and lesser businesses. Yet, for the Indian community, unemployment according to the assistant chief, T. L. Scott, hovered at that time at about the rate of 50 to 60 percent.[7]

The following interviews consider the causes for this discrepancy between Indian unemployment and local job opportunities. These interviews also present views by the Santees on the pressure to give up, on the part of some, their Indian identity.

7. Hudson Crummie, Chief (retired), and son, Santees, 1984

In May of 1985 I first interviewed Hudson Crummie, former chief of the Santees, who served as their leader from 1974 to 1982. I talked with him at other times and the following is a compilation of these interviews.

Q: Wes White told me that the Santees had made big strides under your leadership. Could you tell me more about this?

Hudson: Well, that was nice of Wes to tell you that. I've had lots of help. Helen Amerson has been a big help.[8] We have been able to get some federal help for the community . . . it's through a CETA grant [Comprehensive Employment Training Act]. We got an adult education program through that . . . I think by two years ago we had fifteen people who had earned their high school certificates because of it.[9] And we have had good results in getting more of the younger ones to become more aware of their Indian roots . . . and we had some classes in Indian handicrafts.

Q: Yes, that's good . . . Wes also gave me an article from *The State* newspaper of 1980 that quotes you . . . I think it went this way: "We are tired of the comment that there are no Indians in South Carolina . . . We need the legislation badly to change some attitudes." Is that about correct?

Hudson: Yeah, I seem to recall saying that . . . our recognition is long overdue.

Q: When you became chief you were working full time, I believe. How was it that you decided to get involved in the tribe?

Hudson: It was in the late sixties and early seventies and we were as crushed down as we had ever been . . . our parents and our grandparents had no good education . . . they always took what came along. We let ourselves be taken advantage of . . . we were "criminated" against is a way of putting it. Some of us decided to change things.

Q: What did you do?

Hudson: Well, for one thing, we decided that we no longer wanted to be called the Crane Pond people . . . like "He's from Crane Pond"—saying that with a sneer! . . . You see, there's an old pond near here by that name . . . to us it was like using a swear word. And it made us feel like second-class people . . . so, because of that big oak tree by the church—and the school house—we decided that we would call ourselves the White Oak Indian Community . . . and we made it stick and now no one dares call us Crane Pond people! [pause]

You know . . . I can't get over how some of those folks in Holly Hill think themselves better and still are going to the beach to get a tan like ours.

Q: So, even though you got people to stop using the Crane Pond word, prejudice against Indians still exists?

Hudson: Well, I sure think so, especially in Holly Hill . . . but the younger people don't seem so race conscious.

Q: What else has taken place?

Hudson: Oh, we tried different ways to get funds to help with education, with job training, with help from Columbia. But we learned that folks in Columbia didn't believe . . . or care . . . there were Indians in South Carolina. And we did some politicking but often funds would never get to us.

Q: You mentioned the old school building; isn't that now the tribal office?

Hudson: Yes, it sure is . . . it's our community center, the old school building is. Helen Amerson's office is there. In the segregation era it was our school, our Indian school.

Q: Did you go there?

Hudson: Oh . . . sure did . . . that school goes back a long ways . . . at first we had the first six grades with one teacher . . . a white woman. Then it was raised up to nine grades. But we never got much money to support it. You know South Carolina at one time had three school systems . . . white, black, and Indian, in these parts where there were enough Indians . . . yet people say there are no Indians! Can you imagine how much it cost to keep three systems going! . . . Ours was so poor we couldn't afford a lot of things . . . no playground for the kids . . . we had to make our own swing sets . . . I remember making a flying jenny for the school.

Q: During that era, if a child wanted to go to high school, what happened?

Hudson: Oh . . . well . . . we couldn't go to the white school and we didn't want to go to the black school . . . we were Indians and didn't fit in anywhere.

Q: What happened when desegregation took place?

Hudson: Well, first, our school was closed down . . . and our children had to face new situations . . . new kinds of discrimination . . . I remember, when I was chief, I tried to get some federal funds to pay me to travel from school to school to make sure that discrimination wasn't being used against our children . . . but that never got going . . . You know that blacks get some help from the government so that they can get some jobs they couldn't get before . . . and I bet they get some consideration in schools . . . but Indians don't get any consideration. We Indians need to learn how to get recognized!

Q: Could you tell me what else happened when you were chief?

Hudson: Well . . . one year I got started on a project for the government. My job was to go all over the county to find Indian people who weren't touched by the census . . . if I had a full chance I bet I could've added nearly two hundred onto our roll . . . but the travel money was cut off before I could finish my search.[10]

Q: How did you identify Indian people?

Hudson: Oh, I often went by their last names . . . but that was only a part . . . I'd go by their looks . . . their skin . . . and I looked for high cheek bones . . . even if their skin looked sort of white or black . . . their Indian blood shows . . . and even if they were dark skinned they were Indian . . . [pause] if they had good hair.

Q: What do you mean by that?

Hudson: Well . . . I mean that if they had dark hair that was straight . . . and if they were old and had white hair . . . if it was straight . . . see, that's good hair. [pause] Now if a person is kind of light skinned and they might even have curly hair but if they have other Indian features, then I can tell . . . I can tell that they have Indian blood . . . but often they are passing for white. You see that a lot. Like there is an old woman who lives near here . . . just down this road and across Fire Tower Road. She is Indian but won't admit it . . . at least won't admit to some people. You go see her and you'll see what I mean.

Q: Well, before I do that I wondered if you could give me some background information about yourself.

Hudson: Let's see . . . where to begin . . . [pause] . . . Well, first of all . . . I'm disabled and can't work . . . of course maybe I'm too old to work anymore, even if I could . . . but I did work at the lumberyard for twenty years. You know, it really was a planing mill where I worked and because of that I can't hear in my left ear . . . they didn't supply earplugs. And I'm nearly blind in my right eye 'cause a chemical at the plant got splattered into it.

Q: Do you get workman's compensation for those injuries?

Hudson: Oh . . . [bitter laugh] they paid me half pay for two weeks after the splashing. But . . . no . . . I haven't got any health coverage . . . except from Social Security.

Q: But you must have some kind of retirement coming to you from the lumber mill?

Hudson: Oh, just thirty-five dollars a month plus my Social Security . . . We['ve] got to live on that somehow . . . sure am glad I own that truck and this house . . . and I hunt and fish and that helps us out a lot. [pause] But I can't hunt and fish, except when the government says I can . . . hunting and fishing are the joys in my life but I've never done that just to kill or sell . . . That's what we Indians ought to have the rights to do . . . be able to hunt and fish for food. You know, once we could . . . I remember as a kid I could . . . just like my father and my grandfather could. They used to go to the swamp in the winter with nets to get fish to eat for the family . . . and for other families . . . can't do that anymore . . . we need to get recognized as Indians!

Q: Could you tell me when you were born?

Hudson: Sure . . . I was born in 1917 . . . so that makes me sixty-eight now [1985] . . . but I'm still active . . . I got to do in order to go . . . always into something.

Q: I see that photograph up on the wall behind you . . . of a young soldier . . . is that your son?

Hudson: Yes, that's one of my children . . . that was during the Korean War . . . and there is Stanley here . . . he lives with me.[11] My wife has passed. And I have a daughter who lives nearby. And there's my pickup . . . that's about all I have . . . well, that's a little joke. I've had eight children, six of them boys.

Q: Was your wife from White Oak?

Hudson: Oh sure . . . her name was Edna Platt and my mother's name was Florence Sweat Crummie . . . and I've got six grandchildren and nine great grandchildren. [My father] was a farmer and he worked at odd jobs . . . We lost a lot of our land . . . he died when he was . . . well, around sixty-two.

After one of my interview sessions with Hudson, I drove across Fire Tower Road to the house where the elderly lady lived who he had mentioned "is Indian but won't admit it." She greeted me politely but agreed to talk with me only on the condition of anonymity.

Q: Thank you for allowing me to talk with you and do your portrait, if that is okay?

Mrs. S: Now why would you want to do that? Do I look like an Indian? [with a hard, short laugh]

Q: Well, Helen Amerson asked me to take your picture, if you were agreeable.

Mrs. S: Oh she did, did she! Why though?

Q: She wants a print for the tribal records is what she told me.

Mrs. S: Well, we'll see . . . maybe, but I don't want you ever to put it in a newspaper or anything like!

Q: Well, if that is your wish I certainly won't. Besides what Helen wants, Hudson Crummie tells me you are Indian.

Mrs. S: He does, does he! He thinks he knows everything about everybody! That guy does.

Q: Well, he tells me that your last name is an Indian name. Is he wrong?

Mrs. S: But this is my husband's last name . . . so it's my last name. Did he tell you that my mother was a white woman?

Q: No . . . I don't think exactly that, but . . .

Mrs. S: [Suddenly she laughs with a winning smile.] You know, I can't get over old Hudson . . . he's always trying to get me to sign up . . . on the roll . . . sure my father was Indian . . . but that doesn't mean I'm Indian . . . [pause] you know, I was born here . . . I was born in Eutawville.

Q: When was that?

Mrs. S: I was born in 1904 . . . so that makes me eighty-nine doesn't it . . . you know I got married real young. I was fifteen and came here . . . what they call White Oak now. In this very house . . . been here—well, what's that? That's seventy-four years in this old house . . . all alone now.

Q: So your husband has passed now?

Mrs. S: Oh yes, some time ago . . . we had four children . . . and, now . . . let's see . . . you know I can't recall right now how many grandchildren I have. [She laughs self-consciously.]

Q: Do your children live nearby?

Mrs. S: Oh no. [Suddenly her good spirits disappear.] I had a child die young and a daughter . . . a daughter who . . . well she killed herself . . . but I've got two living children . . . they live down at Charleston . . . I've got a grandson who is doing well . . . he's only seventeen but he's got a good job somewhere near Charleston . . . he builds ladders. And he's getting married in June . . . to an Indian girl from here . . . from White Oak . . . she's older than he is . . . I think she is twenty-two . . . can't figure that out . . . are you staying around here this evening?

Q: Well, I'm staying overnight somewhere. Why is that?

Mrs. S: Well, the local folks are having a get-together tonight . . . in that little building behind the church . . . the White Oak Church of God. Not at the old school, but that screened-in building they use for picnics.

Q: Well, I may hang around and go to it. You think it would be okay if I—as a stranger—went to the party?

Mrs. S: Oh sure, they would be tickled I bet.

Q: Are you going?

Mrs. S: Oh no! When I go to church . . . which isn't often . . . I go to the Church of God of Prophecy . . . that's down Fire Tower towards Holly Hill.
Q: Is that church, like the White Oak Church of God, Indian?
Mrs. S: Oh no [with a touch of disbelief at my apparent ignorance] . . . it's mostly white folks go there . . . besides, they do things differently there.
Q: Could you tell me what you mean by that?
Mrs. S: The Church of Prophecy, well we sing songs . . . with a piano, sometimes with other . . . well like guitars . . . it's well . . . a lot more lively than White Oak!

With that we have a brief portrait session, and I take my leave. That same evening—a Saturday—I return to the White Oak Community and take part in a prenuptial get-together in the pavilion behind the church. I meet the current chief and church elder—Oscar Pratt and his wife—and gain permission to attend the next day's Sunday school and main service of their church.

Also this evening I meet the bride-to-be and briefly talk with her. I ask her if she is getting married in the Indian church. She, quickly without any apparent reservations, answers in the negative. She and her husband-to-be are getting married in the predominantly white church. I want to ask her why, but we are interrupted by well-wishers and, thus, our conversation ends.

The next morning, which is May 26, 1985, I attend as planned the White Oak church and am struck with two observations: first, the church service seems under-attended, as there are many more empty bench seats than filled ones. Second, the minister, Utson Platt, conducts a very reserved, very quiet service. There are times for singing but all without musical accompaniment.

As with many nonrecognized Indian groups within the Cofitachequi footprint, the Santees long ago lost most of their original culture. However, Christianity appears to have played an important role in their survival and spiritual life as Indian people, in their group identity. Further, the White Oak Church of God, in particular, appears to be more fundamentalist than other Indian congregations I have visited.

Not until December of 1991 do I find out more details about the church and the community. At this time, again, I find myself at the church but get there as the morning service is just letting out. From a daughter of Utson Platt, I learn that the church members believe that any musical accompaniment might lead to an overstating of emotions, which might, thereby, lead the service away from its quiet, personal, and spiritual purpose. She also adds that attracting the young of the White Oak Community from her Church of God is a charismatic Church of God that is down Fire Tower Road toward Holly Hill.[12]

On this December Sunday, I meet Willy MacKelvaney, who tells me that he originally came from the Four Holes Indian community—some thirty miles away—but lives at White Oak because that is where his wife, along with her son from a previous marriage, lives. He works in construction but must travel each day close to 150 miles. He does so because the pay is twice that of the wood fabrication mill in Holly Hill that pays the minimum wage up to six dollars per hour. In construction, workers get eleven dollars per hour to start.

Also on this Sunday outside the church I speak with a White Oak Indian woman under conditions of anonymity. She is physically strong looking and appears to be around thirty-five to forty years of age. She drives a red pickup truck with the word *Jesus* on the license plate. A sign with the word *Christmas* is attached to the grille.

Q: I wonder if I could take your picture in front of your truck?

Miss R: Oh, no! I don't let anybody take my picture . . . I don't like the way I look in a photograph! Now don't get me wrong, I believe in being friendly with people . . . but I just don't allow people to take my picture.

Q: Okay, that's fine with me. But could you tell me something about yourself? Do you live around here?

Miss R: Oh sure . . . I went to school right over there [pointing to the former Indian school building]. I went for the first nine grades . . . then I went to Holly Hill for the tenth and eleventh grades [a frown appears on her face].

Q: Why did you not finish?

Miss R: I just couldn't take the way they shamed me . . . It was the students . . . the white students.

Q: Why did they, do you think?

Miss R: Oh . . . it was the way I dressed . . . It was my poor clothing, I guess . . . you see, my mother always dressed me like she did my brothers. I used to work the fields like my brothers did . . . guess I was a tomboy type. Those white kids didn't like that . . . I wore a work shirt and old jeans—but clean ones—to school. [pause] Sometimes I used to think they shamed me 'cause I was Indian . . . can't say for certain about that, though.

Q: What did you do after you quit school?

Miss R: Oh . . . I worked at home . . . you know my daddy has some land—he still has a big garden—and we had farming to do. Then I got a job in Holly Hill at a shirt factory . . . I worked there for twenty-two years, but then it went bankrupt and of course I got laid off. But worse than that was I lost all my money in their retirement program . . . I lost eight thousand dollars of my hard-earned money! [she says with bitterness] . . . but now I've got another job . . . over at St. George [some fifteen miles away] . . . I've worked there for two years now.

Q: How is the White Oak Community doing?

Miss R: Oh, it's different than when I was growing up . . . it's losing its ties . . . as a community. Even blood relatives don't stick together like when I was a child . . . [pause] . . . don't know what will happen . . . some people still live here but [have] got to travel long ways away for jobs . . . like Willy was telling you. You know, he was born at Four Holes but married a White Oak woman.

Q: But you still live here?

Miss R: Oh, yeah. I live down Fire Tower Road.

This ends our conversation. On this cool, overcast Sunday I watch Miss R get into her truck. I am wishing that I could talk her into a portrait of herself and her truck, but I cannot seem to summon up the courage to ask her again. She slowly drives off. It is the Sunday before Christmas Day and there have been, even for this small congregation, a large number of people in the parking lot. Some are still there talking, leaning against their cars and trucks. There are a few children racing around their mothers, who are trying to get their husbands' attention. It is lunchtime and people are getting hungry. In fact, I have hopes of talking with Oscar Pratt, the current chief. I do not see him and decide to go to Holly Hill for lunch.

In the afternoon I return to the White Oak area and to the Pratt's home—a trailer that sits next to a large field that obviously is being farmed. But when I knock I find out from his wife, Ruby Pratt, that he had to go out of town. So she and I get to talking as their dog gives me the sniffs.

Q: That's a beautiful dog you have. What kind is it?

Mrs. Pratt: He's a husky . . . he won't hurt you, he's friendly . . . doesn't he have pretty blue eyes! His name is Smokey . . . I sure love him . . . [there is a pause as a sad look comes over her face] . . . The vet says that we should be giving him heartworm pills . . . you know in this warm part of the world he could real easy get that disease . . . lots of mosquitoes around.

Q: But why don't you?

Mrs. Pratt: [Sighs] . . . Well, oh . . . Oscar says we can't afford those pills . . . they are expensive. We have lots of expenses . . . [her voice trails off as she looks at the dog].

Q: Yes . . . someone told me that your son has some health problems.

Mrs. Pratt: That's true . . . he needs an operation . . . because he was born without a regular jaw . . . so he doesn't have many teeth . . . he can't chew his food! All he can eat is food ground up, or baby food and liquids. [sighs] . . . You know he finished high school and he's looking for a job, but . . . [her voice trails off]. Now my other son is twenty-four and he's doing real good . . . he's got a good job and started a family . . . so now, these are my babies [referring to her handicapped son and the dog].

Q: Have you always lived here?

Mrs. Pratt: Well, it seems like that . . . Oscar is always promising me to build a nice new house . . . but all our money has to go to take care of things . . . and what's left over goes for buying land and for keeping the farm going.

Q: How much land do you own?

Mrs. Pratt: Well, right now it's something over one hundred acres, I think . . . but I think he's looking to buy more . . . he keeps real busy . . . he works over in Walterboro every day and then he comes home and works the farm at night . . . you talk with him, he'll tell you all about it.

Q: Well, thanks for taking your time for me; I wonder if I can do your portrait with Smokey?

Mrs. Pratt: Oh, oh, no! I don't want my picture taken. The only time I will allow my picture to be taken is when I get my driver's license . . . [laughs] . . . Did you know, did anyone ever tell you that some of the folks at the church didn't like that picture you took of them? That was some time ago . . . yes, that was five or six years ago.

Q: No one said anything to me. What was it they didn't like?

Mrs. Pratt: Ah . . . well . . . I'm not too certain . . . can't remember exactly . . . I think it was to do with the way the picture showed how the carpet looked so worn out.

I thank Ruby Pratt for letting me in on things and take my leave. I decide to drive once again to Hudson Crummie's house. When Hudson was chief, he along with the leadership of the Edistos, Pee Dees, and a Greenville urban Indian association joined the Council of Native Americans. However, in 1982 Hudson lost out as chief of the Santees. Now, in 1991, the council has a new director, a Lumbee Indian named Murphy Woods, and Hudson on this day talks about the trouble he has allowed himself to get into because of the new director.

Hudson: Murphy Woods sure knows how to work me with a long spoon!

Q: I'm not sure what you mean by that.

Hudson: Oh . . . it's an old saying . . . it means that one person gets the most out of someone else without having to give up much in return or getting his own hands dirty . . . let the other person get his hands dirty!

Q: Yes, I see what you mean. How does that work with Murphy and you?

Hudson: Oh, it's a long story, and well . . . the law might be getting into it . . . I just can't tell you much . . . it's just that Murphy came to me and wanted to know if I would like to be on the council payroll. He said that he had grant money he could spend on research. Well of course I was interested, but I wanted to know what was really behind it . . . later I found out that Oscar [Chief Pratt of the Santees] and Matthew [Chief Creel of the Edistos] and some of the other chiefs on the council were causing Murphy some problems. That's because they were questioning how Murphy was using council money.

Q: Are there any other things going on?

Hudson: Well, the usual things. I'm getting older and gimpier. White Oak isn't doing so well . . . it's unemployment that hurts us. People have to leave to find work somewhere else. Offhand, I know of three families who left recently . . . to Charleston . . . even to Florida . . . we call them the scattered people.

With this gloomy picture I take leave of Hudson Crummie. I returned to the community a number of times but never did catch up with Hudson who, it seemed, was always on the go in his red pickup truck. One time, a year later, I spotted his truck roaring down a dirt road. There was a plume of reddish dirt spinning up from behind. That was my last glimpse of the former chief.

After Hudson Crummie and for nearly twenty years, the chief of the Santees was Oscar Pratt. I have had conversations—some short, some long—with Chief Pratt at irregular intervals during these past twenty years.

8. Oscar Pratt, Chief (retired), Santee, 2003

My first impressions of Chief Pratt were that he was a quiet, background person who might be difficult to interview. I based this opinion upon observations of him at various Council of Native Americans functions, where he rarely volunteered any comments and quite often kept himself to the side.

However, when we spoke on a one-on-one basis, he became open and outspoken, especially about the difficulties that he and other Indians faced every day of their lives. My most recent conversation was in 2004, when he was no longer chief. The following is a compilation of all these interviews.

Q: Chief Pratt, what do you think is the main obstacle for Indians in this area?

Chief Pratt: [without hesitation] It's the prejudice against Indians. It's not real obvious maybe but when you look at who works at the cement companies—there are three in Holly Hill—and they pay the best wages, you won't find any Indians . . . except for one and he is from North Carolina. With the civil rights law, some blacks can get hired . . . but under a quota system, of course. But when a job comes up, it goes to a friend or family . . . of white folks. When we ask for a share, then they tell us we are not Indians . . . "There ain't no Indians anymore," they say. "Do you want to be called a black, then maybe we can work you in," they tell us. How come the civil rights laws aren't applied to Indians, I ask! If we want a decent paying job we got to travel away from Holly Hill . . . Look at my brother, Jimmy. He does construction work down at Charleston . . . that's close to 150 miles a day he has to drive.

Q: He spends a lot of money traveling that far every day.

Chief Pratt: He sure does . . . he should be working nearby . . . there are many good people right here on Fire Tower Road who would be good managers, supervisors, foremen—like me—but they never get a chance . . . 'cause they're Indians . . . but that's why some folks can pass for white and do.

Q: You say you are a foreman. How did that come about?

Chief Pratt: Well, first of all, that's not at a cement plant . . . by the way, Indians can get hired here at the wood products plant but the best they can get is four dollars or five dollars an hour . . . and [these wages] never go up much! For me, I have to travel to Walterboro every day [eighty miles round trip]. That's where I'm a foreman . . . it's for a company that makes modular homes . . . I've been there a long time and proved myself and now I get around eighteen dollars an hour. I've had better offers up in North Carolina . . . but I don't want to move from White Oak.

Q: Besides your foreman's job, you are a farmer. Could you tell me how that is going? What do you grow?

Chief Pratt: Oh, that's going okay, but I don't make much on my farm . . . I raise corn and soybeans and I've got about one hundred pigs . . . I feed them the corn I raise . . . my cornfield is over by the house . . . here on this land. Besides the pigs, I raise soybeans. [Then with some embarrassment he says] I save off two acres for not planting soybeans . . . you see . . . the government gives me six hundred dollars for not growing as much soybeans . . . as I could [short nervous laugh].

Q: How much land do you own?

Chief Pratt: Well, I started out with some land next to our house and I've been adding land when I could. A lot of that land was owned by my father and my grandfather. A lot of Indians held land but lost it back . . . that was some time ago. For some time now I owned well over sixty acres. Then in 1992 I bought sixty more acres . . . I've got a friend—a white man, a good man—who lent me the money . . . he works for the bank . . . I borrowed fifty thousand dollars for those sixty acres . . . I couldn't have paid for it if he hadn't lent me the money. [He laughs] You know, at work they call me JR . . . you know that guy in *Dallas* who's always buying up land.

Now let me tell you this . . . I've got some black friends, I've got a lot of black friends and they tell me this, that when their relatives or friends moved up to New York they . . . or some of them . . . wanted to come back. But they couldn't because they had sold or lost all their land . . . they had no land to return to. But I don't want that to happen to my family or other Indians who came from here, but moved away . . . you see, there's a lot [of] my people [who] have left here, and if they want to return, then they'll have a place to come back to.

Q: How big a family were you born into? When were you born?

Chief Pratt: Well, my parents, they had twelve children . . . six boys and six girls . . . but only three live around here. I was born in 1940.

Q: So land ownership is very important to you. Does the tribe own any land in common?

Chief Pratt: Oh . . . well, there's that little bit over there next to the church . . . where the old school building is . . . and around it . . . about half an acre maybe . . . not much.[13]

Q: Did you go to school there?

Chief Pratt: Sure . . . we all did . . . course I only went the first nine years, then I went to Holly Hill . . . finally got my high school diploma . . . I went at night to earn it . . . two nights a week I went.

Q: It seems that there are fewer Indians in White Oak than ten or twenty years ago; am I correct?

Chief Pratt: Yeah, that's so . . . some have moved out . . . to find work. Others though have moved out 'cause they thought they could bet-

> ter themselves . . . by not being Indian. [pause] We've got some people who are Indian when they think they can get something, otherwise they are white. Now you got to understand some pass for white when they might have a better chance for a good job . . . I guess that's hard to blame them . . . but if we could get our children to have a better education and get a fair chance at a job and be proud of being an Indian . . . well, that will bring people back to the community.
>
> Then we can live like Indians . . . I don't mean like in teepees and that way. We just need to live a normal life and be looked up to, not down to . . . we just want to be what we is![14]

Chief Oscar Pratt's vision of a thriving community of Indians has not yet materialized. In a 2004 conversation he informed me that he was no longer chief of the Santees and that the White Oak Community continues to grow smaller. But Oscar is fulfilling a long-held promise to his wife. He is building a new, two-story, high-peaked home for his patient wife. In a 1993 South Carolina Educational Television program Oscar stated that he had been married for twenty-seven years and all that time he promised his wife a nice house in which to live. By 2005 the house was nearly finished, though they had yet to move in as the plumbing and electricity were not complete.[15]

The new house sits near their double-wide in a portion of the cornfield. It sits across the flat field from Fire Tower Road, the church, the tribal office, and the white oak tree in plain view of all those who drive by. For the rural area that surrounds his house it stands as a symbol for brutally hard work and determination. For Oscar and his family it is also a symbol "to be what we is."

At the beginning of the twenty-first century the Santees elected a new leader. Chief Roosevelt Scott petitioned the state Minority Affairs Commission for the Santees to be recognized as an Indian tribe. Because of all the historical and other background work done by its leaders and members and by a number of other contributors such as Helen Amerson, as well as Wes Taukchiray (back in the 1980s), Chief Scott was able to put together an excellent petition.

On January 28, 2006, an Associated Press release announced that the Santee Indian Nation—some six hundred strong—had met all the criteria to be accorded recognition as a South Carolina Indian tribe. Chief Scott was quoted as saying: "We're finally getting to be what we really are. Before we acted like we were ashamed to be Indians."[16]

4
The Edistos

Very near the confluence of Four Holes Swamp and the Edisto River, which is called the Pon-Pon by old-timer Indians, are two American Indian communities, one on either side of the river that forms the boundary between Colleton County to the west and Dorchester County to the east. This land up and down the river is at times swampy and at other times hard and crusty; places are overrun with scrubby growth and loblolly pines. The cleared fields do not look fertile. Often mounds of fire ants rise up in the fields. The air can be heavy with humidity. This is pine-barren country, the low country of South Carolina.

For nearly three hundred years of recorded history this land has been home to small groups of Indians. The river was rich in fish and the swamps yielded game for hunters and cypress trees for paddles and canoes. Certain plants and roots yielded herbs for medicines. Many Indians were driven here to avoid the multiple pressures of colonial and antebellum powers. In the 1700s, remnants of local tribes, especially the Kusso (or Cussow), settled in this difficult area. In 1711, the colonial power in Charleston awarded the Kusso a small reservation as "land laid out to the Cussow Indians."[1]

Other southeastern bands arrived in this area. In particular, in 1747, a band of about fifty Natchez Indians who had been driven from Louisiana arrived after surviving for a while in the high country of western North Carolina. They sought land and peace from the colonial government. Historians have referred to this Natchez band and other remnant groups who submitted to colonial authority as Settlement Indians. Other terms, not always intended to be flattering, were used then and into the civil rights era to define Indian identity. For the past thirty-some years, the Natchez-Kusso Indians of the Edisto River have called themselves the Edisto Indians.

Today, in mid-May of 2003, the sun is shining in the low country. The morning is getting warm as I observe a tribal get-together at the new Edisto Indian Medical Clinic/Tribal Center. Unlike their annual March festival with its large crowds, large circle for dancers, drummers, and ceremonies, and another circle for concessionaires, today's powwow is more like a large family picnic. Edisto Indian members have staked out under large pines and pin oaks with plots of land for their cars and trucks. Tables, chairs, and barbecue grills are set up. The air is beginning to float the odors of cooking food. There are one hundred or more people, with the promise of more to come.

This field where the clinic sits was once the site of a school building for Indians. The tribe bought this land of two acres from the school board for the nominal fee of five dollars.

On one side of the open circle stands a large temporary tent where there is a microphone. The chief of the Edistos, Matthew Creel, is talking to the slowly assembling group. I am standing in the shade of a very large, old pine tree next to the medical clinic, which was completed a few years ago. Sitting at a table in the shade is Johnny Creel, a former chief of the Edistos. A large, darksome cloud has hung over him for many years. Leaning against a tree is his son Glenn. We are in conversation. I have known Glenn since first taking pictures of him and his family in 1985. He is now thirty-six years old and a medical doctor, the first to come from the Edistos and perhaps the first Indian from South Carolina to become a licensed practicing physician.

The following interview is based upon our conversation on this day in May 2003 and upon a previous conversation.

Q: What path did you take to become a doctor?

Dr. Creel: I was admitted to medical school eight years ago but not right after finishing undergraduate school [College of Charleston, 1991]. I didn't do so well on the exams the first time so I got teaching jobs in Colleton County. I taught math, science, chemistry, physics, and biology at two different schools during those four years. I kept studying for the medical exams and teaching helped me a lot to prepare for the exams. Finally I did well and got into the Medical University of South Carolina [Charleston]. I graduated in 1999.

Q: What was your specialty for your internship?

Dr. Creel: I decided to go into family practice and I have a practice in Walterboro and have privileges at the Walterboro Hospital and I come here to this clinic twice a month on a pro bono basis.

9. Dr. Glenn Creel, Edisto, 1992

We have another doctor who comes here also . . . and I have been pastoring for seven years now at the Little Rock Holiness Church.

Q: I remember taking photos of you and your wife and child at the Edisto Indian Church of God [in Four Holes]. Do you remember that?

Dr. Creel: I guess so. But I am pastoring in my family's church now.

Q: How did you decide to become not only a medical doctor but also a pastor?

Dr. Creel: I had wanted to become a preacher for a long time and then I had a dream and the dream told me my missions in life.

At this point I am relating this dream as Dr. Creel stated it in a 1993 South Carolina Educational Television documentary:

> Well, I had this dream about going fishing and fish represent souls. Then the dream changed to the Edisto River and on the bank were two young boys, and some woman came along and said something that offended them and they jumped into the water and the water was rough along the edge . . . and I jumped in and began to coach them to swim on their backs and they were okay. After the dream I swore my life to Christ and to medicine at the same time. Up 'til then I didn't know if I was throwing away my life . . . was medicine, as hard as the study of it was, the right thing? Lord, am I in your will? That night of the dream He confirmed that I was going to use medicine to heal the physical and the ministry for the spiritual part of the people.[2]

Now it is back to my interview.

Q: Are you the first Indian from South Carolina to become a medical doctor?

Dr. Creel: Well, I am, I guess, the first to finish medical school and do an internship and pass exams in my specialty, which gives me full licensing including hospital privileges. But I went to medical school with Theresa Williams, who completed medical school but did not complete an internship . . . she can serve in a general practice but without hospital privileges.

Q: Where is she from? Where is she now?

Dr. Creel: She was a Santee Indian but I have lost track of her. She was in a different class than mine and I'm not sure where she is. And, oh, there was a Lumbee . . . his name is Thomas Maynor and he became an MD, but last I heard he went to Nevada.

Q: Did the issue of the Indianness of you and the other two Indians ever come up in medical school?

Dr. Creel: Not really [laughing]. We were all too busy trying to survive, to get through.

Q: Excuse me for asking, but when did being an Indian become important to you?

Dr. Creel: Oh, sometime when I was young . . . in school. But the really bad thing was when someone would ask us what kind of Indian we were. I would usually just say an Indian, or most of the time, just say which Indian was the majority . . . Cherokee or something like that. All I knew was that I was an Indian. I didn't know which kind. Then recently we discovered, we found that the Natchez-Kusso Indians were where we were descended and we adopted the word *Edisto* because we live on the river . . . It touched me to learn of other Native Americans and of their tribes [and how] we are like a united person.

Q: I have been told that drugs are making inroads in Four Holes.

Dr. Creel: Before, it was alcohol and guns that were the big concern. Now it is crack. Within eyesight of where we are standing [at the clinic] there is a crack house. We are getting together with the Ridgeville police to raid it. Crack is destroying things. It is getting to the young people.

Q: Who runs the crack house? Who brings crack there?

Dr. Creel: Outsiders [ominously].

I want to ask more questions of Dr. Creel but other events that day intervene. I want to ask him how the young people get money for crack. One source, not an Indian, tells me that nearly 70 percent of the young men are unemployed at Four Holes. Further, rumor has it that a few women have become prostitutes.

On this day the chief of the Edisto Indians, Matthew Creel, is at the microphone. He is talking to the gathering about his cousin Johnny Creel, Dr. Glenn Creel's father. Johnny, who is now sixty-seven, is a former chief of the Edistos. In a highly disputed election ten years ago, Johnny lost his bid to become chief of the tribe. He lost by one vote to Matthew and, certainly, some bitterness resulted. A few years after this disputed election, Johnny sided with the then-director of the South Carolina Council of Native Americans, who was charged with financial corruption. Johnny's association with this man, as well as his unpopular effort to unseat Matthew, resulted in his disgrace. He became for a long time persona non grata, at least in the Four Holes part of the tribe.

However, on this warm spring Saturday in May, Johnny Creel has been invited to attend this tribal picnic and festive occasion at Four Holes. His cousin the chief, who is up for reelection this year, is now asking Johnny to come up to the microphone. Matthew presents a plaque to Johnny in commemoration of all the work he has done for Creeltown and the entire tribe in more than twenty years of service. Johnny appears somewhat surprised about this ceremony and all its implications. His voice sounds grateful as he thanks Chief Creel and the assembled Edisto members.

As Matthew recedes from the microphone, Johnny says he wants to sing his favorite song: "Make a Joyful Noise." So after a pause, then with a voice deep and oddly somewhat sad given the song's title, he begins to sing his favorite spiritual song. His voice is impressive singing a capella, and everyone is quiet and attentive. As the song progresses, we feel the weight of disapproval rise off Johnny Creel's physical presence, off his sad spirits. The song is both joyful and, oddly, mournful at the same time.

Then it is over and he says as an awkward apology to the picnickers, "I tried as best I can, even though I am not a good singer." As he stands there, first there is silence and then clapping. He walks away from the microphone and comes over to be under the big pine tree with his son, the doctor and minister. He looks content. There is a faint smile on his face as he looks at his son. He looks a lot less tired as he goes over to a table in the shade of the clinic, and his wife brings him some food. It is noon and the picnic is on. I talk Dr. Creel into going inside the clinic for a photo session.

Now is a good time to write more about the history of the Edistos. In the mid-1700s when the Settlement Indians were living near the Edisto River in Colleton County, as a matter of record, about one-fourth of the slaves in South Carolina were Indian.[3]

It was imperative for free Indians, the Settlement Indians, to find land of their own—to find, literally, common ground—however humble. One can assume that becoming part of an established Indian community was also a means of escaping enslavement. Another means of preventing enslavement was to carry an affidavit of Indian descent, a passport for Indians in their own land. Wes Taukchiray found such a document for an ancestor of Eddie Martin, a former chief of the Edistos—an 1854 affidavit of Indian descent belonging to Chief Martin's great-grandfather, John Hozendorff Martin.

John Hozendorff Martin lived near Walterboro, which is near present-day Creeltown. Not far away is the "land laid out to the Cussow Indians." This land, this reservation, awarded in 1711, was lost before the Indian Non-Intercourse Act of 1790. Wes Taukchiray and I both believe this land is now owned by a paper company.

The first settlement of the more contemporary American Indians of this area was called the Osbourne Indian settlement, which existed from about 1840 until the 1920s. Concurrent to this community was Creeltown, which appears in the 1850 census with nine Creels and two Davidsons. By the 1900 census there were twenty-five Creels, four Tracys, and eight Martins, all Indians.[4]

Creeltown is said to be the mother of Four Holes, which is across the Pon-Pon in Dorchester County and first shows up in the 1910 census with five

10. Eddie L. Martin, Chief (retired), Edisto, 1984

households of Indians. Georgia Muckelvaney, an Indian girl from Creeltown, at the age of fifteen identified twenty-five Indians there. Georgia married Gene Davidson and later became the Four Holes historian.[5] Yet some of the Indians in Four Holes came from the Osbourne community, Georgia's husband being one, which could make the Osbourne settlement the grandmother of Four Holes. Regardless, the Edistos can trace their roots well into the Indian past.

Back at the picnic now Johnny Creel has finished his lunch and I join him. The following comes not just from conversations on this day in May 2003 but also from previous conversations going back to 1985.

Q: You were born and reared in Creeltown. When people talk about their past does anyone talk about the Creel name?

Johnny: Well . . . we never thought about it much until Wes White [Taukchiray] told us that he had found out that we were probably related to Natchez Indians [who] might have talked in

Creole . . . or were Creoles from Louisiana. And maybe . . . along the way, *Creole* became *Creel*.

Q: When I first met you, you were working for Hercules, that chemical company. In fact, they call themselves a forest resources company. What were you doing for them?

Johnny: Well, I was harvesting stumps. I had worked my way up to be a foreman . . . There are stumps from a certain kind of pine tree we call "lightners." These are old trees that have been cut down and the people who did it left the stumps in the ground . . . and I was hired to find them stumps because not all stumps have all those resins in them.

Q: Why are the resins valuable?

Johnny: 'cause they get all kinds of chemicals from these stumps. They make turpentine and varnish and even medicines from the lightner stumps. Very valuable . . . but getting scarce.

Q: How long did you work for Hercules?

Johnny: I guess nearly fifteen years and then they decided to get out of the stump business. They offered to sell me all the stump-pulling machines and the truck we used to take the stumps in . . . and I borrowed money and got it and started my own business.

Q: How long were you in the business?

Johnny: I guess it was about four years . . . but a lot [of] bad things happened and I lost it all . . . Now I work for the county . . . I operate a bush cutter . . . for three years now . . . I keep busy . . . even though I have some sugar [diabetes]. I have to be careful and take my medicine . . . yet I still work . . . I like it . . . I get out there and work.

Q: Back in the 1980s you told me that Creeltown had no good sewage system or water supply. Is that still true?

Johnny: Well, we have good water now in Creeltown . . . but not public sewage . . . still a septic system, which sometimes is not good.

Q: Is Creeltown still a safe, quiet place?

Johnny: Yes, it sure is . . . Glenn [his son] is building a house next to mine. That sure is good.

I take a lunch break and then catch the eye of Chief Matthew Creel. He appears in good spirits and seems hardly any older, except for some grey hair, than when I photographed him in 1983 and again when I had this 1994 conversation with him:

Q: Chief Creel, how is the Four Holes community doing?

Chief Creel: Four Holes is a better community since twenty years ago . . . 'cause there is less alcohol being used . . . makes Indian people get violent . . . and the churches are stronger now . . . people are praying more. My church has a good minister . . . for seven, eight years now. He puts his own money back into it.

Q: Which church do you belong to?

Chief Creel: The Givhan's Pentecostal Holiness Church. More people go there now . . . When people accept Jesus, they can control themselves more . . . The other church [the Edisto Indian Church of God] has a full-time minister . . . can't see how they can afford him . . . They also have expanded some.

Q: What else is going on at Four Holes?

Chief Creel: That bar down there by the Church of God is out of business . . . about six years ago. People stopped going because they stopped drinking . . . but [we have had] some problems with the younger males . . . One [was] shot two weeks ago . . . He was fifteen years old . . . A bunch was drinking . . . an older one had a pistol. They were playing around . . . He took all the bullets out, he thought . . . but one [was] left in . . . Then the gun goes off . . . Police say that it was an accident.

Q: Are there any activities for the young people to do?

Chief Creel: Well . . . the young people are in a drumming and dancing group and the kids really like it . . . My older son was in it but he is in college now [Southern University, a Baptist-supported college in Charleston]. Now Matt Junior is dancing and drumming.

Q: What is the major problem facing Indians here?

Chief Creel: Well . . . the economics over the past ten to twenty years is better . . . but the major problem is housing and sewage. Four Holes has a septic system . . . very poor because the soil doesn't give. You know it doesn't seep into the soil and break down . . . It backs up or finds a trench to seep to. We need federal recognition to get Indian money to create a modern sewage system.

Q: Have you gotten any help for this from the local government or the state?

Chief Creel: You can't believe the government [in an agitated voice], but Indian people have to blame themselves . . . They always accepted whatever the government handed down. The government built them a school. It had white teachers. They accepted that.

Q: To change the subject, how many people are on the Edisto roll?

Chief Creel: Almost eight hundred on our current roll, but we need to take out people who aren't Edisto . . . It sure is painful to ask people to leave the roll even if they don't belong . . . You see, a good and proper roll of names is the most important way of recognition as Indians.

Q: What are the Edistos' chances of getting recognition?

Chief Creel: Oh . . . I think that they are good . . . about five years away if things go right.

Nearly ten years have passed since that interview and Matthew Creel and I are again in conversation at the 2003 picnic.

Q: It is amazing to see how young you look . . . how do you do it?

Chief Creel: Well [smiling], I keep busy . . . have been a contractor now for twenty-five years and I keep busy along with Pearl in running the tribe [Pearl, his wife, runs the day-to-day operations of the tribe] . . . and now Matt Junior is working for me in contracting so we'll all keep busy.

Q: This is the first time I have been in the clinic and tribal office and it looks good.

Chief Creel: Yes, we put it up real good . . . and there are other things that go on here . . . and the older community center too. We have an Adult Ed program going on and a program for seniors.

Q: How much land does the tribe own?

Chief Creel: Oh, there are two acres here and one acre at the old community center.

Q: I heard that the tribe has been able to get a sewage system for Four Holes.

Chief Creel: [Looking very pleased] Yes, we got a good system in . . . hooked up with Ridgeville [the closest town, population six hundred]. It cost one million dollars to get it down. We finished it [in] January.

Q: How did you get the money? From a state or federal grant?

Chief Creel: No . . . most of it came from the Methodist Church. We tried the government but didn't do so well . . . and . . . well, the biggest help came from the Methodists.

Q:	Well, good for them. What now is the current enrollment?
Chief Creel:	Well . . . I would have to check with Pearl but it is about 985. All of them are Edistos.
Q:	What is the most important task ahead?
Chief Creel:	We need city water. We are working on that . . . The water tower is okay, but not good enough. But the most important is to get federal recognition. We don't have state recognition either, but that is not as important as federal.[6]

Thus ended our interview. The Edisto picnic continues. It is now into the afternoon and I leave the picnic behind and drive toward the main street of Four Holes, Eagle Drive. On my left is the older community center. Back up that way Matthew Creel and his family live in a well-made two-story frame house. But I take a right turn on Eagle Drive and slowly drive by homes of people I know or once knew. On my right is the rundown, abandoned grocery store once owned by Gene Davidson, now deceased. Next to the old store is his wood-frame house—abandoned, damaged beyond repair in 1989 when Hurricane Hugo pummeled the roof, flooding and ruining the home that his wife, Georgia Muckelvaney Davidson, had so carefully, row upon row in their bright dining room, stocked with Mason jars of colorful vegetables from their garden in the back. All is in a state of decay.

I drive on and see some brick houses and single-wides and a few double-wides and the abandoned block-walled bar. Nearby is a side street and a wood sign painted bright white with clear lettering pointing the way to the Edisto Indian Church of God. Unlike the other church in Four Holes, the Church of God allows membership of those who have had divorces. The church is charismatic and I have witnessed an almost mystical ceremony of the laying on of hands. Beyond is a forest of loblolly pines and beyond that a state road, and crossing that road would lead to Four Holes Swamp, which has meandered its wet way to the lowlands from the sandhills of central South Carolina.

Then I find John Muckenfuss' double-wide and pull into his driveway. John gives me his big smile. He was born July 2, 1938, during the hard times of the Great Depression. I first met John in 1985 and at that time began a series of interviews and took his photograph outside his home of that era—a wood-frame house with peeling blue paint. Also, I photographed his daughter Lurleen (called Snooky by her friends). On one photograph I incorrectly spelled her name "Erlaine." In 1993, after I had finally gotten some of these photographs to him, I received this letter:

11. John Muckenfuss Jr., Edisto, 1992

Lurleen and I thank you very much for the photographs. You and your camera did a great job (smile). It is a great honour for you to use our pictures . . . However, I am looking forward to making an extra photograph.

My family and I are doing fine. I have more grands coming in now. I'm still living at the same spot. But I've purchase a new home back in 1991; almost sitting in the same spot. It is a double-wide mobile-home 28 ft × 52 ft. year model (1991). Hope to see you soon. Remember to make corrections on my daughter's name. It's not Erlaine, but it's Lurleen (Ha-Ha) O.K.?

Kind regards,
John Muckenfuss, Jr.

Now, in this late afternoon in May 2003, I am sitting in the living room of his double-wide. I take his portrait one more time. He is beginning to look his age and not his usual happy self. Today he is alone. His wife, his second, is at the picnic and his youngest child, a girl, nineteen, is at work.

My mind drifts back to 1985 to the photo session with his family. Lurleen had such a winning smile then. Does she still have that big smile?

Q: How is Lurleen doing?

John M.: Oh, she is doing fine. She lives here in Four Holes with her second husband . . . married David Creel first and they had two children . . . Well, things happen, don't they?

Q: How are you doing?

John M.: Well, I'm not doing so well . . . I've got sugar [diabetes] and the doctors say I have hypertension and my cholesterol is too high . . . and last year—in October—I ended up in the hospital with damage to my lungs.

Q: How did that happen?

John M.: I was cooking over there and there was grease in the pan and I was slopping it around and some spilled out and caught fire . . . a big ball of flame came up and [I] got some in my face and in my lungs . . . had burns on my face, my arms here . . . and on my hands. I was lucky to live.

Q: I hope that you have recovered.

John M.: Yeah, from that, but now I am getting cramps in my toes and sometimes in my legs and arms . . . even some muscle spasms sometimes. [He tries to smile gamely.]

Q: How do you like your double-wide?

John M.: Oh, I like it just fine . . . it's got good air conditioning . . . You know, the central kind . . . comes up from those grates, not those window units. You see, back in 1988 our house burned out and we got a trailer and then in 1991 we decided to take one of those consolidation loans to pay off a car and the single-wide and get this double-wide . . . but we can't make the payments and the loan office is going to repo everything . . . We are just waiting . . . months now . . . for them to come and evict us . . . just waiting to see . . . but I have a backup plan.

Q: Can you tell me?

John M: Well, I have a friend with an empty lot that I can rent for a low amount. Things will work out.

Q: John, I have known you for almost twenty years and Wes [Taukchiray] and Roger Manley [a researcher of American

Indians] have interviewed you, and they have told me that you had an interesting childhood; could you tell me about it?

John M.: Sure, I'll tell you. I told them, didn't I! I'll start at the beginning . . . When I was eighteen months old, my parents, who were very young and poor, gave me up for adoption. It was during the Depression. My parents separated and my mother gave me up. But my foster parents treated me good. When I was seventeen, they sent me to Voorhees College [a predominantly African American college]. They paid the tuition. I did okay at first. I majored in business administration because I wanted to work in a bank. But [I] got real slack in my second semester. Didn't do my homework and missed classes. So I failed. Then when I was eighteen, my foster father died and his wife—she and I never did get along—told me where my real roots were. Here in Four Holes as an Indian. Then I found my real family.

Q: But, John, that is not exactly how I heard it. There is something about your life being like Joseph in the Bible. Could you tell me about that?

John M.: Well . . . that is true that many people tell me that I am the Bible Joseph . . . It's because [of] all that I've been through . . . You see, here's what happened to me when I was a baby . . . My mother couldn't take care of me and took me to live with her cousin . . . Now, times were hard . . . and I was sold for money . . . one hundred eighty dollars, I think I was told . . . My real parents were Edistos . . . but my foster parents were black. I was raised for a long time thinking I was black.

Q: When you returned to your real family here in Four Holes, were you angry with them?

John M.: No [in an agitated voice], I was told how hard times were . . . I think, I think I was happy to be where I belonged . . . [His voice trails off.]

Q: The Bible Joseph was sold into slavery by his brothers and yet was able to move up and become a leader. Is there any of this in your life?

John M.: Maybe. [He smiles.] I know that when I was around twenty years old, I decided to do a survey of how many Indian people lived in Four Holes . . . That's important to keep up.

Q: What else happened in your life that you can tell me?

John M.: Well, I remember that I was drafted into the army in 1969 . . .

for two years . . . I also remember being in Texas and segregation was still strong . . . but not in the military. I remember once going into a restaurant with a white guy, another soldier. I remember the waitress saying to him, "I'm sorry, we don't serve his kind," is what she said. I'll never forget it. So I pulled off my hat to show my hair and said, "Lady, does this look like a Negro's hair!" So I got served . . .

I have darker skin than a white but my birth certificate says that I am white. It should say Indian but when I was born . . . they didn't seem to consider that . . . You know when I got out [of the army], when I was twenty-four or twenty-five, I went up to St. George and had my birth certificate changed to read Indian . . . and now . . . now I have an Edisto Indian tribal card and have had for a long time.

Q: So when you got out of the service, you came back to Four Holes. What kind of work could you find?

John M.: We would travel down to Charleston to work at the shipyards and things like that . . . And my father taught me how to fish and hunt and trap, even make a cypress paddle . . . You know he did all that most of his life. He was really good at it.

Q: Well, John, it is getting kind of late in the day. I need to be going.

John M.: Am really glad you dropped by . . . Send me some photos . . . You know, soon I will be sixty-five and maybe I'll get some more Social Security. I want to live until I am at least seventy and by then the good Lord comes for me, I'll be willing to go . . . but not before seventy.

He looks at me very seriously, and then a smile comes across his handsome face. The biblical Joseph was sold into slavery by his jealous brothers. He also had potent dreams and aspirations that came to fruition. But driving him also was the need to forgive and reunite with his family and tribe. John Muckenfuss' life can be seen in this light. The biblical Joseph, it is believed, lived to be 110. Will this be the case for John?

Today, as I get up to leave, the late afternoon western light is bursting into the double-wide's living room. I promise John a book when it is published. Outside of his home the air is moist and heavy. There are two dogs lying on the small outside deck. They look up at me expectantly, but quickly flop back in indifference. I walk to my car through scrubby grass. The air becomes filled with buzzing insects. Beside an outbuilding, I see John's garden.

My story of John is not over. Sometime later in 2003 I sent him some questions and photos, one taken in 1985 of him with Wes Taukchiray, three teenagers, and two children. In December I received this letter:

> Dear Gene: I received your letter today and I was surprised to hear from you. I'm glad you are ok and thanks for the photo of me, Wes and my children. This photo was taken a long time ago. Katie has a Boy 1 ½ years old. Tillman has two Boys and a Girl and he's in N.C. Wes White is all Grey now instead of Black hair. Irvin has a Son weighs over 200 lbs. Leslie has two Girls and I'm the proud father of seven Children and Granfather of thirteen Grand children. Irvin is in jail for child support. He Got over a year to do. No I don't have my double-wide no more. I lost it and 1 ¾ acre of land. I live over on the next lot. Right way my Garden was planted. I bought me a 14×70 mobile home. And I love it better than the doublewide. Write soon.
>
> Thanks,
> John Muckenfuss, Jr.
>
> P.S. the word you asked about has crack hit the commo [community]? Yes, and it's getting bad among the teenagers and young adults. But no fights and drive by shooting yet. But two car deaths.

The day after my 2003 interview with John Muckenfuss, on a Sunday morning, I am driving up a state road through St. George (population 2,200). I am looking now for a landmark to find the road that leads to Laverne Creel Knight's home. I pass by an area called the Indian Fields Swamp and recall that, according to Wes Taukchiray, some Pee Dee and Natchez Indians were given a hundred acres here some 250 years ago to form a reservation. Not far from this swamp I find the correct road and her home.

Johnny Creel has arranged this interview today. Laverne was once married to an Edisto Indian with whom she had three children. Now, though, she is married to a white man who has Alzheimer's disease. Laverne introduces me to him and he gives a wan smile. Here also this morning is her daughter Theresa.

Q: Laverne, thank you for inviting me into your home and talking with me. Could you bring me up to date on your medical condition?

Laverne: Well, when you took my picture, I was recovering from surgery for that blood clot to my brain . . . I remember that I wanted you to take my picture from the side of my face that was on the other side [with a nervous laugh].

Q: Are you still on medication?

Laverne: Oh, yes . . . I still have to get my blood tested all the time . . . The doctors say that I must keep taking the Dilantin and Coumadin . . . got to take the right balance . . . My house is a mess. [She looks around, embarrassed.] You see, I work six days a week. My brother Larry and I grow vegetables, and we take them to Walterboro to a farmers' market. It keeps us real busy but I sure like it . . . but soon I won't be able to work with my brother 'cause I will have to look after my husband . . . Don't know how I will pay for all my medicine . . . You see, I lost my health coverage when he had to retire. Now, my husband will get some Medicare for his medicines, but mine . . . well, the Lord will make a way to pay for mine.

Q: You are going through some hard times. Do you own this house?

Laverne: Oh, yes, I've lived here for nineteen years. But I was born in hard times . . . I was born in 1952 . . . My father was a sharecropper near Moncks Corner. Over there on the other side of Summerville . . . in Varnertown. I was reared in the segregation era. When my parents separated, I went to the Indian school in Creeltown. White kids had their bus, black kids had their bus, Indian kids had to walk. When you went doctoring you had to sit with the black sick people, not with the white, or alone. But my mother knew roots and herbs and did some doctoring. I don't remember how.

Q: What else can you tell me about your life then?

Laverne: Well . . . with my three children I lived on welfare and food stamps, which was just enough to pay for rent and some food . . . I was divorced by then . . . getting enough each month for electricity and clothes . . . very hard to do . . . I did gardening. Back then Indians felt that they didn't belong. We couldn't identify with blacks, and whites would not allow it. Indians were looked down on.

I look at Theresa, Miss Edisto Indian of 1987, whose portrait I did at that time, when she was fifteen. In fact, I have a group portrait of the 1985 contestants when she was runner-up and fourteen. Now, nearly twenty years later, she is the mother of three children and divorced.

12. Theresa Creel with son, Edistos, 1992

Q: Theresa, do you want to say something?
Theresa: Things are different now for Indian women. Sometimes you are treated a lot better if you have nice skin color. I get more respect now than when I was young. Sometimes it is an advantage to be an Indian woman.
Q: I remember ten years ago when I took your picture at the Creel Reunion, you were working at a truck stop at St. George by the interstate and were having trouble with that job.
Theresa: Yeah, I sure didn't like that job! [with a look of disgust] I didn't work there too long . . . The men would come in drunk a lot. Drunk men are hard to put up with. They were too nasty to me . . . really nasty.
Q: Would you change anything now, if you could, about your life?
Theresa: Yes, a lot [very sadly].
Q: It seems to be painful to think about what has happened to you.
Theresa: Yes, very painful.
Q: Could you talk about it?
Theresa: No, I can't [in a most definite way].

At this point we go outside for a photo session. We find a shaded area beside a high hedge under some trees. I take some photographs of Laverne and

Theresa together and then separately. Hovering way back by the house is the afflicted husband, slowly moving around. I am using fine-grain film to convey detail and subtle tones. Sometimes Laverne and Theresa are smiling, sometimes sad. They seem to want me to pose them and I want more spontaneous arrangements; perhaps we achieved some compromise.

Q: Laverne, you have a nice yard here.

Laverne: Thank you, I sure like it here. I've got a nice garden out behind the house. We are near Indian Fields Swamp. Did you see the sign? Some Indians used to live near here, long ago.

Q: Yes, I saw the sign. Tell me . . . do you have an Edisto Indian tribal card?

Laverne: Oh, yes. [very emphatically with pride] We both do.

Q: Are you going to vote in the next election?

Laverne: Oh, sure . . . but I want Enola Gay [Clark] to run. She would make a good chief. She's really good at being a leader. She listens to your troubles.

Q: How did she get her first name?

Laverne: Oh, she was born in 1945 about the time they dropped that atomic bomb on Japan. Her parents named her after the airplane, the plane that took that bomb.

Q: Theresa, back when I first took your picture, what was it you wanted to be?

Theresa: [A big smile on her face and then a laugh that seems ruthful] I wanted to be a photographer's model. I was fifteen then. [Her smile turns to a look of sadness.]

Q: You have three children now, but what are your plans after your children are grown up?

Theresa: Oh . . . I'm not too certain . . . maybe get some schooling . . . I never finished regular high school but I've got a high school diploma 'cause I passed my GED [proudly].

Q: Good for you! Maybe it is not my business to say this, but if you could find someone to look after your children, you could start taking classes sooner. [Her mother hears this and starts to move away from us and soon disappears into her home.]

Theresa: [A little uncertainly] Yes . . . okay. I will try to get some schooling . . . to get a good job.

Is she saying this just to please me? But we part and she gives me a big smile and I promise to send them prints. Then she heads to her mother's house and

I get into my car. Her stepfather comes around the house and gives me a pale, even empty, smile. It seems oddly fixed on his face.

Then, a sadness comes over me as I drive along the highway toward Varnertown, which is the subject for the next chapter. I think of Theresa and all the others I have talked with in the past two days. What secrets are there haunting Theresa?[7] Somehow I am reminded of the words of an elderly lady in Ingmar Bergman's film *Smiles of a Summer Night:* "You can never protect a single human being from suffering."

Her mother's destiny seems fairly clear to me. Perhaps this is what will happen. Laverne will look after her husband until she can't. He will be put in a nursing home and she will go back to raising and marketing vegetables with her brother. But Theresa's future is very unclear to me—I feel a mystery there.

Then, as I drive along, I think about Matthew Creel and how, probably, he will pass on to his son the family business and one day, probably, Matt will be chief. Johnny Creel's destiny seems clear also. Finally, he will find some contentment. He is again within the arms of the whole tribe. His son, the medical and religious leader, will work out his destiny there near the deep river of the Edistos, the Pon-Pon, and perhaps one day he will lead his united tribe into federal recognition.

As I motor down the flat roads of the Carolina lowlands, I think of John Muckenfuss, the Joseph of the tribe. Roger Manley, the researcher of Indian people, tells me that John has a vast untrained memory—a memory of at least 450 names of Indians but in no certain order. I hope this story with the photographs of John will honor him. I am sure that when he reads it, he will let me know.

5

Varnertown

On an overcast, chilly day in December 1938, the Farm Security Administration photographer, Marion Post Wolcott, age twenty-eight, came to Varnertown. Apparently she was not aware of the name of the village, because she recorded in her notes that she photographed the Clark family "near Summerville, South Carolina."[1] More precisely, Varnertown is over ten miles east of Summerville on alternate Route 17 between Carnes Crossroads and Moncks Corner.

Records show that Ms. Wolcott had been in Robeson County, North Carolina, during early December. On Christmas Day she was headed south and passed through Columbia in a rainstorm. The area of Summerville is some ninety miles south of Columbia, placing her at Varnertown in the late part of that month of 1938. Until then she had been in the South only four months, mostly in West Virginia.

Yet here she found herself at a farmer's home on Mimosa Lane. She took a series of seven photographs. One is captioned as "Indian Family near Summerville, SC, Dec, 1938."[2]

In this photograph are Geneva Varner Clark, age thirty-three, the mother, and three of her sons. We know it was a cold day, as Mrs. Clark is dressed in a long overcoat. She has tilted her hat-covered head to the right and snuggled into her thick and soft collar. Her arms are crossed in front with her hands tightly tucked under. Oddly, her left foot (in sturdy-looking shoes) is up on its toe. Immediately to her left is Melvin, age six, whose right shoulder and arm touch his mother's coat. To Melvin's left there is Hamp Jr., age twelve, holding their dog Smokey by the collar. On Hamp's head is a billed cap of a type typical of the Depression era. It reminds me of the cap worn by Henry Fonda in *Grapes of Wrath*. The cap throws his eyes into shade. As he leans sharply over to his right to hold the dog, his left foot extends far out to the left to keep his balance.

To the mother's right there is a fairly large open space and then there is Joe, age nine. Joe is capless as he stands fully upright with both hands buried in his pockets. His feet are spread apart, more than the others', and are planted firmly on the ground. His face looks grim compared to the others'. Missing from this photograph are Robbie, age four, and the father.

Behind the family is a clapboard house with a set of short steps leading to a porch. Four unsturdy-looking posts hold up the porch roof. On the right side of the house is a mud chimney.

The photographer also made a vertical picture featuring the mud chimney with the three boys plus Robbie. In this image Robbie is sitting on the side of the porch, facing the camera with his feet dangling down. He is wearing a white sweater and, oddly for the weather, short pants. His bare legs are crossed at the ankles. To his immediate left is Joe and then there is the chimney—wide, tall, crudely supported with posts and cross members. There is a large corrugated pipe rising from the top. Immediately to the chimney's left, the viewer's right, is Melvin, who is sitting on an extraordinary wide ladder, and then Joe, leaning up against the ladder, in a casual pose. His legs are crossed at the ankles.

This photographic image, more than the others, is a work of art. The visual composition is taut, with no wasted space, with formal structure, and filled with texture and detail. It reveals not just documentary information but also emotional depth. It raises the same question all good photographs did in that era: What will happen to these children?

But where was their father, Hampton "Hamp" Clark, age thirty-four? According to Robbie Clark, sixty-seven years later, his father was inside, not wanting to be in the photographs. In a seeming contradiction, Robbie, who was age four at the time, told me that the photographer was a man: "If there was a woman there, she sat in the car." Robbie went on to say, "I saw a puff of smoke after a flash . . . I was scared of the smoke and flash . . . My dad was watching out the window at him taking the pictures . . . He [the photographer] asked my mom her race and she said Indian . . . but my dad never liked pictures [of himself] . . . My dad was in the house with me . . . but the man taking pictures begged me to come out and let him take the picture . . . and my dad told me to go ahead . . . so I did and I set on the porch."

Robbie also reported that his father was a good farmer, raising corn, cotton, sugar cane, and vegetables. Robbie's mother was to have one more child, another son. By 2005, all but Robbie were buried about one mile away

13. Robbie, Melvin, and Joe Clark, Varnertown Indians, 1997

from Mimosa Lane in the Williams Cemetery with many other Varnertown Indians.

In November of 1997, fifty-nine years after Marion Post Wolcott came to Mimosa Lane, I first visited with Robbie Clark, his wife Ethel, and their extended family. The old clapboard house no longer exists, yet the Clark's current house also suffers the signs of aging, looking much like the original.

On this bright, warm autumn day, I take photographs of Robbie and his two older brothers, Melvin and Joe. They are standing against a tall wooden fence. The shock of time, of aging, never ceases to move me. Robbie is sixty-three, Melvin is sixty-five, and Joe is sixty-eight. As I take pictures I notice that on the fence behind them there is a small sign with a black background and in white block letters a single enigmatic word: *Hoover.*

After this session I wander around in the large yard. Behind a wall, I discover stacked in separate orderly piles tricycles, bikes, car parts, sinks, old toys, pipes, and odds and ends. It is the debris of some fifty years of use and accumulation. It is as if the family refused to separate themselves from any memories by stacking all the physical evidence into squared-up piles.

Then it is time to have a family group photograph. I am reminded of my own childhood when my immediate family would travel from near Pittsburgh, Pennsylvania, to Elmira, New York, for an annual family reunion marked by photographs, of course, done by a distant cousin. The large camera would be on a tripod. My cousin would dive under a large black cloth in order to check focus and composition. Then in a theatrical gesture he would whip the dark cloth from the camera and the top of his head (upon which sat a floppy black hat). It was as if he were a stage actor trying to attract the attention of his audience. Perhaps these events started my interest in the medium.

By comparison, I am using my little 35-millimeter camera. I suppose that to the Clarks, I would show none of the dramatics that my cousin once did. Now, there are twenty Clark family members gathered together. But this figure does not include their extended family, which numbered fifty-seven at the time. This number sprang from Geneva Varner Clark and her husband Hamp Clark.

Some last names in this family are Varner, Clark, Dangerfield, and Burbage. These names are part of the eight names associated with being a Varnertown Indian.

A typical and useful proof of Indian identity is the historical record. A family name, however Anglo-Saxon it may sound, is often a key ingredient of the historical records. For example, in the St. James Goose Creek Parish (which includes Varnertown), the last name of Tan is connected with being Indian.

Born around 1815 was a John Tan. One of his children, Valentine "Tine" Tan, was born in 1853 and still living in 1900. At that time Tine Tan was listed on the federal census as being Indian.[3]

And the Tan name is connected to Geneva Varner Clark. Her sister Mary Varner married a Henry Tan, who it is assumed was a relative of Tine Tan. William Varner married Mary "Mamie" Williams, also Indian, in the nineteenth century, and their son Raymond married Emma (or Ethel) Varner. Their son Carl Varner was born in 1930 with a birth certificate that states "Indian" as his "Color or Race."[4]

This is not the end of the story. William Varner and Geneva had a son named James Ben Varner, who married Jessie L. Broad, and their daughter was Annie Belle Varner (born in 1912), who married Sidney Clark in 1928. A few years later their child was listed in *The School Directory of South Carolina: 1935–36* as a student in the Pine View (Indian) School.[5] This school, a small, one-room elementary school, was situated north of North Charleston. Sidney and his family moved south from Varnertown to work as laborers at the Carolina Nursery and Florist near the school.[6]

William and Geneva Varner had another son named William Richmond Varner, who married Mary Jolly. Their daughter Geneva "Neva" Varner married Hampton "Hamp" Clark, the family in the Wolcott photographs. Furthermore, genealogical records appear to indicate that Robbie Clark and his family have Indian heritage on both sides of the family. His father Hamp Clark was probably the great-great-grandchild of a William Clark who in 1807 obtained two sworn affidavits of Indian descent on March 23 of that year. It is also important to point out that, according to Wes Taukchiray, William Clark was the son of an Indian woman living in the Charleston area and a member of the Catawba Nation.[7]

There is at least one other source of historical evidence to draw upon establishing Varnertown as a predominately Indian community. In 1896, *The State* newspaper published a letter by a McDonald Furman. Furman referred to an "Indian Church" at Varnertown (now the Gateway Community Church). In this same letter he referred to the Varnertown Indians and Indians elsewhere in scattered places in South Carolina, using a racial epithet meaning "Indian" in that era, that is, "redbones."[8]

These historical data are presented to help establish what the Varnertown community has always known—they have Indian roots. However, as the twentieth century unfolded not all of the Varnertown Indians asserted their Indian identity. Of course, some had for a time been "marrying out to white," as the term is sometimes used. But in more recent times some Varnertown Indians would "pass" for a white person and then for a variety of reasons return to defining himself or herself as Indian. One such person is the Reverend Arthur Clark, born in 1942 on Christmas Day, the son of Annie Belle Varner Clark, who has been mentioned already in this chapter.

On a humid, slightly overcast Sunday in May of 2004, I find myself outside The Full Gospel Mission Church at Cross, South Carolina. Cross is a rural village, some twenty miles from Varnertown, where a number of Varnertown Indians now live. I arrive at the church just after the morning service and introduce myself to Pastor Clark, who invites me into his church office. He tells me that his wife and he are looking after their grandsons today.

Q: Many thanks for taking your time to talk with me and answer my questions.

Arthur: Oh, it's nothing . . . anything to help out with our goals.

Q: I drove through Varnertown just now and talked with William Varner as to where I could find you and he gave me excellent directions.

Arthur: Yes, of course, I know William . . . he runs his own business. He's in the same business most of us are in.

Q: I asked him if he belonged to your tribe and he said that he "has enough to do as it is." What is the business that you mention?

Arthur: Well, I'm a carpenter and builder and of course a preacher. And my father was a builder . . . but he was a farmer first. He had . . . oh, around 150–200 acres . . . cotton was the main crop, the cash crop . . . and corn. And my granddaddy on my mother's side was a carpenter. Oh, I would say that the majority of men [of Varnertown] build houses or are farmers . . . William, the man you talked to, he's my cousin.

Q: A few years ago, I photographed Robbie Clark and his family . . . they are related to you, aren't they?

Arthur: Oh, sure they are kin . . . my uncle was Hampton Clark (we always called him Hamp), who is Robbie's father.

Q: Well, you keep busy: a carpenter/builder, pastor, and chief of a tribe . . .

Arthur: [correcting me] I was chief but no longer . . . it just takes up so much time . . . The position is open but Lisa Leach is the tribal administrative officer . . . you ought to talk with her sometime.

Q: Well, I'll try. What is the name of the tribe?

Arthur: It is the Wassamasaw Indian Tribe of Varnertown and Cross, South Carolina. At last count it was 165 [members].

Q: You have a tribal building?

Arthur: No, not yet . . . but we have land to build on . . . that'll come [the building]. You know, when I was chief I drove many times, for three years, up to Columbia for meetings . . . to work on state recognition. There were thirteen tribes trying to get recognition . . . then after three years it became around twenty . . . tribes would split off from each other. Finally, we had come to one standard [for state recognition] to be called a tribe: You've got to prove one hundred years of history as a tribe. In my tribe there are eight names associated with being a Varnertown Indian [he names some].

Q: Now, living in Varnertown, how many people are there?

Arthur: Well . . . [He looks at his wife, who has come back to the church office from their home] I guess there are about two hundred people . . . now about eighty or ninety of those are Indians . . . you know my mother is ninety-four years old, her name is Annie Belle Clark, and she is living history . . . see that's one hundred years right there . . . We had an informal organization in Varnertown . . . all that time. My mother could tell you a lot . . . and there's Ellen Varner, she's in her eighties and she has many stories [to tell].

Q: Most of the Varnertown Indians are proud to be Indians?

Arthur: Well, that's a good question . . . it's kind of hard to answer exactly . . . you know there's a lot of the older ones . . . they say, "I've passed for white all my life—I'm not going to change now" . . . But there's a lot of the younger ones who don't want to pass for white; they say, "I want the people to recognize me for who I am" . . . That's great because that makes sure that it will live on.

Q: I guess if the older people have their way, then being an Indian would die out?

Arthur: Yes, that's true . . . you know, I myself once thought of myself that way . . . My birth certificate says "white" on it . . . and I used to think "why not see it that way," but then that's not who I really am. I need to let people know who I really am . . . now, when I fill out forms, I put down "Native American."

Q: I suppose that the Civil Rights Act has had an effect on all this?

Arthur: Oh, I think the Civil Rights Act is fantastic for African Americans especially . . . but some people bend over backwards to make sure African Americans have their rightful place, but we have to fight the government, we have to fight individuals, we have to fight everybody just to get recognized. Our ancestors were born here and we are still trying to get recognized. Now with the [formation] of the Minority Affairs Commission we are with African Americans, Asians, and Hispanics, so we are all under the same canopy, and now when we want change we have the power backing us . . . There is a commission within the commission to approve of a tribe . . . it really should be Native Americans approving recognition by other Native Americans. Yet there are some people [Indian wannabees] who want to take advantage of the situation nowadays . . . But I think it is a shame for a person who is born Native American to prove they are Native American. Other ethnic groups don't have to prove anything, but we have to prove everything.

Q: But if your group gets state recognition, that will help, don't you think?

Arthur: Yes, of course. You know, there are three groups in this area. There are the Santees (right where we are, here at Cross, we are only eight miles from Eutawville), the Edistos, and us, the Varnertown Indians. Over the years there has been a lot of intermarrying but still all three are distinct groups . . . culturally there is a little difference . . . all of us are trying to get recognized.

Q: I understand that Will Goins has helped your group to get your petition organized and in other ways.

Arthur: That's true . . . he has been a big help for us, and others. His latest publication is *The People Speak* . . . I think you have at least one photo in it.

Q: Oh, I've not seen the publication. What stage is your petition in?

Arthur: Well, we've got a lot more work to do on this . . . Lisa is the best person to talk with on that.

Q: I wonder if you could give me directions to the Williams Cemetery. I would like to go there today and take some photographs. Would you like any prints that might help with your petition?

Arthur: Oh, yes. That would be wonderful. [Arthur and his wife then give me exact directions to get to the cemetery where so many of the Varnertown Indians are buried.]

Q: I know that I'm holding you up for lunch but one last question. Could I get you and your wife to allow me to take a few photographs?

Arthur: Oh, sure . . . is it okay to have our grandchildren in the picture?

Q: Oh, that's great. Let's go outside where the light is better.

And that is what we do. His two grandsons are excellent subjects, especially the older one. He begins to make faces for the camera. He even sticks out his tongue at times. Once, he pulls out his cheeks and crosses his eyes. His grandparents stand proudly behind the boys and may or may not see the antics. We finish the session outside the church and they all walk over to their home. I notice a large veranda to the front of the house. Like the house Oscar Pratt built for his wife, it looks new and stands out from the landscape.

Later that day, at the cemetery, I find the headstones of so many of the people I have heard about. There is Robbie Clark's mother, Geneva, who died in 1975, and his father, Hamp Clark, who died in 1968. Hamp was born in 1904 and "Neva" in 1905. There alone is proof of the Varnertown Indian

14. Stella and Arthur W. Clark with grandsons, Wassamasaw, 2003

lineage for at least one hundred years. These and other such thoughts flutter through my mind as I make my visual documentation.

However, the most striking scene I witness is the grave site of a young boy by the name of Joshua Shane Clark. He died at the age of eleven. I see his tombstone and then ten feet of a stone checkerboard pattern filled with tiny statues, all leading to a large statue perhaps five feet in height of a dancing nymph with two tiny children at her feet. The nymph is without clothing except for a long ribbon, which seems to spring from a small stone replica of a tree. The ribbon winds up the dancer's legs and across the front of her and then swoops behind the figure to her other upraised arm.

Suddenly a strong breeze kicks up and it begins to rain. For a second, it seems, I see the ribbon moving in the breeze. It is all in my mind, of course.

Are the statue and ribbon made of stone or some acrylic resin? For some reason, I dare not touch.

Just outside this *tableau vivant* of death and grief are a jumble of flowers, old burnt-out candles, and statuettes. Marking, circling, the limits of the entire scene are chairs and even old automobile tires. There is a feeling of great anguish.

It was only much later that I learned young Joshua had been driving down a county dirt road, at speed, in a three-wheel all-terrain vehicle. He came suddenly to a road-wide washout, a giant pothole, and in a split second tried, like a young Evel Knievel, to jump the gully, only to land short. His head pitched forward to smash on the metal handlebar. He died shortly after.

This terrible event has cast a shadow on the Clark family. Joshua was the grandchild of Robbie and Ethel. His mother's name is Robin. In 2005, I spoke with her about the incident. She told me that her son was in the care of a cousin and the cousin had a boyfriend who owned the three-wheeler. Joshua was not watched closely by the adults at the time. Robin later sued the county for not having filled the gully. Then she went on a search for the right statues to use at the grave site. Finally, she found what she was looking for in Georgia.

Those statues, those nymphs, represent beautiful maidens dwelling in the mountains, forests, meadows, and waters of some mythological time—this at least is the dictionary definition of a nymph.

Now, as I write this, the memory of the grave site still gives a powerful feeling. An outside source told me that one member of the family, an aunt, was so affected by the events that she would sit for hours at the grave site and even began to talk with Joshua (or at least his spirit). But later she gathered herself together and ceased her visits.

The story of this Clark family does not end here. In April of 2005, I received a phone call from Ethel Clark. She and Robbie were very angry because of an inflammatory, to them, article on the Varnertown Indians that had just been printed in the *Charleston Post and Courier.*[9]

It seems that the author, Bo Peterson, made reference to the 1938 photograph by Ms. Wolcott of Robbie's family and repeated the complete caption printed on the back of the photograph, including a racial epithet that Robbie's family takes with great offense (a different epithet from the one referred to earlier in this chapter). This epithet is considered by the American Indians I know, and by Wes Taukchiray, to be particularly offensive to this day. In fact, for some it is a fighting word. Out of respect for the individuals who have befriended me in my work, I have chosen to not include this racial epithet.

If readers want more information, I refer them to the rather offensive book *Almost White,* by Brewton Berry.[10]

The *Post and Courier* writer took it upon himself to offer a fairly common definition for this epithet, presumably as a lead to his main story. Regardless of the writer's motives, it infuriated the Clarks because of the historic denigration associated with the term: a person of mixed racial heritage trying to pass as white. Robbie Clark and all other Varnertown Indians who I know have always stated that Robbie's mother never tried to pass as a white person. She was always known to assert her Indian identity. The Clarks felt angry and helpless to do anything to correct the newspaper article, they told me.

On a positive note, the article, titled "Local Tribe Reclaims Its Roots," announced to the public, correctly, that the "Wassamasaw Tribe of Varnertown, Cross, South Carolina" had been awarded formal state recognition as an Indian group, stating, "The recognition doesn't count for much [materially]. It allows the Wassamasaw to label their work as tribal crafts for sale; it can open up some services and the possibilities of grants. No state funds are attached."[11]

Yet there are positive psychological effects. When the recognition was announced to whoops and cameras snapping, Richmond Clark was quoted as saying, "It was weight lifted off your shoulders." The recognition also gives to the Wassamasaw a formal seat on the state Minority Affairs Commission.

Although the name Wassamasaw has only been used recently, to the best of my knowledge, this is no "pop-up tribe"—a term used to describe the sudden rise of small local Indian groups. In fact, the tribal name comes from a historical swamp about twenty miles from Varnertown called the Wassamasaw Natural Area. It is a ten-acre swamp, a tiny portion of the extremely long-limbed Four Holes Swamp, with a two-acre island in the midst of hardwood trees such as tupelo and bald cypress with some maple, oak, and sweet gum.[12]

According to the historian Gene Waddell, this region was the territory of one of about eighteen independent tribes, once collectively called the Cusabo, in the South Carolina low country between the Santee and Savannah rivers. As a piece of speculation, the present-day Wassamasaw may have their tribal roots with the Sampa Indians, who according to Waddell's map were located in early contact times in this immediate region.[13]

For Robbie's family, who has just become aware of the Wassamasaw swamp, historical research of this kind is of no great importance. What seems to be more meaningful is the recognition of the Wassamasaw and the history, pride, and well-being of their immediate family.

Here is a combined 2001 and 2005 question-and-answer interview conducted with Robbie and Ethel Clark:

Q: Did you, Robbie, attend the Varnertown School?

Robbie: Yes, I attended that school from 1940 to 1944. I did not get much education, nor did my brothers. My dad never went to school . . . We quit school to work with our dad because he needed us to help him on the farm. The farm was good . . . We never went lacking for food. We might not have had all nice clothes like others did but we were happy just being at home helping our dad. And he would always help the older Varners out when they come to him for help . . . That's the kind of man he was . . . We used to get mad with him because he would [help others out] and they would not help him at all. We would say no, but Daddy, he'd say we had plenty of food.

Q: Ethel, did you go to school?

Ethel: I attended the Indian school in Summerville. It was called the Red School. I attended it from 1936 until we moved to Lincolnville . . . can't remember the year 'cause I was small. But I went to school at Ladson, and I quit there in 1946. When we moved [from Summerville] that's when everything and everybody became a problem with us and still some to [this] day.

Q: What kind of problems did you have?

Ethel: I had no problems with anybody when I lived in Summerville . . . not until my mom moved to Lincolnville . . . that's a very small little place. Then that's where I had problems . . . they would call us Indians and then bad names. We would tell our mom what they would say. She would tell us, you know what you are so try to get along, and we tried but that didn't help. So we did what we had to do and that was to fight.

Q: Robbie, did you have similar problems as a child?

Robbie: I did not have any trouble as a child because my dad always kept me and my brothers close to home . . . because he did not let us visit anybody's home because he did not want no trouble with other kids [even though] they were kin.

Q: Did your children ever have problems with others in regard to being Indian?

Ethel: Well, we once had some problems with kids who were kin because they would pick at our children . . . I could not understand that 'cause we are all kin . . . so we kept our kids at home and would not let them visit or play with those kids on that side of the road . . . anyway our children had a good childhood and happy children also.

Q: Do your children have birth certificates that say "Indian"?

Ethel: Yes, all our children do and some grandchildren. You know, I once had a Santee Indian tribal card . . . it's out of date now. Now Robbie and his brothers, they were all born by black midwives and they would put down on the birth certificate whatever they might think the baby was . . . back then there wasn't a place for putting Indian . . . my birth certificate just says "Baby Driggers" . . . that was March 31, 1931 . . . I don't know what Robbie's mother's birth certificate says but she always said she was Indian. You know our daughter Geneva is named after Robbie's mother.

Q: Robbie, what were your best memories of childhood?

Robbie: I liked staying at home and working on the farm with my dad and brothers . . . and my mother. We had it hard. I think how much my mother loves her kids and tells us how life was all about that and that makes me happy even today. She passed away in 1966 [actually it was June 27, 1975] . . . my mother would tell us how to treat people of all races well . . . but the best was when I had children of my own.

Q: The worst?

Robbie: Knowing that I would grow up and have to work outside in the world . . . no longer helping my dad on the farm and not knowing what it was like to work with other people out there . . . because working on the farm [was all I knew].

Q: Ethel, what are your best memories?

Ethel: To live at home with my mom and three brothers and having fun and knowing my brothers were there to help me with things I needed help with. I grew up with my three brothers and I grew up to be a tomboy. We had a good life with just the four of us with our mother.

Q: The worst memories?

Ethel: I did not know my dad. Because he passed away when I was three. And that made me angry. Because my brothers saw him and knew him but not me. Then my mother married Henry Clark. That's how I know about the Clarks, but that's when we moved to Lincolnville and we had a hard life . . . with him . . .

he never done anything right and was mean to us. He had a farm and we worked on it. And he was mean to our mother . . . Robbie's dad would tell my stepfather about it [to stop being mean].

Q: So through your stepfather is how you met Robbie?

Ethel: That be true.

Q: In 1997, when I took the family photograph, I remember one of your daughters was a student learning to be a dental technician. Did she finish her training?

Ethel: Dusty is not one of our children; she is my granddaughter. She had to drop out of school; she's married and has two children. Now she is a manager of a Scottsman store.

Q: How are your other grandchildren doing?

Ethel: All are very happy and doing fine: three are in grade school, one in high school. Becky Harwell is in college. Robbie Burbage works and has three children. Chad Burbage works and has two children. Erin Burbage is a housewife and has two children. Thanks for asking about them.

Q: I want to ask you, what do you think about that *Charleston Post and Courier* story about the Indians of Varnertown?

Ethel: There are mistakes in that story and the writer never called us after it was printed. We could have gotten it straight. Here's what Robbie and I think: They want to make a name for themselves, that's all they want.

In summary, even though there are many Clarks and other Indians with Varnertown roots who assert their Indian identity, there are other Varnertown Indians who repress this identity. Further, not all people living in Varnertown have Indian roots. According to Arthur Clark, the former chief, there are many people of Filipino background who moved here, some seventy years ago and since then, from Charleston, where they first found work at the naval shipyards.

However, there are other Indian influences on this core community. Foremost is a long-standing community of Indians who once lived in and around Summerville—today, no coherent group there is asserting its Indian identity. Any such assertion appears to be on an individual basis. One such case is that of Bubber Harmon, who owned a thriving business in downtown Summerville. Unfortunately, a fire in his apartment over his sporting goods store and restaurant, the Tee Pee, abruptly ended his life in the 1980s. He was well known for his assertion of Indian identity.

Another "neighbor" to the Varnertown community is Frank Pye. He lives in a village about halfway between Varnertown and Summerville on Crazyfeather Lane. He was born in the White Oak Indian Community (north of where he lives now by thirty miles). Frank became active with the Edisto Indians around 1964. Although not born to this tribe, they adopted him. How this came about, I once asked Wes Taukchiray. He said that Frank was a very hard worker for the tribe and "thinks like an Edisto; he is an Indian all the time." Because of his hard work for the Edistos and because he has made himself indispensable, Frank Pye has been the tribe's vice-chief since 1988. I believe that Frank acts as an inspiration to the other low-country Indians who for whatever reasons do not belong to an established tribe.

For Robbie and Ethel Clark, they appear to exist in a sort of tribal limbo. They have chosen not to join with the Wassamasaw because of long-standing differences within their Varnertown community. Yet they have indicated a desire to belong to some other tribe.

But what is not of the future, but of the present, is the reality that a tribe, some 120 miles to the north and east of Varnertown, has become established as the Waccamaw Indian People—centered in Conway, South Carolina, near Myrtle Beach—and they are the subject for the next chapter.

6

The Waccamaws

In February of 2005, *The State* newspaper ran a photograph of Chief Harold D. "Buster" Hatcher shaking hands with the state archaeologist, Jonathan Leader, after the South Carolina Commission for Minority Affairs voted unanimously to formally recognize the Waccamaw Indian People as a tribe. Chief Hatcher is leaning across a table, as is Dr. Leader from the other side, with their hands meeting halfway.[1]

Some 250 years have passed since the Waccamaws of South Carolina had official or historical tribal recognition. Disease, enslavement, and warfare pillaged a group that still had some six hundred members around 1720.[2] In 1755, Cherokee and Natchez raiders killed some Pee Dee and Waccamaw people who were living in settlements indicating that traditional tribal identity was becoming unglued.[3] Those Waccamaw Indians who had not been enslaved and who had not become "Settlement Indians" were escaping to join inland tribes, especially the Catawba. This entire process further weakened Waccamaw identity.

In 1752, the King of England ordered all owners to free their Indian slaves. Owners solved this potential economic crisis by labeling their Indian slaves as "Negro," a term that has had a profound impact on Indians for centuries, even until this day.[4]

In the antebellum era of the nineteenth century there were some free Indians, as there were other "free people of color," living in small groups—often near rivers—in the Waccamaw region. One such group was the Dimery Settlement, located five miles from the Little Pee Dee River in Horry County, South Carolina. Records indicate that in 1813 a John Dimery bought three hundred acres in Dog Bluff Township for fifty dollars. Chief Hatcher states that, in that era, Indians did not generally have Christian names, but in order to register anything in the courts, they had to assume one. Hatcher goes on to state in a 2005 letter:

> Another interesting fact is that John Dimery allowed many Native people to live on his land, but there is no record of anyone ever paying rent or leasing any portion of the land. This leads me to believe that the Indians who lived on or near there pooled their money to purchase the land and did so with John Dimery as their point of contact. These people likely lived on the land and for all purposes except legally, owned the land. However, since they had no rights as far as the government was concerned, their land was simply given to Joseph Lewis [a non-Indian] sometime after the Revolutionary War. That would have been after 1776 and the land was purchased by John Dimery in 1813, at most some 37 years later. This doesn't seem to me to be enough time for the community to disband and be rebuilt.

Hence, from the preceding it can be inferred that there was an Indian settlement at Dog Bluff well before the 1813 purchase and that John Dimery was in fact an Indian taking on a Christian name. Furthermore, after the purchase more Indians assumed Christian names such as Hatcher, Cook, Cooper, Turner, and others, and these surnames became associated with the Dimery Settlement.[5]

The people were farmers (cotton, corn, tobacco) and day laborers, with some tradesmen and craftsmen. News articles from 1887 refer to an existing Indian, Christian church. At its height the church had a congregation of over one hundred. According to Chief Hatcher, the settlement reached a high point of over one thousand men, women, and children.

At some point in the nineteenth century a school was created for the children of the settlement. This school later became known as the Pine Level School (Indian) and ran into trouble during the worst times of the Great Depression when in 1934 local county school officials, with the apparent reason of saving money, decided to merge Pine Level with an African American elementary school, calling the new school a "colored" one.

Vander Hatcher, husband of Gertrude Dimery (the granddaughter of John Dimery) and grandfather of the present Chief Hatcher, filed a lawsuit against the county. Just prior to the lawsuit Hatcher and some others in the settlement withdrew their children from the "colored" school and attempted to enroll them in the local white school. These children were not accepted and both the parents and their children were beaten and driven off, several times, before the lawsuit was launched.

The school board's response to this suit was to designate a group of individuals (of unknown race) to look, as a physical measure of identity, at each child and to decide their fate, their race being based upon facial features, color of their skin, and other traits. By this procedure, "In at least one case a brother attended a 'colored' school while his sister, with the same mother and father, attended a 'white' school."[6]

However, later, the Dimery Settlement was able to gain back the Indian identity at the Pine Level School. According to official records, in the 1938–1939 school year there were forty pupils, with the "Head of School" listed as Eugene Cooper, presumably a Cooper from the Dimery Settlement. However, by 1954–1955, the enrollment was down to eleven pupils, reflecting the slow demise of the settlement.[7]

The struggle to define one's Indian identity on the education front was but one portion of a larger problem. During the Jim Crow era of the twentieth century the law required that legal records such as birth and death certificates and school and marriage records list people as "white," "black," or "mulatto," with the term *Indian* not being officially recognized. Even beyond the Jim Crow era, it was not until 1987 that Indian graveyards were officially protected. As some Indians have noted, "We are the only race in this country that must prove who we are and are the most regulated people in America today."[8]

This historic struggle to define one's self as a human and Indian in the Carolinas, over the years, faced not only legal barriers but also stringent economic and social ones. This was especially the case with marriage between Indians and whites. The subject of miscegenation was fraught with alarm and repression. A newspaper article from 1905 gives a good insight into this topic, specifically here in Horry County, and not only for that era but well into the twentieth century:

> An investigation was held last Saturday in the court of Magistrate Joseph W. Johnson in the case of Julius T. Hatcher, who is charged in the warrant as being of the Negro race and intermarrying with a white girl. Absolutely no proof was made showing the presence of Negro blood in Hatcher's veins, but he was bound over to the court of General Sessions along with the Rev. Carroll who married them. The girl who married Hatcher was not included in the warrant . . .
>
> The Hatchers are a dark-skinned people, but if there is any Negro blood in them, no one knows whence or when it got there—if anything it may be Indian or Spaniard. But they are good citizens, perfectly honest, industrious and hard-working people . . . There are those who will

> testify that the girl in the case is not of the highest social standing, that she too is of a dark complexion, and should it be admitted for a minute that Hatcher is tainted with Negro blood, yet the fact that he sought a wife among those of his own class, will be his best defense. If he had attempted to marry a white girl of high social standing, his case would be different in the opinion of the people.[9]

This incident seems to reflect that the nature of intermarriage has both social and economic textures, to wit (in so many words): a dark-skinned person may marry a light-skinned person—that's maybe okay—but only as long as they come from the same economic class. But we will not tolerate a mixing of lowborn with highborn! No, sir!

Now it could be argued that this occurrence took place one hundred years ago and so much has changed since then, hasn't it, especially considering the effects of the civil rights era? Well, perhaps. But I need to cite another incident that took place in Horry County and happened to another Hatcher. This Hatcher is the current chief of the Waccamaw Indian People, although he was not chief at the time the following happened.

It was in 1972 at a restaurant in Myrtle Beach, the famous tourist spot. Buster Hatcher had just returned from a tour of duty in Vietnam. While in Vietnam he received a combat wound that still had not healed. He entered the restaurant with his girlfriend, to whom he had just proposed marriage. A man greeted them. Buster's own words tell what transpired: "My girlfriend was not totally white-skinned, but light-skinned. Well, this man in the restaurant said to my girlfriend, 'Oh, you can eat at the table but he'll have to eat at the counter' and he came back to me with a paper plate and paper cup and then he said to my girlfriend, 'What are you doing eating with a half-n—— . . .' Now that wasn't the thing to do!"[10]

Personal examples of racial prejudice continue into recent times. Chief Hatcher has told me of other instances of such prejudice to him—and even to his son—into the twenty-first century. These occasions are brought out in the interviews to come in this chapter.

Beyond the personal attacks, an adversarial relationship between the Indian people of the Southeast and their local and federal governments has continued into the twenty-first century. Why?

According to some Waccamaws, "fear of land lawsuits, and recently gambling, have caused many elected officials to deny our existence. The federal and state laws were amended to guarantee the blacks the same freedoms as the whites. This has never been done for the Indians."[11]

It was not until 2004 that the term *Indian* was defined by the state of South

15. Chief Harold "Buster" Hatcher, Waccamaw of South Carolina, 1993

Carolina. Chief Hatcher states that there are over six dozen previous references to the term *Indian* in South Carolina law without a stated legal definition. He writes, "This was a problem for South Carolina Indians whose identity had become obscured over the years as the terms *mulatto, white* and/or *black* were used to describe us but none matched our appearance."[12] Therefore local businesses, restaurants, banks, and so on based their determination as to race or ethnicity upon their own measure of appearances. Yet the government (state or local) based its determination upon official documents.

Hence, Indians did not know which laws or customs applied to them and which did not. Chief Hatcher worked over five years as a volunteer investigator with the Horry County Human Relations Council and discovered that the very law that established the council specifically omitted Indians. After failing to bring some change, he resigned.

Harold D. "Buster" Hatcher was born in 1949 in Conway, Horry County.

At the age of eighteen he joined the U.S. Army and rose to the rank of chief warrant officer. He spent most of his twenty years in the military with the 82nd Airborne Division. He earned a Bronze Star, a Purple Heart, and the Vietnam Cross of Gallantry plus "about thirteen other medals of lesser significance" before his retirement in 1988.

In 1994 he and I conduct the first of a number of interviews, counting the e-mail kind. We are in the living room of his home along Old Altman Road, about five miles from the center of Conway, a town of thirty thousand, and fifteen miles inland from Myrtle Beach. His two sons come and go out a screen door as they visit with neighbors. The phone rings occasionally. At first I have some trouble adjusting the mic of the tape recorder. In fact, I feel somewhat intimidated as Chief Hatcher wears, I believed at the time, a somewhat suspicious look on his face. But as we begin to talk I become more relaxed, as I think he does.

Q: I got hold of you through a reporter who wrote an article about you. From what he said you have not lived here all your life?

Chief Hatcher: I was born in Conway but we hopped around a lot when we were real young . . . Conway to Socastee to Myrtle Beach to an area on 378 called Pee Dee . . . then I joined the Army. I quit school in the ninth grade. I spent twenty years in the military all over the world . . . and then came back to the same road as here and then I built this house.

Q: How old were you when you moved out of Conway?

Chief Hatcher: I was five at Socastee, seven or eight at Myrtle . . . wouldn't go to school . . . had a big problem going to school . . . teachers used to call me names and the kids called me names.

Q: This was during the segregation era; was it a white school?

Chief Hatcher: Yes, I don't know why they decided to send me to a white school . . . I guess because our hair didn't look like blacks' . . . didn't have an Indian school so they had to put us somewhere . . . and anywhere they sent us would be wrong.

Q: How many were there who had that same problem?

Chief Hatcher: I think I had it worse than most because my skin was darker . . . and I had two sisters and usually the good-looking sisters are accepted the most . . . people don't usually be too mean to them . . . my brother and I, especially me—he was not as dark-skinned as I was . . . I caught it from everywhere . . . But at the time I didn't know I shouldn't. I thought that I was less than human . . . I really did . . . I thought that was the way I was supposed to be treated . . . and when I went to school there was fighting on the bus and I was called—I don't like these names, but . . . was called "brass ankle," "half-nigger," "croatan"—that was considered half-black at that time—"high yellow." I didn't really know what all that meant at the time.

Q: You could tell the way they were saying it that it was a put-down?

Chief Hatcher: Well, I don't know that I did . . . but when someone would spit on you and gang up on you and beat the daylights out of you . . . I knew that you weren't liked very well.

Q: This was worse than the way kids often act?

Chief Hatcher: I was different . . . I was like a sore thumb . . . I knew that people didn't like me, including the teachers . . . I look back and don't know why they would call me "dirty" . . . so I didn't like it because I was always getting my tail end kicked every time I went to school, so I would not go to school. And my Dad would put me on the bus and then I would get to school and then I would walk home. Twenty-nine days I went to school in the second grade in the whole year.

Q: How did your dad handle all this?

Chief Hatcher: I think he tried to do things that [he thought] would help me. He bought some kind of cream . . . that some of the black folks used . . . to help you turn white. I was supposed to keep that smeared on my face all the time. I don't know if it would work because I wouldn't use it. I look back [and see] he was doing what he thought would help me . . . he did it out of love . . . but the one thing that would have helped me the most was that if the teacher [in second grade] would have been at least neutral. But she joined right in with the kids. She would stand up there in class and if I would make a mistake she would call me stupid . . . it just wasn't a good situation.

Q: How did this make you feel?

Chief Hatcher: It made me feel that I was less than everybody else . . . I felt that I shouldn't be there . . . that it was for the higher-class people . . . It's kind of hard to explain . . . but we moved from Myrtle Beach to an area called Pee Dee . . . I went to second grade there . . . They didn't pick on me like at Myrtle . . . they were more diverse people at Pee Dee. About then at that time my mother and Daddy had separated . . . only went [to school] there one or two years . . . Then we moved to over near Highway 90 and I began to go to Waccamaw Elementary . . . the principal there, Miss Rusk [was a] beautiful person—and I was accepted. People treated me like everyone else . . . Then I went to junior high and it started again . . . much bigger place than Waccamaw . . . and people would call me names . . . but by then I knew what was going on and there was fight after fight . . . and I got pretty good at it too!

Q: Is this still in the segregation era?

Chief Hatcher: Yes it was . . . I was still in a white school. I graduated from there and went to Conway High School and there were a lot of fights there . . . They had a demerit system and if you had twelve demerits you were expelled for three days . . . by the end of the first six weeks I had been expelled three times . . . and it was all fights. Now in the army all the colors are green—now I know some black folks may not believe that—but I believe it . . . I was treated fairly, at least not the way I was treated around here . . . In the army a fellow taught me something . . . Those folks who have to call people bad names were just ignorant and I knew I couldn't change that and so my attitude started to change.

Q: Do the children nowadays face that anymore?

Chief Hatcher: My sons Doug and Dalton are not well liked . . . because I'm not so well liked . . . now there is a group of people who would do anything for me and then there is another group that doesn't care for me. [pause] And there's still people who, well . . . [show their prejudice] . . .

Q: Tell me about this.

Chief Hatcher: Well, when I go out I usually wear a feather . . . not too long ago I went to a restaurant . . . not bothering anybody . . . and this fellow came up to me and said: "Why do you wear the feather?" I said, "To show I am proud of my heritage." He said, "Well, I'm a white man and I don't wear anything to show how proud I am." So I said, "Will you wear a tie to church?" "Yeah, I wear a tie." I said, "Well, that's part of a white man's dress and this is an Indian dress." So he said, "Well, maybe I'll just take that feather off of you and stick it somewhere!"

Q: So things like that still happen?

Chief Hatcher: You ought to go and read the law books of this state. I had to sue the state . . . and I don't know if this state is any different than any other . . . but I sued to have my birth certificate say what it should have said long ago. It says "Indian" now . . . but at the time it said "white." When I was born, being white was the thing to be . . . people didn't want anything but being white.

My mother always told me I was Indian. I knew—at seven or eight—I was Indian but I can tell you this . . . there is more to being Indian than having dark skin, black straight hair. There are things about the way you believe . . . and I am sure that for whites there are attitudes which show that it's not just about skin color . . . the things you believe and the way you feel, an inner voice . . . that maybe comes from genes . . . The knowledge is there but hidden and we have been trained to ignore it . . . while our actions are tailored to be more acceptable to society.

A sparrow in England and a sparrow in Myrtle Beach will build their nests in the same way. They will [use] the same tying techniques, build them the same height in the trees and so forth. The two nests, several hundred miles apart, will look the same, and even contain the same types of building materials. This is so, not because one of the two sparrows taught the other, but simply because both are sparrow.[13]

Q: Are both your parents of Indian ancestry?

Chief Hatcher: My mother is part Indian and my Dad was . . . well if he wasn't full, he was awfully close. I don't think there are any thoroughbreds anymore.

Q: How many siblings do you have?

Chief Hatcher: Well, I have three brothers and five sisters. My father and mother had had me, my sisters Iris and Reba, and my brother Doug. And then when my mother remarried, to a white man, she had five children. They are of course my siblings, though my half brothers and sisters are not active in the tribe . . . because they are born of a white father and have light skin . . . they have never felt the sting of the hatred that the rest of us did.

Q: Do your brother and sisters from your father and mother's marriage belong to the tribe?

Chief Hatcher: Yes, Doug belongs . . . and Reba and Iris are very active in the tribe. They are some of the best support I get . . . because this is a thankless job.

Q: When did the tribe form?

Chief Hatcher: The tribe formed before historic times! But, legally, it was chartered in South Carolina in 1992. I have learned through the past years that there are people who will use my words to hurt us and will write articles and so forth saying that I said we were not a tribe before 1992, then challenge our over one hundred years of community.

Q: How did you get started in getting a charter?

Chief Hatcher: Well, I retired from the army in 1988, and I built this house by 1989. And then I was working as a mechanic in Conway—I have a degree in auto technology. I really didn't have to work but I wanted more . . . I wanted to have some extra things . . . and this company came up for sale . . . and I wanted to buy that company and make something out of it . . . but when I tried to register it as a minority-owned company [the birth certificate became an issue] . . . Now, all the time I was in the military all my records said I was Indian . . . ah, everything said I was Indian . . . I never thought about the birth certificate—never crossed my mind.

Well, when I tried to register that company . . . I ran into wall after wall . . . Now you shouldn't step on someone else's head to climb above . . . but there is a debt owed to black people and there is a debt owed to Indian people and I believe that. But I don't believe it is owed by the everyday working Joe . . . This country is not really divided by race but amongst dollars and pennies—and we just hang the racial thing on it because we don't know any better. The black people believe the whites have everything and the whites think the blacks want everything and neither one is true . . . I had paid the same dues that black people have had to pay . . . and if there is an advantage for them, then there should be one for me . . . but when I went to get it, it wasn't there. "Well, you're not black," [they said]. "But I'm not white," I said. "Well, it doesn't matter."

Now if you go back to the census of 1910, you were either "black, white, or mulatto." Okay, at that time *mulatto* meant something other than white or black and all my people were from Dog Bluff and they were considered mulatto [Indian] . . . But now it means a cross between black and white.

Q: Dog Bluff? In Horry County?

Chief Hatcher: Yes, close to the Pee Dee River . . . they had an Indian school there in the 1800s and probably into the 1900s. There were a bunch of Turners, Hatchers, Dimerys . . . all these people were known as Indian people and all attended the Indian school . . . now all of them are white . . . If you go to one, he'll tell you he's white . . . it's what they want to be.

Q: Is there an economic advantage to say they are white?

Chief Hatcher: Not now, I don't think . . . now it's the thing to be Indian.

Q: So the people who still live there at Dog Bluff don't want to take part in the tribe?

Chief Hatcher: Well, they think what I am doing is stupid . . . because they think it's dumb to wear a headdress . . . if however someone comes to us and says that he is missing out on some of his culture and wants to do something about that, then I want to help him.

Q: Well, in regard to your company, were you able to have your birth certificate changed?

Chief Hatcher: Oh yes, I did . . . I sued them . . . went to court . . . I did all the work myself, my own legal work . . . oh, I filed it, I served a copy on them . . . that was the Office of Vital Statistics of South Carolina. They told me initially to go to North Carolina and join a tribe there, "Then you can come down here to file an ID card, and then we can work with you." I told them that I wasn't born in North Carolina . . . I told them I wasn't going to settle for anything less than getting my certificate changed.

I got my documents together . . . I got a certified anthropologist to write a document and I got sworn affidavits from my mother and aunts . . . and I was surprised 'cause the state didn't fight me in court, they just sent me a consent order and said that all I needed was a judge to sign it and Judge Kay Hern in Conway did . . . She said that it was the first time she ever saw this done but was happy to sign it . . . So they changed the birth certificate and then I went to the Governor's Council on Small Business and tried to convince them the necessity to recognize Indian people and Indian businesses, and they did and they certified my company. And from all that, I thought there were other people who would run into the same situation . . . and that's when I decided to open up this organization [the tribe].

So I advertised in the paper and several people showed up and we got us a charter and headed on out . . . for a nonprofit corporation.

Q: Are there any people practicing Native American religions or beliefs?

Chief Hatcher: Absolutely. We have a fire keeper in training. His name is John (Sleeping Badger) Cox and he is being trained by Earl Many Skins. Earl is a Lumbee and a very spiritual man and he comes over here often to be the teacher. [Note: Earl (Many Skins) Carter, an American Indian fire keeper and teacher, is interviewed in Chapter 8.]

Q: Does your tribe have any regular spiritual meetings?

Chief Hatcher: Yes, every full moon at least five have a fire . . . It's open to everyone . . . and every regular meeting we have our fire keeper come to do a purging and smudging . . . and if I give a feather out I always make sure it gets smudged . . . We want to bring back as much tradition as we can . . . I'm not a deeply spiritual person but I have the feeling that the ancient people had it and it kind of surprises me sometimes because I will think and do something and then I will end up reading a book and it is the way the Indians used to do.

Q: Do you see other cultural differences from other groups?

Chief Hatcher: Ah . . . yes, you know that the ancient people believed that a prayer could not reach heaven if it were not taken up on smoke, tobacco smoke fanned with an eagle feather . . . Well okay . . . now, the eagle is a protected bird and I don't think you should kill an eagle ever but on occasion you'll find an eagle along the road or a hunter accidentally kills an eagle, then these eagles are put into a repository and the claws and beak and feathers are made available to American Indian people to be used in religious ceremonies. But they are not available to me.

Q: Where are these repositories?

Chief Hatcher: There is one in Colorado and another in Atlanta . . . now if you are a member of a BIA [Bureau of Indian Affairs]–recognized tribe then they are available to the tribe . . . Now one of the problems in South and North Carolina and Georgia is that Indian people were once slaves and once you are taken into someone's house as a slave, you lose your identity as an Indian.

Now, the BIA comes back and says we will recognize Indian groups if you can show a continuous tribal control since European contact . . . and I get irritated when the BIA tells me I can't be an Indian in my own state for policies I had no control over, like slavery. And I'll fight that until the day they bury me . . . I'm not going to buy it. They are going to have to back up.

[I will argue this] until the BIA or the federal government or somebody says you don't have to be a BIA tribe to be recognized as an Indian and as an Indian you would have the right to worship the way you used to worship . . . And I have people who do want to worship with eagle feathers.

Ten years after our first interview, in 2004, I met with Chief Hatcher at a restaurant in Aynor, South Carolina, that is near Dog Bluff and the once-populous Dimery Settlement. We were meeting to discuss the latest developments in the efforts of his tribe to obtain state recognition. We also were going to visit what remains of the Dimery Settlement, including a large fenced-in Indian cemetery.

Q: How well is the recognition process going?

Chief Hatcher: Yesterday, the Commission for Minority Affairs and its Indian Ad Hoc Committee settled on the criteria for Indian groups to meet . . . It's established the standards to go by for a group to be recognized as an Indian tribe or as an Indian group . . . but it's been a long process . . . Do you know what Governor Sanford told me once when I paid him a visit? . . . He said, "What can I do for you?" I told him, "We have been put aside, we need to be included in the Commission for Minority Affairs, that's the first step. The second step is to set criteria that only legitimate Indian people can meet." He said, "Well, I won't help you, but I won't fight you on it."

Now he did say he would sign it if it came across his desk, but he wouldn't help to get it there. Now that man [the Governor] is a Republican but so is the Lieutenant Governor yet we get along good . . . he's written a letter to try to help my tribe get recognition.

South Carolina has sticking in their gizzard [a fear of] claims for land and gambling[14] . . . I've worked with Governor Campbell and Governor Beasley [both Republicans] and even Governor Hodges [a Democrat] and it was like hitting a brick wall. But I talked with Governor Hodges and told him if you look at the statistical abstracts you'll see that Indians earn 30 percent less than whites for the same job, same educational level. And the poverty level is five times greater for

Indians than whites . . . when do we become human beings? He said, "I can't do anything about it but I'll set something in motion so that we can." So he established the Governor's Ad Hoc Committee on American Indian Affairs.

So we started our meetings . . . that was ten years ago and there were six to eight groups . . . then in a few years there were eighteen groups and now [2004] there are twenty-one . . . some call them "popcorn" groups . . . a lot of them have sure sprung up.

Q: How many will meet the criteria as a tribe, do you think?

Chief Hatcher: Edisto, Varnertown, we will, the Santees will, don't know about the Pee Dees . . . David Locklear [long-time chief] has been inactive . . . not sure what will happen there.

Q: Well, that's good that standards for being Indian have been established, but I wonder now that things have changed a lot if you still get any bad vibes from non-Indians?

Chief Hatcher: A couple of years ago someone came in and vandalized tombstones and cut down a cedar tree at the Dimery Cemetery. Then later some lady wanted to see the cemetery and asked where was the cedar tree. She said, "Most Indian cemeteries have a cedar tree . . . they thought cedar was a sacred wood."

Here's another story . . . I've an aunt by marriage who is dark-skinned and Indian [she lives near the cemetery] but wants to pass as white. Well, she demanded that the newspaper, which had an article on the vandalism, retract the name "Indian" in reference to the Dimery Cemetery vandalism. Well, the newspaper refused to do so and said that the Dimery Cemetery was well known as Indian. So when her brother died about six months later and she buried him, she buried him outside the fence . . . no mixing down here.

So we finished our lunch and interview and headed down the road to what was left of the famous Dimery Settlement. Chief Hatcher showed the way to Dog Bluff and the cemetery, where I took photographs. He showed me his father's grave site and his grandfather's grave site. My final question that day was: Are you related to John Dimery, the founder of this once-thriving Indian community?

Chief Hatcher: Yes, he's my great-great-granddaddy . . . You know, I remember when my Daddy would take me to visit someone older than him or someone he respected . . . He chewed tobacco . . . and

> when he would go up to this person he always took a chunk of that tobacco off and gave it to the person he was visiting . . . I don't know if that is a direct link to the old thing about [Indians] giving tobacco to your elders . . . but that's what he did . . . I don't know if you ever heard about a potato bank?[15] Well, he'd show us how to do it . . . just so many things I learned . . . because he did it.
>
> I've been asked if I was raised in an Indian environment and I don't know if I was but I have found out today that [what my father showed me] was a Native tradition.
>
> You know, I'm not all that spiritual . . . I'm more a politician . . . but there is something about the fire circle and the way it's done that is very important to me.

This concluded our 2004 interview. In 2005, after his tribe had been awarded tribal recognition, he told me via e-mail the following:

Q:	What is the tribe's current enrollment?
Chief Hatcher:	Four hundred.
Q:	What is the progress at your tribal grounds? Any building? Will you hold this year's powwow there?[16]
Chief Hatcher:	The grounds are going well but money is a problem. Yes, we have a tribal office trailer and a house trailer on site for the groundskeeper to use. We have sewer and electricity and water. And yes, we will hold the powwow there if I can get the grass planted in time.
Q:	Have you changed your opinion about the chances of the Waccamaws achieving federal recognition?
Chief Hatcher:	I now believe that we can meet the standards after looking and researching for the past ten to thirteen years.[17] I believe that there are ways of making the case that will be acceptable to the BIA. However, G. W. Bush is not Indian-friendly and we will not submit while he is president. He has already said that there will be no new tribes while he is the president. That certainly indicates Indians in the recognition process will get a fair hearing, huh?

So ended my conversation with Chief Hatcher. It seems fairly clear that now, in the twenty-first century, the most easterly reach of the Cofitachequi confederation included the region of the Dog Bluff Indians, the Waccamaws of South Carolina. Also fairly clear—from the hindsight lens of this current century—is that the Cofitachequi also included the tribes along the Great and Little Pee Dee and the Lumber rivers of South and North Carolina. This will be the subject of the next two chapters of this book.

However, before going there, it is important for the reader not to confuse the Waccamaw Indian People of South Carolina with the Waccamaw Siouan of North Carolina. Located in the southeast part of North Carolina, the Waccamaw Siouan have enjoyed state recognition since 1971 but not yet federal recognition.[18] I have been asked by the tribal council to print their resolution (somewhat abridged due to space limitations): "Be it resolved: that the Waccamaw Siouan Indian tribe . . . has no association or relationship with the Waccamaw Indian People of South Carolina. Be it resolved: that the Tribal Council of Waccamaw Siouan Indian tribe does not recognize the Waccamaw Indian People of South Carolina . . . as an Indian tribe or tribal entity."

Feeling uneasy concerning my agreement to have their resolution, by itself, in this book, I contacted Chief Hatcher of the South Carolina Waccamaws and asked his side of the issue (also abridged):

Chief Hatcher: I don't know the answer to your question except that . . . the last mention in the history books indicates that [the Waccamaw Indians] lived just outside of Aynor [South Carolina] in 1751 . . . It seems to me that with the Waccamaw River flowing from Lake Waccamaw [North Carolina] to Georgetown [South Carolina] we would all be kin.

Our resolution . . . is that we believe in unity and that we recognize and honor all tribes who have met the standards of state and federal recognition in order to further the spirit of unity and the status and well-being of all American citizens including its natives.

Chief Hatcher's efforts have resulted in a positive communication with the Waccamaws of North Carolina, and they are working on their differences.

In conclusion, for the past several years Chief Buster Hatcher of the Waccamaw Indian People of South Carolina has been trying to organize the various tribes and groups and their leaders. The aim of his group, called the South Carolina Indian Affairs Commission (SCIAC; not to be confused with the state's Minority Affairs Commission that determines tribal status), is for all Indian people to be included under an umbrella group for the purposes of gaining more political (and hence more economic, health, and educational)

16. Some Indian leaders, State House, Columbia, South Carolina, 2007

benefits. We keep in contact on a regular basis through e-mail and through his SCIAC newsletter, which he edits with humor and clarity. (Please note that Buster has been so busy with SCIAC affairs that he has resigned from being chief of the Waccamaws, but I will continue to refer to him as "Chief.")

I need to draw the reader's attention to the group photograph taken in 2007 at a powwow (sometimes spelled "Pauwau") on the state-house grounds with the South Carolina House building in the background. The importance of this group portrait is not just factual but also symbolic. It reveals, first, that it is no longer necessary or wise to hide one's Indianness and, second, that a serious common goal of all tribes encountered in this book is to gain tribal recognition.

Some of the members of this group, in addition to Chief Hatcher, are the current leaders of tribes that have gained state recognition recently. One of the tribes so represented in the photograph is the Beaver Creek Indians, a group/community not included in the text since I had no contact with them during the principal phase of my research.

This leads to the cover photograph, a sequence of three images of the same person, Kristin Barron, a member of the Beaver Creek Indians. This arrangement of images shows at the factual level a very lively dancer. Including this sequence in the book helps convey a number of ideas: First, Ms. Barron is the current princess for her tribe and through her photograph her tribe obtains visual recognition not otherwise revealed in the text. Then, the movement of her dancing steps also conveys that the movement of Indians asserting their identity is not just the business of the middle-aged but also a concern of the youth. Finally, the sequence helps reinforce the idea, found in the first shot of Kristin standing, that the state looks friendly (formally at least) upon the Indian community. Consistent with this assertion is the fact that on this day the governor of South Carolina, through one of his representatives, marched in the opening ceremonies and read a proclamation in support, in essence, of the assertion of Indian identity.

7

The Pee Dees

Deep into northwest North Carolina, in the Blue Ridge Mountains, and into the Piedmont (at the foot of the mountains) begins the Great Pee Dee River but called here the Ladkin. The Ladkin River travels irregularly through varied terrain as it heads south and east. Along its route artificial lakes have been created with such names as High Rock Lake, Badin Lake, and Lake Tillery, all in North Carolina. It is at this last lake the waterway receives its new name, the Great Pee Dee. Perhaps coincidently this general area marks the northernmost reach of the Cofitachequi chiefdom, whose upper boundaries then turn westward toward the Catawba River in North Carolina.

But as the Great Pee Dee is headed southward toward the South Carolina border, it passes by contemporary towns with such precontact names as Cheraw, Pamplico, and Pee Dee. This last town probably was called Vehidi, at least it was so labeled in 1567. As the river gathers width and volume, it joins its smaller sibling, the Little Pee Dee. Then downstream the Pee Dee is joined to the Waccamaw River. Together they roll to the ocean at Winyah Bay.

But it is along the upper reaches of the Little Pee Dee where many of the present-day Pee Dee Indians live. This river starts as a tiny creek just over the North Carolina line in Scotland County. The river works its way into South Carolina not far from the town of McColl. Here lies the largest concentration of American Indians in the Pee Dee region. In the 2000 U.S. census there were 350 American Indians in McColl (or 14 percent of the population of 2,498).[1]

Then for some forty miles this rivulet, the Little Pee Dee, runs parallel to but north of its bigger sibling. But as it grows some muscle the river makes the nearby land swampy. At times occasional piles of tan, grey, or white sand are visible. Yet not far from this apparently unfruitful drainage are flat fields of soybeans, cotton, tobacco, cucumbers, and other vegetables.

As this big creek progresses from Marlboro County to Dillon County it becomes deeper, wider, and greener. Roadways pass over it by way of narrow bridges. In season, near these bridges, a sweet smell of wild plants fills the air. Are they honeysuckle or Carolina jasmine? I am not sure.

Then in Marion County, the Little Pee Dee runs into the much wider Lumber River, which comes down from Robeson County, North Carolina. Yet the larger river gives up its name to the Little Pee Dee, which now becomes a real river and rolls along for fifty miles until it joins up with its bigger namesake.

However, it is on the land that the Little Pee Dee traverses (before joining the Lumber) in Marlboro, Dillon, and Marion counties where most Pee Dee Indians live. According to the 2000 U.S. census, there were in this tri-county region 1,716 American Indians reported. By comparison, in 1990 the figure was 1,244.[2]

Over the years, leaders of the Pee Dee groups have indicated that there are many more Indians living in this region than show up on the census. Poverty, rural isolation, the urge to avoid discrimination by "passing" are often offered as explanations to account for the uncounted numbers. The rise in the recent census figures appears, in part, to reflect efforts by leaders to have more Indians assert their identity and be counted on the census.

In 1985, I met with David Locklear, then chief of the Pee Dee Indian Association. He lives in McColl, Marlboro County. He took me to some of the rural areas of his county and also Dillon County. In these rural areas poverty commands people to live, in many cases, in marginal conditions very similar to those of the 1930s Great Depression era.

Many work the fields as day laborers or sharecroppers or tenant farmers. Some live in unpainted wood shacks or run-down single-wide trailers. It is as if the clock of American "progress" stopped for these people in, say, 1935. For them the passage of fifty years has meant, apparently, nothing.

On that summer day in 1985, I did a photograph of Mary Jane Hunt and her seven children. They all had just returned from picking cucumbers for a local farm owner. The four boys and the mother are wearing blue jeans, which at the knees are coated with the dirt of the earth. They are sitting or standing on the crumbling wood porch. In the background, where James and Johnny are standing, there is a window visible with two glass panes missing.

The mother, the eye always returns to the mother with her long, straight black hair, is scratching her dirt-encrusted hands. Her legs are draped down off the front of the porch. We see her bare feet and, then, their yellow-brown dog plopped down by her feet, panting in the heat. Everyone, even the dog, is looking in different directions other than at the camera except for Josh, who is sitting on the porch at the right of the frame and closest to the camera. His arms are crossed at his belly. He has dark curly hair and grey eyes. There is a look of both curiosity and concern on his face. Will he ever go to school? Will he finish his education? I ask myself. Except for the fact that the photograph is taken in color fifty years after the program ended, it could easily enough pass as a 1935 Farm Security Administration (FSA) image. It seems to breathe of hard-work poverty, of bare-bones existence.

In 2000, 24 percent of Dillon County's populace lived below the poverty line. Marlboro County is not much better at 22 percent. These figures are considerably above the national average of 14 percent.[3] Of course, this figure is nothing to brag about.

This is not to say that all Pee Dee Indians live in such dire conditions. Some work, or have worked, in small industrial plants found in or near a few larger towns such as Dillon, the county seat named after a large landowner, with a 2000 census population of 6,316. Some Indians find work in service occupations associated with Interstate 95. Others have gone on to finish high school and attend local trade schools.

This region is primarily agricultural and hence roles and opportunities are more fixed, it seems, than in more urban areas. Since, according to the 2000 census, there are 679 American Indians in Dillon County yet only 85 in the town of Dillon, the only town of any size in the county, the figures tend to support that in this county, as with many others, American Indians are a rural population.

On the day that David Locklear took me into the rural areas, he pointed out families here and there who, living in remoteness, most likely have been missed by the census takers. Added to their obscureness are those families in which, for example, the wife might be of Indian background but the husband would be white. Even if the census taker found the house, the odds favor that the wife would claim the race that her husband claims. In fact, I met such a family that day.

Furthermore, laws against miscegenation could come into play in obscuring Indian identity. Although both North and South Carolina had miscegenation laws, the laws were less enforced south of the border well into the twentieth century. Hence, many couples from North Carolina would cross the line to get married and settle in South Carolina,[4] and in so doing they often obscured their roots, their identity.

But what are the early Native American roots of the present-day Pee Dees? First of all, this geographic region was once a part of the eastern province of the Cofitachequi chiefdom, and according to some sources, the Pee Dee's main village was Vehidi on the Great Pee Dee River. But then de

Soto marched through here with the captive Lady Cofitachequi in tow, and after him came Juan Pardo, and after his expedition then came the European traders, and then the incursions of the colonists. The Pee Dees, as well as other speakers of probably a common language with different dialects, found themselves squeezed between the Carolina colony and the Cherokees. By the 1700s, remnant bands resettled primarily in two areas: in and around the Pee Dee Basin area and near the Catawba River.[5]

According to the Smithsonian's *Handbook of North American Indians,* refugees from other tribes also joined up with Native Americans in the Catawba region. These bands of Natchez, Saponi, Tuscarora, and Yamasee not only joined with the Catawbas but also some splintered off to the greater Pee Dee Basin area. Many "disappeared for a time and reappeared as part of the Lumbee."[6]

According to Wes Taukchiray, certain surnames are connected to present-day Pee Dee Indians. These names are Chavis, Locklear, and Cumbo (the last being extinct since 1905). He asserts that in tracing these names back in time he has found a connection to some Saponi Indians (and Cheraw and Tuscarora Indians married in) who moved to the Lumber River area in a period of fifteen years after 1763.[7] Where did the group come from? According to Taukchiray, they came from areas of North Carolina, having moved there earlier from Cheraw Town (present-day Cheraw is in South Carolina on the Great Pee Dee) as part of the Catawba Nation, where they lived from 1729 to 1753.[8]

Taukchiray goes on to say that in the 1910 U.S. census there were fifty-five people who lived along the North Carolina line in Dillon County, South Carolina. They were counted as Indian. All except for the very young were from North Carolina, according to him.[9] It should be added that numbers of South Carolina Pee Dees, in present times, have migrated to North Carolina.

Given the lack of exact historical records one could argue that the roots of present-day Pee Dees come from several sources. The first source would be the original Pee Dees, some of whom were probably able to survive by seeking refuge along creeks and swamps and amongst unwanted land. Second, some came down from North Carolina, as Taukchiray argues. And, third, the remnants of other tribes who worked their way to the Pee Dee region should be factored in. Finally, the fact of intermarriage with non-Indians should be considered.

In the twentieth century American Indians were sometimes recognized, but they were generally ignored, and their welfare, villages, and schools were underfunded.

As with many other Indian communities in the Carolinas, there were grade schools set up for Indians in the Pee Dee area and, of course, separate schools for whites and blacks until the end of segregation. In northern Dillon County, the Leland Grove Indian school operated from 1934 to 1970. A highly respected teacher—James K. Braboy, a Lumbee—once taught there. Today this white wood building still stands as someone's home. Nearby is an Indian cemetery, as is the Leland Grove Free Will Baptist Church, which is predominately Indian. No more than a long city block away is the Little Pee Dee River. A few miles to the north, just south of the North Carolina line, is the Pee Dee Baptist Church, also Indian and also near the Little Pee Dee.

A third predominately Indian church also located in the upper part of Dillon County exists as a Methodist Church, which was the church that James Braboy attended. Over in Marlboro County, I once visited a church that had until recent times been considered a predominately Indian church.

The existence of separate schools, churches, and communities has contributed to isolation from non-Indians. But with the civil rights movement and official integration of the public schools, this isolation began to break down, at least for school-age children.

Whatever exactly has taken place over the centuries to suppress Indian identity is slowly changing. In the past twenty years more and more Pee Dee people of Indian heritage are willing to talk about their and their families' experiences in being Indian. In 1993, Jo Kitchen, a member of the Marlboro branch of the Pee Dee Indian Association, recounted (in a South Carolina Educational Television documentary) some of her parents' experiences when they went to a white school: "My mother and father had a hard time. They could go to school with whites but when they did they would have to put up with different things that would happen to them . . . like they could not face a white child [not allowed to] . . . They would have to turn their back to them in class . . . and things like that. So it was hard for them to say . . . actually say they were Indians . . . now things are different . . . We [Indian parents] are getting [our children] interested in their heritage."[10]

In this same television interview another Pee Dee Indian, Virgie Montoya, a member of the association's council, had this to say: "I don't think they lost their pride . . . I think they are still proud of their heritage. And it never was a popular thing to be an Indian and it still is not. I think the people are becoming educated about the Indian heritage, the culture, and we are trying to instill pride in our people."[11]

To assist in this regard the Pee Dee parents have formed an after-school Indian dance group called the Wind Walkers. If the students do not get passing grades, then they are not allowed to take part in being a Wind Walker ("no pass, no play"). Karen Garris Montoya, Virgie's daughter and administrative assistant to Chief Locklear, is the adult leader of the dance group: "We were at a powwow. And we had come home and were sitting around talking . . . and we thought . . . you know, our kids can do that. So a friend of mine had made a tape of competition songs and chants . . . like the flag song and the hover song. So we called the kids up and said we have something we want you to do . . . and that's how it all got started."[12]

This concludes my section on the Marlboro County branch of the Pee Dee Indians. When I first went to the Pee Dee region in the 1980s there was a single group, the Pee Dee Indian Association, but with a vice-chief or "sub-chief" for Dillon County. By 2005, this single association had become fragmented into more than one Pee Dee group.

Going back now to 1985, I have an appointment to meet with Joe "Stump" Hunt. He is the vice-chief of the Pee Dees of Dillon County. Joe lives in a predominately Indian village called Oakland. This community is located on a hard road north of Little Rock by some ten miles and east by a few miles from the Little Pee Dee River. The nearby land is agricultural. Within five to ten miles are the three Indian churches already described. Joe owned, at that time, a convenience store next to his house. Many years later when I came to visit, the store was missing, having been replaced by a volunteer firehouse. Living in this village for most of his adult life, Joe is a wealth of local history and personal experience, which I hope to portray faithfully in this narrative.

It is June 1985. Joe is taking me to visit with relatives and friends living all over northern Dillon County. As we drive along we talk about the time we first met, in 1984, at an Edisto powwow when I took his portrait with a cigarette dangling from his mouth. The photograph has a bit of the "Marlboro Man" look. He is trying to talk me into showing the photograph to a tobacco company so both of us can make money from the picture. I decline the idea as unacceptable since my father, who contracted emphysema from a lifetime of smoking, had died of a stroke five years previously. The smoking of tobacco plays a large role in Joe's narrative, as we will see.

We go over back roads as he gives me a tour including a visit to the old Indian school and the three Indian churches. We talk about the Little Pee Dee River and how the Hunt surname is associated in this area with being Indian.

Finally, we stop at a small farmhouse where I meet his cousin Tom Hunt and his wife, Bessie. Tom is sixty-two years old but still very healthy looking, being strong boned and muscular. He is wearing bib overalls. Like Joe

17. Joe S. "Stump" Hunt and grandson, Pee Dees, 1984

he seems to like to dangle a cigarette from his mouth. He has worked for the Smith family, the landowners, for fifty years, since the age of twelve.

Tom: When I was ten I was in this car with Mr. Smith and some others. I think maybe we were going too fast. We were crossing over the Pee Dee when we crashed into a fence and into the railing and then we went into the river. I can still remember what happened . . . it's still clear to me . . . we were into a deep part and the car [was] upside down. And I would have drowned but Mr. Smith got me out and saved me . . . he pulled me up and onto the side of the river. But now that's all I can remember. But I know'd he saved my life. And when I could, I started working for him and all my life for that family . . . I work for Mr. Jamie now [the son of Smith].

18. Bessie and Tom Hunt, Pee Dees, 1985

Q:	How big a farm is it?
Tom:	Oh, it's around ten thousand acres of land. Now Mr. Jamie doesn't own it all . . . he leases some and rents some . . . but it is big! We live here on it . . . but it is like ours.
Q:	So you are still working?
Tom:	Oh sure. But not full time anymore . . . My wife and I work our garden and we keep chickens . . . We keep it going.

After this conversation, I take some pictures of Tom and his wife near their garden and then some by the chicken pen. Joe and I then go across a dirt road to Tom's son's house, which is more of a shack than a house. I make a mistake and ask to take photographs before getting to know the son and his wife. The wife refuses to allow me to take pictures of her or the house. She seems angry, but not necessarily with me. Tom's son speaks with me a little but there is a great difference between father and son, who appears bitter, unlike his father, who seems to be content, even perhaps happy. I learn that the son, like his father, works for the Smith family but is not doing so well. I ask him whose motorbike is it that I am looking at and he tells me that it is his but all that he can afford, in an angry way.

Joe and I decide it is time to leave from this part of the county. We head back toward his home, where I meet his wife, Flonnie, who, like Joe, likes to smoke. Then Joe begins to recount his life story.

Q: Have you lived here all your life?

Joe: Oh no, I was born over in North Carolina, in Scotland County, but that's not far from here . . . near Laurenburg . . . We were Tuscarora Indians . . . not Lumbees . . . the Lumbees came later.

Q: How did you get your nickname of Stump?

Joe: [Laughs] Oh, that came from the midwife . . . you see [laughs again in a self-conscious way], I had a fat rump and I've been told that she held me up in the air and told everyone that I ought to be called "Hump" Hunt. And I guess maybe some people called me that at first . . . but all my family . . . I mean the young ones, couldn't say "Hump" right. Instead, they would say "Stump" and that's what I grew up with . . . that's what stuck! [We both laugh.]

Q: So, when were you born?

Joe: Let's see . . . I was born July the first in 1932 . . . so pretty soon I'll be fifty-three years old.

Q: I understand you own a convenience store.

Joe: Oh, sure do. That's next door . . . I mean there's a house in between us but it's that block building over there . . . I built that building. But I sure would like to sell it. My back has been bothering me . . . I've got a pinched nerve, the doc said. And it's long hours . . . I can make, or used to at times, six hundred dollars a week. Flonnie used to help out but she can't anymore . . . She got disabled . . . that store can be a lot of problems.

Q: And you keep busy with the tribe, also?

Joe: Sure do. I'm a sub-chief for the Pee Dee Indians of Dillon County . . . been sub-chief since 1976.

Q: Could you tell me some of your earlier experiences as an Indian?

Joe: Well . . . it's hard to know where to begin. Let's see . . . well, when the Korean War began, here in the Pee Dee there were only two races to mark on the official forms . . . that be white or colored. Now there was another place to mark, that was "other," so if you were an Indian you could mark that, but there was no official place to mark Indian, you see. Now for me when I was called up to go, to be drafted in the army, I marked "other" on the form at the center. But there at the center was this woman, a secretary I guess, who called me a gypsy.

Q: Why did she do that?

Joe: Well I don't rightly know . . . except maybe 'cause she like a lot of people had to label people. I was neither white or black so she felt I had to be something she could name.

Q: What did you say to her?

Joe: You know, I can't remember. I must of told her I was Indian. Anyway, it turned out I didn't get drafted after all . . . 'cause I got out because I was the only surviving child. [Joe changes the subject.] You see, in the 1950s, Indians could not vote, just like blacks. When Eisenhower came in . . . he managed to get "colored people" . . . you know, blacks and Indians . . . the right to vote, if you could give proof that you had reading ability. And then there was lots of vote buying . . . 'cause some folks thought that the right to vote could also mean the right to sell their vote.

Q: When you were growing up, how was Indian identity officially established?

Joe: Oh usually at birth . . . by the midwife . . . it depended on if she knew the family . . . sometimes what you looked like . . . things like that . . . all this makes me think about another thing that happened to me.

I was in a hospital . . . it was in 1964, in Mullins [South Carolina]. See, I had been working on someone's furnace—I've done all kinds of jobs—on this furnace there was a sensor unit and it blew up on my face . . . It got some of my head and my face, even my lashes. Lucky for me, I had closed my eyes . . . but for a short time I couldn't see a thing. Anyways, I got to the hospital . . . to the emergency room. They said I had third-degree burns and after that they took me to a room. Now you see, I have frizzy hair and when I woke up in the room, I could see that I was thought to be a black man because the guy in the other bed was black. Well, I put up a big protest . . . I told them, I was an Indian and shouldn't be in that room. At first they didn't pay any attention to me until someone who worked in the hospital knew me and knew I was an Indian and told the folks there that it was truth . . . So they took me out of that room and put me in a room with a white man.

Q: I guess there wasn't a room just for Indians?

Joe: Of course not . . . you see, you get better care if you are considered to be white [as if in defense of forcing the room change].

This ended our conversation at that time. We walked over to his convenience store. It had the appearance of a 7-Eleven–type store with some basic food items, beer and other drinks in refrigerators, and lots of snack-type foods. There was a woman employee attending to several of the local, very Indian-looking, children who were wandering around the aisles looking for something to buy that would fit their budgets. I bought some grapefruit juice and peanuts for my road trip back to Columbia. Joe "Stump" Hunt and I said our good-byes, at least for then.

On the day before Thanksgiving of 1991, six years after our initial long conversations, I return to Joe's house. We have set up this time for a family reunion–type photo session. Joe introduces me to the members of his extended family. He shows me his first great-grandchild, who is less than a year old. Slowly the family assembles for a group portrait that covers four generations of twenty-three Hunts.

After the photography and as people begin to drift apart, Joe invites me to an outside building where he uncovers some homemade wine, more like moonshine. "Isn't it good!" he says. For me it tastes awful and in fact, it has a bitter taste, but I lie, saying, "Yes, it's, well, quite original." But this leads to an interview.

Q: Stump, how are things going?

Joe: Well . . . not too bad, not too great either. Don't know what you know but I've been put into jail . . . right now I'm on a work release program. You see, I was sent up two years ago. I got a five-year sentence and just got turned down for parole. I'm released during the day to work and for this weekend I was able to get off.

Q: Stump, I didn't know anything about this; what sort of work are you doing?

Joe: Oh, me and Aaron Oxendine got us a little business doing a drywall business . . . sort of a general contractors business. We call it S and S Contractors . . . over in the Florence [South Carolina] area.

Q: But what happened to get you into jail, in the first place?

Joe: It's a long story, okay! But this is what happened . . . Oh by the way, did you notice how good I look! I've lost most of my pot gut [patting his stomach]. I feel real good too . . . of course I still smoke some . . . okay, here's what happened. Well you know that convenience store I use to own?

Well, I was always trying to sell it and I got someone to buy it but he couldn't keep up the payments . . . really it was more like a lease. Anyways, I still owed the bank money on it . . . it's been a while since we last talked . . . Well, I began to sell moonshine. And also I turned a lot of the day-to-day running of the store over to younger people. Then in 1989, some SLED [State Law Enforcement Division] people made a raid on the store and they found some moonshine . . . I wasn't there at the time. But they weren't finished 'cause they did another search, then another, and then they "found" a small can and inside the can they pulled out some packets of cocaine. And so I was charged with possession of five one-gram packets of cocaine. Gene, I swear I never saw that can before in my life!

Anyways a prosecutor gave me some choices . . . here's what he told me. If I would plead guilty to moonshine selling I would have one year in jail and . . . or . . . fifteen hundred dollars. Or, he offered that if I pleaded guilty to a drug charge, I would receive three years probation and [a] five-hundred-dollar fine . . . don't know why the drug charge wasn't as bad as the moonshine one; that's what I was thinking.

But when the time came for sentencing . . . 'cause I had pleaded guilty to the drug charge . . . the judge gave me five years in the slammer! You see, I had no lawyer and I didn't get in writing the choices those law people had given me . . . boy, did I make a big, big mistake!

Q: Stump, sorry to hear of all this. [I change the subject.] Just how "Indian" is Oakland?

Joe: Oh, it's about half Indian and half white. But a lot of those that pass for white are really Indian . . . 'cause, well, they think they'll be better off.

I take Joe back to his home and head through autumn fields to find my way to Columbia. It is late in the day; the light is at its "golden hour." As I drive along, I see cotton fields, which have recently been picked. Along the way, I see large carts made of thick wire. These carts, sitting randomly about, are now empty of cotton except for tiny bits clinging to the wire sides. In the fields, there are fragments of white cotton, now colored a gold hue from the late-in-the-day sun.

Nowadays machines are used to pick the cotton but a black-and-white image made in 1935 by Ben Shahn, an FSA photographer, comes to my mind. It is of three people, one a young boy with a cap turned backward, bent over to their task of pulling the long, large bags that trail behind each person as they pick cotton by hand, laboriously.

But soon this image disappears and the reality of the moment takes over. Quickly, the golden hour is changing. The color of the sky and the color of the leftovers of cotton in the fields and on the wire carts have turned first a pinkish glow and then into a magenta hue, a color that happens just after the sun goes down.

Oddly, a feeling of sadness comes over me. I slow down at a country crossroads and try to find a radio station to listen to. Suddenly, I find a faraway station playing a Neil Young song. I can hardly make out the music, the lyrics, but it brings to mind one of his songs of how drugs are undermining his rock group. For that song the punch line is "every junkie's like a setting sun."

I think of Stump Hunt and what he has told me, about his troubles. He has always struck me as basically a good person, a natural leader, someone not afraid of hard work. Was he pushing coke? I don't want to believe it!

A dozen years have gone by and it is now May 2003 when I come to Oakland again. It is a Sunday and as I drive up to Joe's house, I can see several signs of disrepair. He is not at home and his neighbor tells me Joe is at his church, the Pee Dee Baptist Church. I pass by the Leland Grove church and over and then north of the Little Pee Dee. I find his church, where I visited many years ago to take photographs and, afterwards, to have an exhibit of photos. As is usual, there are a few people, mostly teenagers, standing around the front of the church. I ask for Joe and someone goes into the church. As the doors open and close, I can hear the sounds of the church's gospel group singing.

Joe "Stump" Hunt comes out with one of his daughters. She does not look well, with her skin looking blotchy and dark areas under her eyes. Joe though, the great survivor, looks his usual self but older, like me. We shake hands.

Q: Stump, did you get my postcard asking to see you?

Joe: Oh sure, I knew you were coming. Glad to see you. You remember my daughter, Polly?

Q: Yes, back when we took the family pictures, right? [We shake hands] How are you?

Polly: Well, not too good. My cancer has come back. I was doing real good for a while. I took all kinds of medicine. I thought it was gone, at least . . . well, you know . . . under control. But it sure has come back. [Her voice trails off, she looks away.]

Q: I'm very sorry to hear this. [pause; in fact, I am lost for words] Ah, Joe, how are you doing?

Joe: Well, I'm doing pretty good considering. Got into a bad accident. Way back, in, in, it was in '93 . . . soon after I got out of jail. I was working for a contractor and got hurt real bad.

Q: Could you tell me about it?

Joe: You see, I was standing behind a dump truck on a kind of a platform. Back behind me was a fall off down to a concrete floor. So I'm standing near that fall off and then the dump truck started to move backwards and pushed me off. I fell about twenty-five feet . . . someone measured it later . . . and I broke my left leg and my elbow . . . see my arm. [He pulls off his Sunday coat and pulls up his sleeve. There are scars everywhere, not just on his elbow.] They had to put in a steel plate in my leg. [He pulls up his left trouser leg to show the scars.] It took me years to get the right medical attention . . . before everything healed.

Q: Why did it take so long to heal?

Joe: Don't rightly know. [His voice trails off as if he wants to change the subject.]

Q: Well, how is Flonnie doing?

Joe: Oh, she passed. She died let's see . . . eight years ago. She's buried out behind the church, in the graveyard.

Q: You've been through a lot. Could the three of us go out there and you show me the grave?

So, Joe "Stump" Hunt and his dying daughter and I go to the family grave site. There we find a gravestone with Flonnie's inscription on one side and Joe's not-quite-finished inscription on the other. Embedded into the grainy granite is a color photograph of Flonnie and Joe together, both with slight smiles on their faces. The photograph, after eight years, is still clear and bright with accurate colors. Perhaps it has been varnished to protect it from the sunlight.

As I am inspecting the photograph, I look up and see Joe and Polly lighting up cigarettes. Since Flonnie was also a smoker, I want to ask if she died because of it. I can't get up the courage. Instead I think how for centuries and centuries tobacco has been used in sacred ceremonies and rituals to help with cleansing the spirit, with bonding of relationships.[13]

But now, are these historic good uses turned around as excuses to overuse it? I put this question out of mind and ask if it is okay to take some photographs of them at the grave site. As the light wind whips Polly's long, dark hair about and as she and her father continue to smoke, they agree to the photo session. I begin to take pictures of the two talking in unposed ways and angles. Then we do some posed images. I get them to stand next to the gravestone. Polly then moves, kneeling on top of the earth, to be over Flonnie's actual site, closer to her deceased mother, perhaps. Joe squats down where he will permanently reside.

I am looking for an expressive image that will somehow reveal the human truth of this moment. Then it is over and Polly painfully gets up and slowly walks back toward the church. Joe and I head to the parking lot where we talk for a while.

Q: Stump, tell more about what has been happening to you.

Joe: Well . . . you know [with a sort of embarrassed look on his face] . . . two years after Flonnie died I got married again . . . ah, that was in 1998. But things didn't work out right . . . We had known each other . . . for awhile, but she was quite younger . . . and we soon got separated.

Q: Joe, I have known you a long time and I feel that I need to ask you one more time about what happened at your store back in 1988 or '89. What exactly happened?

Joe: Oh, okay . . . I don't mind talking about that . . . shoot . . . that seems so long ago. Here's what happened: The cops came to my store. I wasn't there when they first came. I had a woman working there at the time and I came over right away. First, they wanted to arrest her for selling beer to a minor. Then they started to search my store. They searched that store five times, I counted them! And finally they found a lid of coke . . . I've done some bad things in my life but I never, ever sold cocaine!

But they claimed I had cocaine in a can and they arrested me. Now here's the thing. Everyone assumed that that white powder was cocaine, but no one did a lab exam of it . . . to prove it. But I pleaded guilty so as to get that girl off the hook . . . that was part of the bargain. And I got a six to ten sentence and served three years . . . got off 'cause of good behavior. So that's the real story . . . I didn't want that girl to get into deep trouble for selling beer to a minor . . . so now all that's over.

With that we wander back to the church porch where there are some people standing around, and after this I go into the church service with Joe. The church is nearly full and the choir is singing again, in fast-paced modern gospel style. Many people turn to look at us, smiling, as we take seats near the back. Joe whispers in my ear that one of the younger singers is his granddaughter. He looks very proud, pleased, and even happy. His church, it certainly seems evident, has welcomed Stump Hunt back into its arms.

After the gospel music has finished and as the preacher comes to the pulpit, I excuse myself. I try to be as invisible as possible but I can feel some eyes following me. Having attended many Indian church services, I know it is very common for people, mostly men, to come and go throughout a service. Yet I feel somewhat guilty for leaving so soon.

Outside, there are still some people standing around in the shade of the porch roof. A few are smoking.

As I drive away and get on a country road and as I leave the Pee Dee region, I keep thinking about all that I have heard about this Sunday morning. His wife's death, his daughter's impending death, Joe's story of wrongdoing, of retribution, of serious injuries, and his acceptance back into the embrace of the church—all I rehash.

Joe "Stump" Hunt has lived an abundant life. He has had a staggering number of experiences; he has always clung to his Indian roots; he is leaving behind seven children, thirty-two grandchildren, and fifteen great-grandchildren. With all the good and the bad and the inconsistencies, Stump has led a life affirming life.

This story of the Pee Dee could end here but it needs updating. In 2005, I sent an e-mail to Carolyn Chavis Bolton, chief of the Pee Dee Indian Nation of Upper South Carolina, congratulating her and her council on the hard work that led to formal state recognition. I also included some questions. Her response is summarized here.

She told me that the process to obtain state recognition took three years before finally the state "said that we are here." She also told me that most of her tribal members are from Dillon County although some live in Marlboro County. She also stated that David Locklear is no longer chief of the tribe in McColl, with which her tribe is not connected.

I had asked her if her tribe had any common land or community building. She told me that raising funds is very difficult, being that Dillon has only small towns, and therefore they don't have any common land or community building. She said that she had been chief for four years and it has not been an easy job: "I guess that I'm not one of the good old boys."

She concluded that state recognition has not resulted in anything for the

Indian people, at least as far as money is concerned. Recognition, she said, "was kind of like saying, 'Yes, you are here—now go away.'" But this will not happen, she also seems to be saying!

Having her group achieve state recognition has resulted in, among other acts, the issuing of tribal cards, which is a precious prize to someone who qualifies to hold one. The Pee Dee long ago lost their official tribal identity, and the issuing of tribal cards now is a mark, a signpost, that their identity is being affirmed. In 2005, when the Pee Dees of Dillon County received state recognition, Chief Bolton exclaimed to a reporter, "I don't have to prove who I am anymore."[14] This statement is at the very root of the assertion of Indian identity in the Carolinas. The tribal card is the physical manifestation of this identity.

To complete this chapter on the Pee Dee, in January of 2006, the Pee Dee tribe based in Marlboro County and led by Chief James Caulder (about two thousand members) received official recognition as a tribe by the South Carolina Commission for Minority Affairs. On the day of the announcement, Chief Caulder was quoted as saying that back in 1958 he applied for a driver's license and the person checking his application said, "You've got the race wrong here. South Carolina ain't got no Indians." He went on to say that "today erased all of those years of being identified as 'other' or 'white' or 'black.' It gives myself and my people the opportunity to say 'Hey, we are Indians and we are proud.'"[15]

Twenty-five years ago at the start of my research in South Carolina, only the Catawba Indians enjoyed state recognition and they were then in federal limbo. Now at the beginning of 2008, though, there is one federally recognized tribe (the Catawbas) and there are five Indian tribes recognized by the South Carolina Commission for Minority Affairs. In addition there are six recognized Indian groups and one state-recognized special-interest organization, the American Indian Chamber of Commerce of South Carolina. There are other Indian groups seeking recognition now in the wings; please refer to the appendix for greater details.

In a *South Carolina Indian Voicé* newsletter, Buster Hatcher, the editor, cautions his readers that as important as formal recognition is, it is not the end all. He says, "The issues and attitudes that faced us in the nineties are still here. Recognition does not magically make them disappear . . . Recognition, in my view, is merely a step in solving the problems. We can speak with a louder voice now, but we will have to speak."[16]

With these words to conclude the South Carolina segment of this book, it is now time to cross the state line and go to Robeson County, North Carolina.

8

The Lumbees

Across the somewhat arbitrary state border from the South Carolina counties of Dillon and Marlboro are the North Carolina counties of Robeson and Scotland. Here in these two North Carolina counties, well over fifty thousand people identified themselves as American Indian in the 2000 census. Most are Lumbees, although some (about 2 percent) call themselves Tuscaroras, a tribe that thrived in the early history of this region.

In this same census nearly forty-seven thousand members of the Lumbee Tribe are listed in Robeson County alone. If one were to count the Lumbees in the adjacent counties of Hoke (to the north) and Scotland (to the west), then an additional seven thousand people are added to the Robeson County numbers and the total would be fifty-four thousand Lumbee Indians.

These figures make the Lumbees the largest tribe east of the Mississippi River. In fact, only seven other tribes in the United States are larger. These are the Cherokee (when all bands are combined) with 281,000; the Navajo with 269,000; the Sioux at 108,000; the Chippewa at 106,000; the Choctaw with 87,350; the Pueblo with 60,000 (counting nineteen groups); and the Apache with 87,000.[1] All of these other tribes are among the Bureau of Indian Affair's (BIA) federally recognized tribal governments. There are 562 such Indian tribes.

However, the Lumbees are not federally recognized—or not in any meaningful way. In a manner defying logic, common sense, and most ethical principles, the 1956 Congressional Lumbee Act both recognized and then terminated BIA federal status. Explaining this part of the Lumbee story, in depth, is best left to others who have written extensively on the subject. Regaining meaningful federal recognition has been a major goal for the Lumbees and their efforts have also included a petition to Congress for educational assistance.[2] However, the tribe does enjoy state recognition, accorded by the

North Carolina General Assembly in 1885, as do six other North Carolina tribes.[3]

There is a total membership of sixty-seven thousand in North Carolina state-recognized tribes. Counting the entire population, there were one hundred thousand American Indians living in North Carolina as of the 2000 census, dwarfing the Indian population found in South Carolina.[4]

For the Lumbees, being such a large tribe, there has been a considerable focus of attention on their history and struggles that, in turn, has resulted in numerous books, articles, and legal decisions. In searching the Internet recently, I found 137 books concerning the Lumbees. Some of these books have been written by Lumbees, with one being a standard on Lumbee history, *The Only Land I Know,* by Adolph Dial and David Eliades.[5]

Yet perhaps one of the best and very compressed summaries of the chronological and legislative history of the Lumbees can be found at Lumbee.org. The article "Lumbee," written by Dr. Linda Oxendine, a Lumbee Indian, references recent archaeological evidence that shows Indians were living along the Lumber River (once called Downing Creek) as long as fourteen thousand years ago.[6] She goes on to write that the precontact history of the Lumbees is not perfectly clear. As a result there has been widespread speculation of the tribe's origins. In the nineteenth century a local historian held that the Indians in Robeson County were descended from a mix of the "Lost Colony" of Europeans of Roanoke Island and Native Americans from an adjacent island, the Croatan Island. Hence for a period of time Lumbees were referred to as Croatan Indians. However, this term, which once had positive connotations, evolved into the twentieth century to have quite a negative meaning.

Dr. Oxendine cites a number of scholars who believe that the Lumbees are descended from an eastern Siouan group called the Cheraws. In particular she notes that John Swanton, an ethnologist of the Smithsonian Institution, concurs with the Cheraw descent theory, but he also infers a genealogical influence from other Siouan-speaking tribes of the precontact and postcontact eras. She also cites other scholars who maintain that, as was common in the Southeast, remnants from other local tribes would find refuge in and near the swamps of this part of North Carolina. The swamps were extensive then. Now the land has been drained by developers and landowners to provide large acreage for commercial tobacco growing.

It is interesting to note in the history of the Lumbees that in 1715 the Cheraw Indians participated with the Cofitachequi Indian alliance in the disastrous Yamasee War. In this conflict, targeted against the traders as well as colonists in the Charleston, South Carolina, area, the Cofitachequi alliance suffered a severe defeat by a combination of the colonists and their Indian allies.[7]

This tie of the Lumbees/Cheraws with the Cofitachequi alliance is significant to this narrative as it gives evidence that the extent of the Cofitachequi chiefdom included what is now called Robeson County as well as, perhaps, other counties in southern North Carolina.

Evidence seems to indicate that in the precontact and early contact periods women played a balanced role with men in economic, social, and, in some cases, political matters. Cofitachequi had gone beyond a simple hunter-gatherer economy to a more settled agricultural and trading economy supplemented by the traditional domain of men, that of hunting, fishing, gathering, and protection of the tribe.

Although men were important in the newer economy in helping prepare the soil for farming, in digging clay for pottery, in gathering materials for basket weaving, it was women, primarily, who worked the fields, who made the pottery, baskets, and clothing, including the preparation of animal skins, and who practiced herbal medicine. In some cases, women even took part in warfare.[8]

However, as the colonists took over the Carolinas the power and varied roles of women began to be diminished. This loss of balance between men and women is attributed especially to the growth of the deerskin trade. In return for this commodity, Native men acquired guns and a craving for liquor. That is, hunting and the search for additional hunting grounds appeared to lead Native men away from the balance of village life. In consequence, Native culture became more and more patriarchal, like a mirror of European culture.[9]

Native society had lost its balance. This reminds me of the film entitled *Koyaanisqatsi,* which is based on the Hopi Indian word meaning "life out of balance." Although this film concerns itself with contemporary America it could have been applied to the era in question.

But I need to return to the present-day Lumbees. In this regard, I wish to make reference to another book, *Pembroke: A Centennial Retrospective 1895–1995,* written by Lumbees Bruce Barton, Cynthia Hunt, and Linda Oxendine. It is a detailed source of information concerning the Robeson County town of Pembroke.

The already-mentioned Dr. Oxendine is the chairperson of the American Indian Studies department at the University of North Carolina at Pembroke. Mr. Barton is the founder and co-editor of the Lumbee weekly newspaper *Carolina Indian Voice* (no longer in business). Ms. Hunt earned a political science degree from the university and is a paralegal for the Indian Law Unit of the Legal Aid of North Carolina Pembroke office. This unit serves not only Robeson but also other counties in the region, which include some Lumbees as well as Haliwa, Saponi, Waccamaw Siouan, and Coharie Indians.[10] The state of South Carolina has no such legal unit servicing its American Indians.

The Indian Law Unit, along with the Lumbee Regional Development Association (LRDA), is still hard at work in its efforts to obtain BIA recognition for the Lumbees. Very active in this endeavor is Ms. Hunt, who in addition to her work for the legal services unit has contributed to the discourse concerning Lumbee Indian identity and the BIA recognition struggle through her writings. In addition to work on the Pembroke book, she has written a six-part series for the *Carolina Indian Voice.*

Written in 2000, this series of articles has the title "Looking Back While Walking Forward." She talks of a 1934 federal law called the Indian Reorganization Act (the Wheeler-Howard Act). To simplify, the Lumbees, in order to receive benefits under this act, had to compile a list of its members who were of one-half or more Indian blood.

The government sent a Dr. Carl Seltzer, an anthropologist, to Robeson County in 1936 and 1937. Using a very dubious science called anthropometry, he interviewed 209 applicants and declared that only twenty-two met the criteria. These individuals came to be known as the "original twenty-two." In 1938, the twenty-two were informed that they were "certified" but not entitled to any rights or status as members of an Indian tribe since the government was not holding any land in trust for the "Siouans" (i.e., Lumbees).

Cynthia Hunt's response to Seltzer's study is written in her May 25, 2000, article: "The Study included a long intense process which included pseudo-scientific anthropometric analysis of head shape and measurements, skin pigmentation, hair, ears, nose, lips, teeth, and blood type measurements. This was a mockery to the tribe and an affront to the pride of the Indians of Robeson County."[11]

However, in 1972 the Eastern Carolina Indian Organization (ECIO) in representing the original twenty-two was able to gain assistance from the Native American Rights Fund. Bolstered by this support, the ECIO made a case that the termination language in the infamous 1956 Lumbee Act did not terminate the rights of the original twenty-two, whose benefits had been granted to them before the 1956 act was passed.

In 1975, *Maynor v. Morton* affirmed this argument yet the survivors of the original twenty-two and their attorneys were never able to secure any benefits from the federal government. Ms. Hunt concludes this particular article by saying that "for all the significance and benefits *Maynor v. Morton* was to the tribe, the bottom line is that this was just another instance where the federal government treated Robeson County Indians in an unjust and unfair manner."[12]

Be that as it may, the Lumbees, I have been told, are actively seeking another road, perhaps also a very high hill, through a direct congressional bill for federal recognition.

Although Ms. Hunt has stated in her writings that she made trips to several Western tribes in search of support for the Lumbees, she was unsuccessful except for one Indian from the West, Elmer Savilla. He wrote an article for *Indian Country Today (Lakota Times)* titled "A View from the East: Who Should Cast Stones at the Lumbee Nation?" In this article he urges readers to call or write in support of Lumbee recognition. He concludes: "The objections based on mixed-blood are not valued objections, because at this period in our history which tribe can point to its full membership as being 4/4 Indian? The simple truth is that there is no longer a tribe without mixed-blood members . . . Politically we need their numbers . . . However the most important reason is a moral one: because it's the right thing to do."[13]

But what is the cost, the psychic cost to humans who are rejected by their government and by, in some cases, members of other tribes? In his book *Killing the White Man's Indian,* Fergus Bordewich quotes Cynthia Hunt, who talks about "recognition psychosis": "I feel as if I'm not a real Indian if I don't wear feathers. Just thinking about it, I get all bent out of shape. You're told all your life that you're Indian, but sometimes you want to be that kind of Indian that everybody else accepts as Indian."[14]

One of Ms. Hunt's co-authors in their book on Pembroke, Dr. Linda Oxendine, has a somewhat different slant on "recognition psychosis":

> Lumbees know who they are. But they don't know why they are. A lot of people define Indian identity as traditional religion, tribal land, and language. Along with that, there is a tendency to believe that when Indians adapt they become less Indian. Lumbees are Christians, private landowners, and speak English. But adaptation is the essence of being Indian. Before contact, tribes borrowed from each other. After contact, they borrowed from the whites. Tribes were always changing. Total adaptation was not the goal, but people did what was necessary to make life good for themselves, or what they had to do to survive.[15]

In addition to the Legal Aid of North Carolina office and the Lumbee tribal headquarters, the town of Pembroke is the home of the University of North Carolina at Pembroke. This university has gone through a long evolution in name, size, and scope. First established in 1887 as the Croatan Normal School with fifteen students, this school came into being for the express purpose of training Indian teachers. This training would then raise the literacy rate of the Indian population of the region. In 1909, the school's name changed to the Indian Normal School of Robeson County. A few years after that it changed to the Cherokee Indian Normal School of Robeson County. This name lasted until 1941 when the state legislature changed the name to the Pembroke State College for Indians.

Over the years courses were added, enrollment and degrees increased. In 1940, it had its first four-year graduates with baccalaureate degrees. Prior to 1945 only Robeson County Indians were eligible for admission. After 1945 any Indian was eligible. In 1953, white students were admitted. A year later when the Supreme Court outlawed segregation, Pembroke State was opened to all qualified applicants regardless of race.

In 1972, the university became part of the University of North Carolina system. Because of its growth it is one of the largest employers in the area. By 2003, of the total enrollment, 22 percent are American Indian, 21 percent African American, and 50 percent white. A school that once prepared Indian teachers to teach in Indian schools now sees most students majoring in other areas.[16]

The department of American Indian Studies at Pembroke has a wealth of courses, twenty-six in total, on Indian art, literature, history, religious traditions, social work, and sociology. Majors can earn a bachelor of arts degree in American Indian Studies from a faculty of ten teachers including Dr. Oxendine.[17] The number of students who major in American Indian Studies is an unknown figure to me. However, in 2006, I was told by a student that the courses are very popular with Pembroke students, who usually fill the classes.

Yet, as best as I can determine, no other department at Pembroke requires any of its students to take any American Indian Studies courses. This observation, if correct, is not intended to be critical but, rather, an effort to reveal the radical change in the original purpose of the college.

Now this brief story of the Lumbees takes a different turn. It is my belief that Indian identity among Lumbees, as among many of the groups discussed in this book, can also be revealed by an examination of the varied traditions of Indian herbal medicine and faith/spiritual healing.

In 1979, Mary Margaret Steedly interviewed a Lumbee healer by the name of Vernon Cooper, born in 1906 just over the line in South Carolina but living most of his life in Hoke County, North Carolina. This interview led to her paper "The Evidence of Things Not Seen: Faith and Tradition in a Lumbee Healing Practice" and to her graduate degree in folklore from the University of North Carolina at Chapel Hill.

In her paper she classifies Vernon Cooper's technique as a medical practice that combines touch healing, traditional Indian herbal medicine, and Christian faith healing. Cooper's father was a tenant farmer but he had a distant relative who was a medical doctor born in England who migrated to the South. According to Cooper: "He was a doctor when he come over here and found out that the Indians know the herbs, so he lived along with them. And then his son, he just was a root and herb doctor, he just went along with the Indians, they learned him and he'd help them."[18]

Cooper then goes on to reveal his techniques of diagnosis by touching the affected area and gently probing with his hands and by visualization: "Most of the time, when I put my hand on a person, I see the condition, The Lord will show me the cause of it. Sometimes it'll be a shadow or a negative . . . I see things that's not pleasant, and I used to be crazy enough to wish there was some things that I couldn't see. That was wrong. I was that weak. I was wrong . . . So many times I can feel that pain coming out . . . Well, the Lord ain't going to kill me with their pain. I may suffer a few hours, but it's got to go."[19]

Arvis Locklear Boughman and Loretta Oxendine (both Lumbee Indians) interviewed Vernon Cooper for their 2004 book *Herbal Remedies of the Lumbee Indians.* In this quotation the reader gets an excellent picture of Cooper's approach to healing: "We come out of the earth, and there's something in the earth to cure everything . . . Maybe it takes some herbs. Maybe it takes some touching. But most of all, it takes faith."[20]

But where did Vernon Cooper first learn his skills? According to the book *Wisdom Keepers: Meetings with Native American Spiritual Elders,* in the chapter "Vernon Cooper, Lumbee," he received his healing gift in 1917 from his grandmother at her deathbed: "She said this ability was a gift that had been given to our family for four hundred years. She told me, you will be the last one with that gift in our family. There will never be another one. You'll finish out the four hundred years. When my daughter was born I prayed the prophecy would be changed, that she could become a healer, too. But it wasn't to be . . . I've passed on what I could. But the gift of healing with your hand—that can't be passed on."[21]

Before he died Vernon Cooper passed on what he could of healing abilities to other Lumbees, including Daystar Dial.[22] Although I did not know Vernon personally, I certainly knew about him and to this day regret never having met him. At this point it is time to move from the particular and personal to the general and impersonal.

According to the 2000 census, Robeson County had a population of 123,350, with 38 percent Indian, 33 percent white, and 25 percent black. Also note that 23 percent of the population lives below the poverty line.

There are three cities: Lumberton is located to the east of the county along I-95 with a population of twenty thousand. In the center of the county is Pembroke with a population of 2,400 and to the western edge of the county is Maxton with a population of 2,550.

In fact, with apologies to Charles Dickens, the following is a tale of two cities, Pembroke and Maxton. Recently I wondered how these two towns compared to each other, at least in terms of available statistics. From a search on the Internet some curious facts emerge.

The American Indian population of Pembroke is 83 percent of the total, whereas in Maxton the population is 8 percent Indian, 25 percent white, and 64 percent black. In regard to educational level, 22 percent of the population of Pembroke has earned a bachelor of arts degree but only 12 percent of the Maxton residents have such a college degree.[23]

Yet in terms of income, the median household income for Pembroke is $18,355. In Maxton, this figure goes up to $23,143. But why these discrepancies? In looking more closely at the available data (circa 2000), the difference in income, at least in part, seems to be accounted for in the type of employment found in these two towns.

The largest sector for employment in Pembroke is the education, health, and social services category, at 34 percent of the employed population. In Maxton, the largest employment takes place in manufacturing, at 35 percent. In other words, the manufacturing sector pays more and employs more than do education, heath, and social services combined, or at least as I read the figures.

Perhaps I am dwelling too much upon statistics and the comparisons that come from these raw facts. With that in mind, I return to the part of this narrative that focuses upon individuals. On a warm day in June of 1985, I was driving Wes Taukchiray from Pembroke to Maxton, where he was living at the time. Maxton is about twelve miles west of Pembroke and about an equal distance from McColl, South Carolina, to the south.

On the edge of Maxton lived an elderly Lumbee couple, Will and Roberta Locklear, with whom Wes was boarding. Their house was a single story, not too large, and the outside wood was natural, unpainted. From notes made later that day, I will report my conversation with Roberta in the present tense. According to my notes, my conversation was with Roberta only, as her husband rarely talked.

I am sitting on the steps of the front porch facing Roberta, who is in a rocker, and shoeless, in recollection. Her husband Will (or Willie to some) is also on the porch, sitting somewhat behind me. Wes has gone to his room. It is late in the day and this side of the house is in the shade, thank goodness.

Roberta asks me if I would like a glass of water, which I accept and gulp down. Southern summer heat and I don't agree with each other. Although Roberta is sitting in a rocker, she seems seldom to actually rock in it.

The conversation, at first, is typical. It is about the weather, the possibility of good crops, how I got to know Wes. There are pauses between our comments. The air is calm. I then find out from Roberta that she was born on Christmas Day in 1925.

Then, oddly, without any prompting, I begin to tell Roberta about a disturbing dream I had the night before. It, the dream, concerned itself with a conflict between my wife and me. I tell Roberta about this dream in some detail. Will listens but says nothing. There is a long pause, and then she says, "You must follow back the dream."

I am sitting there trying to figure out what this comment could mean. Somehow, to my mind, to follow back a dream implies a pathway, clues, or looking up perhaps Freud on his dream-interpretation theories. But my dream, so vivid the next day in my mind, seems to lead nowhere. There is another long pause on that porch in Maxton on this very warm late afternoon.

Finally, I ask her what she means by that expression. She says, "Well . . . first you must talk with God, and if you are able to, then He will tell you to follow his wishes. [pause] And He will also tell you not to fear what might happen from a bad dream . . . that's what I think."

I try to absorb this. Wes comes out onto the porch. The screen door gives a light bang. He leans against the wall. He now has on no shoes or socks. He thanks me for driving him from Pembroke to Maxton. The scene reminds me of some of the photographs that Marion Post Wolcott took of Lumbees in 1935 before driving into South Carolina. Now, fifty years later, there is this elderly Lumbee couple and a white man, looking like an adopted son, whose life has become devoted to the history and genealogy of Indian people.

Now, so many years later, I realize that as a photographer, I missed out on the opportunity to make a good photograph. But, then, I was still somewhat numb from my dream and what Roberta Locklear had to say about it.

I say good-bye to the Locklears and Wes, and soon I am on the road heading away from Maxton. Roberta's faith is strong, mine is not. In ways my fretful dream has, in reality, already taken place. This comes to me as I drive along those darkening country roads of the Pee Dee Basin. The dream was not predicting of the future, as some people think dreams are, or "wish fulfillment," but a reworking of the past. Roberta had been correct it seems. I have no reason to fear the dream, because I have already lived through it.

On another day in 1985, in autumn, I find myself on a road west of Maxton. I am just south of the hard line between the two Carolinas. I take a break at the roadside flea market outside Pageland, South Carolina. I am walking about. Working one table are three people who look to have Indian roots. Upon asking this, all three tell me they are Indians from Robeson County who come here to sell goods. The woman, who looks older than the two men, is wearing a dark red dress and is shoeless. She is short and thick and has dark-brown, intelligent eyes. She reminds me of my wife's mother, who had some American Indian roots. I want to talk with her more, but potential customers come to her table.

I drift over to the next table behind which sits a young woman who also looks Indian. Since there are no customers at her table I strike up a conversation (from which I write notes later on in the car):

Q: Could you tell me where you live?
A: Oh, we live in Pageland, now. My mother . . . she's the manager at Hardees in Pageland . . . She's gone to open up but will be back soon . . . I'm just looking after things 'til she gets back.
Q: Where did you live before Pageland?
A: Well, we all, there's my mother and I've got two sisters and a brother, come from Robeson County . . . My mother separated from dad . . . ah, well . . . four years ago . . . I'm fifteen [she volunteers] . . . my dad's last name is Chavis.
Q: I believe that name, Chavis, is usually Indian?
A: Oh, yes! I'm 100-percent Lumbee [she says very proudly]. My mom's Lumbee . . . course my dad is . . . but mom remarried, just got remarried . . . [pause] He's a white man.

Then I get back on the road. As I drive along westward, now toward Rock Hill, South Carolina, I think about how the Lumbees have survived. I think it is, in part, because they are practical, so adaptable, some say so feisty, and proud of their heritage.

Many years later, almost twenty years, it is spring of 2004. I am again on the road. I've just been to the Catawba reservation and am headed to Waxhaw in Union County, North Carolina, which is about five road miles east of the

Catawba River. Waxhaw is also about twenty miles south of Charlotte and around one hundred miles west of Pembroke.

Waxhaw was named after the Washaw Indians. They were probably members of the Cofitachequi alliance. Waxhaw has about the same population as Pembroke and Maxton at 2,625 but with different demographics. The population is 80-percent white, 17-percent black, and less than 1-percent American Indian.[24] An important part of American Indian culture here is Earl Carter, sometimes called "Many Skins" by those who know him well.

Earl Carter is a Lumbee Indian who has chosen to live in Waxhaw. I first met him at a Catawba Festival in 1990 when he was discussing with Elizabeth Pyler, a Catawba, her medical problem. It has been my experience that some people refer to him as a "Native healer," a term that seems to make him feel uncomfortable. Others call him a "fire keeper," a term that seems to agree with him more. Out of respect, most call him "Mr. Earl."

The use of these terms seems to bring out what I perceive to be a natural shyness. I am in fact very pleased, even honored, to have been given an opportunity to interview him and to do his portrait once again. On this May day, I find his home on a road just outside Waxhaw at the beginnings of a rural area. He is sitting on a lawn chair outside his house on an acre or so of land. I see a neatly cultivated, good-sized garden, a yard that is unkept, by middle-class standards, with weedy areas. There are a variety of trees including some walnuts and a small stand of bamboo.

Mr. Earl is nearly six feet in height, I think, and he has a deliberate way of walking. When he speaks it is with a deliberate, soft voice with numerous pauses. He tells me that he is fatigued of late due to the contracting of Lyme disease a few years ago with which he continues to struggle. I ask for permission to record our conversation on audiotape. He agrees.

Q: Tell me about the Lyme disease; how did you get it?

Earl: Well three years ago . . . see . . . I go to the woods. There's a spiritual area nearby and I got some ticks on me and I didn't know it. And when I did find them . . . one imbedded here and one under my arm and I found one back here in that big muscle [points to leg]. They had to cut that one out . . . [pause] then I got paralyzed . . . [pause] I was paralyzed for a while.

Q: I bet that was scary.

Earl: Oh, yeah . . . I lost about 130 pounds. [pause] I had fevers . . . then I couldn't walk for a long time . . . then I got a walker, I got that and then I graduated to a walking state [long pause], then I come back.

19. Earl Carter, Lumbee fire keeper, 2004

Q: I won't take much of your time . . . there's no medicine for it?
Earl: No . . . oh, ah . . . the doctors give you stuff but it still always kills something else [laughs]. Doctor knows how to take you apart and put you back together . . . but he don't know your system.
Q: Did you use any of your knowledge about herbs and medicine to help [yourself]?
Earl: Oh, yes!
Q: That's how you recovered?
Earl: Yes . . . probably was . . . but I don't tell them [laughs]. They'd scoff at it and say, "Oh, it's nothing but weeds." But I would say there is no such thing as a weed . . . I would not cut down nothing unless it's in the way . . . nothing . . . [pause] like those blackberries . . . someone says, "Why don't you cut down those

briars in your yard?" . . . Man, there's a lot to eat and lots of jelly. Also, the blackberry stems and roots are an astringent.

Q: But it takes a person like you to know all that; this is not taught anymore?

Earl: No, this is not taught anymore . . . Some people have asked me to teach them and then they say, "Oh, I wouldn't take any of that old weed." I say, "Oh, okay" [laughs]. Some people see weeds. I see medicine.

Q: Do you use tobacco in your ceremonies?

Earl: Yeah, and . . . [pause] no chemicals put on it . . . no nothing . . . all natural. We use the smoke. Smoke takes bad things away . . . like washing your hands . . . [pause] and cleansing the spirit . . . We use it in a pipe . . . it's a pipe prayer.[25]

Q: I took a picture of you at the Catawba Festival and I had [a copy] ready to bring from New Jersey . . . well, my excuse is that in my rush to pack my camera stuff and everything, well, I forgot the print.

Earl: [both laugh] There's a saying: "Instead of Alzheimer's disease, I have old timer's disease?"

Q: [both laugh] Yeah, I think you have it right for me. My memory is not as good as it used to be, that's for sure. Let me ask you, when were you born?

Earl: Nineteen forty-one . . . They [in his tribe] call me "old man." Some people call me "medicine man" and I say, "Don't call me that, you don't need to call me that."

Q: What about the term *healer?*

Earl: Well . . . I don't ever like to be called that!

Q: Buster Hatcher had you over [to the Waccamaw's] to teach someone from his group the proper way of building a fire . . . the word he used was *fire keeper.*

Earl: Yes, well, there is . . . [pause] . . . Well I can't explain it . . . You lay your wood in there in a certain way and you pray . . . all around in four different directions . . . just lay it in . . . You don't tuck it in . . . just lay it in . . . like a baby . . . laying it in like a baby. And . . . ah . . . there's no way I teach that man about it . . . just ain't grasping it . . . [pause] and one thing, if something is handed to you, you think you can be a fire keeper in a day . . . but you ain't [voice trails off].

Q: How long have you been a fire keeper?

Earl: All my life, I reckon.

Q: Where were you born?
Earl: I was born in Robeson County.
Q: So you are Lumbee?
Earl: Yup.
Q: How did you find yourself in Waxhaw?
Earl: Well . . . I says . . . well, I always had girlfriends and whenever I would bring them home, my mother would say, "Did you know that girl is kin to you?" . . . and I would always listen to that story "go west, young man, go west" . . . so I came west and I met my wife here and we've been together almost forty-five years.
Q: Is that right; do you have children?
Earl: Yeah, we have two boys . . . and [audiotape not clear] grandchildren.
Q: What do they do? Has either one followed in your footsteps?
Earl: No . . . and one reason . . . I wasn't told to teach . . . except how to treat people and stuff like that . . . where with ceremonies and stuff . . . I've not taught them . . . [pause] but I've got to teach my granddaughter . . . she's just been born.
Q: So you've got to take care of yourself, so that she's got [time] to become mature enough to absorb what you've got to teach her?
Earl: Yeah . . . and . . . but I don't know if her mom is goin' to like this or not.
Q: How do you know that this is going to happen or should happen?
Earl: 'cause this was passed to me by my grandmother . . . then it's to pass from me to a granddaughter . . . so when she gets daughters, then it is passed to a son.
Q: I see, I understand . . . woman, man, woman, man?
Earl: That's right . . . my grandmother and I would go out . . . pick herbs when I was little . . . and 'cause she couldn't get down [to the ground] . . . she would say, "Earl, get me the arrowroot over there" . . . I would say, "Grandmother, there's some right here." And she would say, "No, I want that one" so I would go and get that one. She would say, "You'll understand when you get fifty" . . . and I didn't start nothing until I was about fifty . . . I stayed away from it . . . 'cause I was afraid of it . . . and ah . . . so I understand now . . . what I got to do . . . see [showing me by example] I pick seven [grass leaves] . . . I go pass seven and pick

[the next] seven . . . what that does . . . it leaves some for the seventh generation. Man don't do that now, he tear up everything . . . now. I have a grandson and it bothers him to see trees pushed over and everything . . . but I'm not giving it [his gift] to him.

Q: Does it bother him that he is not in line to get it?

Earl: Well no . . . it bothers me that he wants to do it . . . Well he probably wants to do it and will do it . . . [pause] See that place where it's been bulldozed . . . he took a fit . . . and up near Waxhaw, they cleared it off . . . it had all kinds of animals in those woods . . . now they are going to make it a cemetery!

Q: I thought you were going to say that they cleared it off to make a [housing] development.

Earl: It always bothers me when I go down that run and it's gone . . . I hate to lose all my stuff here . . . I've got black walnut trees, a cane bed there . . . that makes cool air come through [laugh] . . . but that stuff [bamboo canes] can get away from you.

Q: How long have you been living here?

Earl: Oh . . . ah . . . I've been living here ever since I have been going around to powwows . . . well, that's forty-three years.

Q: Is it okay to go over to the tobacco patch and take some photos? [After some photos, we return to the chairs.] Now, your healing has to do with touching, doesn't it?

Earl: Yeah . . . but not all time . . . not all the time.

Q: It depends on the circumstances?

Earl: Yeah . . . you know . . . if you are tuned to it, it works without touching [he slowly waves hands near my head] . . . Do you feel that energy?

Q: Oh yes . . . it's calming.

Earl: Uh huh . . . I do that . . . [but] some people misunderstand . . . they say, "Oh-huh, that's weird . . . he's a weirdo." I've been called a witch, I've been called a soothsayer . . . all kinds of stuff. But I say, "No, I don't play no games."

Q: My wife would appreciate what you do, because she studied a Japanese technique like what you use, called Reiki.

Earl: Uh huh . . . Reiki . . . yeah. We wouldn't call it Reiki . . . we just call it healing touch.

Q: She's been taught that when something hurts [in someone else] she goes like this [I gesture with my hands as if to shake off something] to get rid of it; do you ever do anything like that?

Earl: Yeah, yeah, I tell you what it does . . . it [the pain] gets in me. I've got to get rid of it . . . the pain they feel, gets sometimes in me and I got to get rid of it.

Q: How do you?

Earl: Oh there are different ways . . . [pause, as if he is debating whether to give me this information, his technique] . . . When I'm clear of it then I can listen to the universe sing.

It is a beautiful expression! By now I am sure that our conversation and photo session have tired him. I leave to head toward Charlotte, then to the northeast.

After getting home to New Jersey, I send Earl Carter the promised portrait from 1990 although none yet from the more recent interview. I also enclose a large glass jug. My wife had an extra one; it is similar to the one Earl uses for growing herbs.

This completes the chapter on the Lumbee Indians. In the last chapter, I will attempt to complete the circular structure of this book by bringing the narrative back to the Catawba River, back to the geographic area that was once the core of the Cofitachequi alliance.

9

The Red Road

I wake up at the first luminous sign of morning. It is March, and approaching the spring equinox, on a Friday in 2006. I am in the narrow bed that I have made from the conversion of my elderly Toyota into a sort of travel van. I am camped out in a North Carolina state park about five miles outside of Pembroke. Looking out the rear window, I see in the dim light the sacred circle some twenty yards away.

The circle itself is approximately ten yards across and is made of slender wood posts roughly waist high and connected by slender wood railings. There are four gates opening to the four major points of the compass: east, south, west, north. In the center of the circle is a carefully arranged stack of wood in a shallow pit. At sunup the chief fire keeper, Earl Carter, will light the wood. Following his lead, his assistants and others who have gathered will begin their annual spring equinox ceremonies, which Mr. Earl has led for the past fifteen years.

Once afire the wood will burn continuously for three days, periodically being replenished with fresh wood by the fire keepers. Nearby, about twenty yards to the west of the sacred circle, is the social circle with its fire that has been burning since Thursday. It too will be kept alive throughout the ceremonies, the "Gathering."

Just to the north of this scene is a large ball field. Beyond is a parking lot and then a lake with numerous ducks and other birds and along one edge an amphitheater. Here at this outdoor theater for a number of years the Lumbee Indians staged a play that dramatized a part of their history, that of fabled Henry Berry Lowrie. This play, called *Strike at the Wind,* was first produced in 1976 but in the past few years has not been staged, I am told. The wood structure—bench seats and stage—has a bit of a run-down look. Later, on this day, I find there two park employees hard at work repairing the theater in preparation for the musical drama's revival.

To the west of the two circles is a swimming pool and beyond that a golf course. To the south of the circles, behind a stand of trees, are the grounds and building that house the North Carolina Indian Cultural Center. In all, the park contains over one hundred acres and was once land given to the Lumbee Tribe to be their reserve.

Different people tell me different stories as to how this became, in the 1930s, Lumbee land only to be lost to private interests and then taken over by the state of North Carolina. Now, even though it is a state park, everyone I have talked with seems to feel that it is truly Lumbee land, their unofficial reserve.

Last night, Thursday night, I sat with a small group in chairs around the social fire and was told bits and pieces of this Lumbee land story. I had arrived just as it was getting dark and met first with Earl Carter. Another person I met with was Harvard Chavis, one of the fire keepers, who makes his living as a contract metalworker. He travels to construction sites up and down the Atlantic coast mostly working on tall buildings. He is an engaging teller of stories including those of near accidents that occurred on some of his jobs. Recently he was working in New England and made a visit to the Harvard campus. The first name of Harvard is a tradition in his Lumbee family, with three generations of men so named.

Also there last night was Phil Hewitt. He was mostly quiet at the time but I found out from him that he came south to go to college at Pembroke to major in American Indian Studies. I also met Melanie Locklear, who works with young people in Robeson County with substance-abuse problems. Melanie told me that although she is a Lumbee with deep family roots in Robeson County she was reared in the Washington, D.C., area. She came to Pembroke to go to the college. I also discovered that she is a niece of the late Grace Lowry, the Lumbee who started the Council of Native Americans of South Carolina.

Although the conversations were good and lively, I was tired from my long trip, which included car problems. I excused myself and crawled into my van to sleep.

Now it is Friday morning and I see some people emerging from a large, round tent. I later find out this tent was designed after the Mongolian yurt (whose fire is considered sacred) and adapted by Earl and Phil. It can fold down to fit in the back of Phil's small pickup. At the top is a hole, and a small amount of smoke twists up in the crisp March morning air.

I see Mr. Earl walking slowly up toward the two circles. Then Harvard emerges from his van that he has parked nearer to the circles than my van or the tent. He has kept the fire going all night at the social circle. I ask him if he uses an alarm clock to wake him at the proper times. No, is his answer; he tells me in a casual way that somehow he knows when to wake up to keep the fire going.

The sun is not up yet. Some people begin to assemble around a picnic table as someone fires up a cookstove and starts the coffee brewing. Everyone is dressed in warm clothing. Then I see a car coming slowly across the ball field toward us. We would be in deep center field if there were a ball game going on. The person in the car has brought boxes of breakfast food. People are drinking coffee and nibbling on rolls; some are smoking. A full breakfast will come later. There are nearly twelve people now.

Then everyone begins to follow Mr. Earl to the sacred circle. They assemble near the east opening. Outside of the circle on its west side is a wooden bench where I settle down to watch.

Earl Carter, the chief fire keeper, begins the ceremony. In late February I had called him seeking permission to attend these ceremonies. Mr. Earl told me that I could attend as long as I promised to not take photographs of any ceremony or use my tape recorder during a ceremony, or take notes, and finally not at any time to describe in detail any ceremony.

So today I simply watch. I will not, of course, report any details. But what takes place this Friday morning in March, as the sun rises over the pine trees, is, for me, moving. The lighting of the fire and the entire ceremony take some time but how long I am uncertain.

At this point then I feel compelled to digress from what is taking place before my eyes to discuss a contentious issue associated with the rise of a variety of spiritual ideas and practices such as I have been observing on this day and have observed in the past. I have been informed by an anthropologist of Indian people that some Plains Indians, as well as other scholars, believe that certain Native rituals practiced by contemporary Indians in the East and Southeast are merely expropriations of stylized, stereotypic versions of Plains Indian rituals.

Put in other terms, it is their belief that such practices as the fire ritual, powwows, "sweating," smudging, and the use of prayer ties and belief in the sacred directions are all products of New Ageism and/or Pan-Indianism, and presumably false.

It is assumed, by me, that their critique of such practices stems from the long history of repression of Native beliefs and practices, which tried to stamp out Native rituals. For example, as early as 1646 in Massachusetts there was an enactment by the "General Court" (a Puritan legislative body) for both the suppression of Native religion and the creation of a "missionary reservation" where Indians who had been converted to Christianity could be segregated from any influence from their nonconverted kinsmen.[1]

This sordid history of religious repression and forced assimilation extended into the twentieth century until 1978 and the passage of the American Indian Religious Freedom Act. The act contains a number of provisions; its core legal basis is that American Indians have been denied their First Amendment constitutional right of free exercise of religion.

Now, how does it apply to the issue at hand? It is my position that critics of the use of Pan-Indian rituals by American Indians need to reevaluate their position. This assertion is based upon two separate considerations. First, not all scholars believe that Native religious practices were completely eliminated from Carolina Indian culture. Second, southeastern Indians have kept their identity alive due, in great part, to their ability to adapt from many sources, including Plains Indian practices.

Based upon my readings and interviews and the work by Frank G. Speck as reported in 1944 in "Catawba Herbals and Curative Practices," I make the assumption that the knowledge and application of herbal medicine by various southeastern Indians is in fact a form of spiritual practice.[2] For example, please note the longtime knowledge and use of herbal practices by the Lumbees described in the previous chapter. I suggest that in support of my argument the reader should review current articles such as "Native American Healing."[3]

However, I will concede that many of the practices and ideas that I have witnessed have their origin in Indian cultures, for example, Lakota, that perhaps have been less negatively influenced by religious repression. Yet that being said, I have come across a source—the *Encyclopedia of Native American Religions*—that states the practice of the sacred fire is a southeastern tradition basic to the religious practices of the Cherokee, Chickasaw, Creek, Seminole, Yuchi, and other southeastern tribes.[4] Is this a practice once in existence, then erased, and now restarted? This source is not clear on the matter. The ceremony that I have witnessed at the Lumbee gathering appears to be consistent with the description as portrayed in this source.

But what about other practices that do probably come to the Southeast as part of a national Pan-Indianism movement? Is this a blasphemous disrespect for the many different American Indian religions, as some critics believe?

I am very uncertain of that. But when I search the Internet concerning the issue, I discover from what appear to be reliable sources that the diffusion of traditional practices is not usually held to be negative. In fact, most sources seem to encourage such practices, as long as they are practiced by Indians.[5]

Since this issue is contentious I have contacted one of my Catawba sources. She tells me the following: "Since we do NOT have any written history as to what was done before European contact, they are right to a certain point about having lost a lot of our knowledge about rituals. But regardless of the cause for the Native American spirituality resurgence, it is happening now . . . A few years ago a Lakota holy man [Harry Charger] came to the reservation and met with a few Catawba men and taught them some rituals."[6]

From the foregoing I am assuming that the diffusion of traditional Indian spiritualism has been going on for some time throughout North America. However, this diffusion has resulted in threats to American Indian spirituality from non-Indians who for whatever reason are not content in just learning sacred rituals but try then to pass themselves off as American Indian holy men. Some even go so far as to "teach" the ways to others.

These actions on the part of non-Indians are explored in an article titled "The Ripoff of Native American Spirituality," by Big Thunder and Red Jacket. In this article the authors take as especially threatening to Indian spirituality the practice of charging money for the unwise to learn Native practices: "These people have many New Age sites up and think they are justified in demanding high payment for bogus healing by 'medicine men.' "[7] This practice, it seems to me, gets back to that crucial issue: Indian identity.

So now it is time to get back to the Lumbee gathering. The fire ritual is over and the participants are moving away from the sacred fire area to the social circle area. I join the group at the social fire and the picnic table nearby. They invite me to eat some of their breakfast, but being a veggie I have brought my breakfast: corn cereal, banana, soy cheese, and milk—my regimen broken only with their wonderful, real coffee. Some show an interest in what I am eating, and I extol the virtues of soy. This must be boring, as people drift away.

As the day progresses people come and go. Some stay to take part in the noon ceremony, others just watch. I get permission from Mr. Earl to use my camera and tape recorder as long as I do so far away from the sacred circle. The social area is fine as long as I ask permission.

I begin to talk with Jim Carter, who is married to Earl Carter's sister but not related to Earl by blood; the fact that their last name is the same is coincidental. Jim is a middle-aged Lumbee who with his wife has two grown children. He asks me some questions about photography and volunteers that he

20. James Carter, Lumbee, 2006

would like to learn more about it. He has a point-and-shoot digital camera but is not pleased about the results.

At this, I go to my van where I keep a backup camera. Although it is a fixed-lens camera with no working meter and no auto focus, the sharp lens with aperture and shutter control might make it a good camera for Jim to learn with. I rarely use it and since it was given to me, I think that it will make a good gift for someone who can possibly make use of it.

I return to the social area and demonstrate to Jim all the controls. After all this instruction Jim agrees to a more formal interview and my use of an audio tape recorder:

Q: Jim, would you consider yourself a traditionalist?
Jim: Well, [I] wouldn't call myself that. I [have] really only started to get in contact—always knew I was a Lumbee, always knew

I was an Indian—but I never practiced any Native ways until about ten years ago. I started going to sweat lodges and stuff like that.

Q: Where was the sweat lodge?

Jim: In Cherokee . . . I started in Cherokee until I found people around here, about five years later, that were sweating . . . I started sweating with them . . . and these ceremonies here . . . I come here and the sacred fire each year.

Q: What got you started ten years ago to [make you] examine your Indian identity?

Jim: That's kind of interesting . . . I was working for a substance rehab program . . . We as a staff were going to do something as a retreat . . . and one of my bosses suggested to do a sweat lodge—I had heard of them vaguely—so they got in contact with some people in Cherokee and that's when I started . . . I think I am the only one who continued it of that group.

It was something I connected with very strongly . . . I felt it was a part of me . . . something I was missing . . . I've continued ever since.

But I don't consider myself a traditionalist . . . I don't go to powwows . . . ah . . . all I do is come to this Gathering and sweat lodges and I read a lot on Native American spirituality . . . to me it is a simple religion—for me—not a whole lot of ritual into it, unlike some churches, very little dogma, you must stay within means, you have to respect the traditions, and the spirituality as a way of life.

It's simple because it's back to nature, and the Native ways seem natural—the sweat lodge, coming out here around the fires, and praying in the medicine wheel . . . it, it seems the right way.

Q: It seems uniquely Native, not something that came from another culture . . . has the feel of authenticity?

Jim: Yes, right! It's something that has been passed down from generations . . . connected to traditions . . . that I thought were lost here . . . Some people have practiced it . . . have lost it when practicing; it was illegal to practice it! . . . Back in the forties and fifties . . . that recent! . . . I just wish more people would take part in this . . . but you know it isn't for everybody.

Q: There's an old saying: "There is no necessary magic in numbers."

Jim: Yeah . . . that's true . . . good solid core of people here.
Q: How old are you?
Jim: I'm . . . ah . . . fifty-two . . . 1953.
Q: Do you have children?
Jim: Two . . . They are adults . . . twenty-five and twenty-seven . . . they come here . . . my daughter was here today for a while. My son has been to sweat lodges with me . . . I've introduced it to him . . . but don't know if they are ready to practice it yet . . . We don't talk about it a whole lot . . . just every once in a while . . . They know where it's at . . . might wake up and start practicing it.
Q: Is your wife involved in this?
Jim: No, she's not involved.
Q: Melanie told me the churches here are pretty much segregated; is that true? Was she exaggerating?
Jim: Not really . . . this whole area is—some people think—more segregated than ever . . . the whole area . . . although some churches have mixed races . . . We're unique in Robeson 'cause we have Natives, Europeans, Hispanics, and blacks—so we have four different races . . . It would be nice to see everyone working in unity, but it don't happen that way. But some churches are branching out and have all races . . . there are some nondenominational churches in this area. I go to a nondenominational church.
Q: Does your wife go there?
Jim: No, hers is a traditionalist Baptist . . . We have a lot of preachers in her family. Her father, her uncles, cousins . . . She had a brother who preached at one time—he doesn't now though . . . and then there is Earl.
Q: Does she resist your way?
Jim: Oh, no! She supports me. And my mother, she's religious and supports it [his Native ways] . . . she understands . . . There is a lodge supported by a lot of the churches . . . a sweat lodge—called "unipi"—it tries to help people cope with substance abuse.
Q: Speaking of substance abuse, have the members of this Gathering overcome substance abuse?
Jim: Well . . . I'll leave that up to them [to tell you] but I'm in [a] twelve-step recovery fellowship . . . I've been in recovery so long that I have a whole, big area of support . . . people here at

the Gathering, in lodges, people at church, and a whole lot of other friends . . . I've been in recovery for eighteen years.

Q: So you were in recovery many years before you got back again to your Indian identity?

Jim: Recovery led me . . . the fellowship opened up other doors to me . . . to venture out and try new ideas and it led me in the door of Native American spirituality . . . that's exactly what it did for me!

Q: I noticed last night that here [at the social circle] there was no drinking, no partying.

Jim: Well, we won't have it! That type of behavior—we won't deal with it . . . because people who drink or do drugs . . . well it brings bad energy to the circle . . . we here are trying . . . seeking ways to change . . . we welcome anybody as long as they are not high on chemicals or anything! . . . Anyone on drugs or alcohol becomes unpredictable.

Q: Last evening you mentioned *The Source;* could you tell me again what you said about it?

Jim: It talks about how the Jewish religion and Christianity and the Muslims . . . how they have clashed . . . how they came about . . . it teaches me a lot . . . I read more now than ever since being clean and being on the Red Road.

Q: Is that what the Red Road means, being clean?

Jim: Ah . . . well . . . not necessarily . . . the Red Road just means that we are walking in Native American spirituality. And some people get sober through that . . . that path . . . just like some other paths . . . Some people sober [up] through churches but the biggest way for people to get rid of alcoholism or drug addiction is through the twelve-step fellowship . . . that's my belief.

Q: And the Red Road helps support this?

Jim: Yeah . . . because there is no conflict . . . all of them go hand in hand . . . if people would take out the dogmas from different religions . . . and stuff like that . . . then some people get caught up in the details though and take out the spirituality of what the Creator meant to be . . . and that is when you have your conflicts between the religions.

This concluded my interview with Jim Carter that day. However, I did ask him days later by way of e-mail to clarify for me his definition of the

Red Road. In his return e-mail he stated: "In 1994 my teaching on the Red Road began [at Cherokee with his introduction to the sweat lodge] . . . To tell you a little about the seven sacred directions . . . the sacred color blue represents the Creator, green is Mother Earth, red is for the east which stands for new beginnings, yellow [is] for south which stands for new growth and unconditional love, black stands for the Thunder Beings which bring rain, and white . . . stands for wisdom. I try to practice these principles every day: think of others before I think of myself and by practicing prayer and meditation each day to improve my relationship with the Creator. . . . The seventh sacred part . . . is in our heart. It's the living spark the Creator put in all his creations. I call it the soul or spirit."

My conversation with Jim Carter at the Gathering took place on Friday during the day. That evening, with others sitting around the social fire, the topic of the Red Road came up again. During this conversation we talked about each person's individual choices, their freedom to follow a given path. Jim then observed: "Yes, we may be free to choose a path, but we don't necessarily choose the outcome." A wise observation, I think.

The next morning, Saturday, after the Gathering has completed the sunrise ceremonies, some people gather at the social fire. Mr. Earl fires up a smudge pot and smudges himself. He then passes the pot to the others, who follow the ritual. The pot is then passed to me and I hold it in my left hand and with my right hand waft the smoke at my face and chest. Then I start to bend over to smudge my legs, as the others had. But then a woman who is standing next to me takes the pot from my hand and she bends down and smudges my legs for me.

"Let me do this for you . . . you are an elder and we must look after our elders," she says. Normally, given my personality, I would be upset with the implication that I am too old to bend over to perform the ritual. But I am not offended; in fact, I feel a rush of gratitude for the pleasure of being honored for my age, for a change.

As it turns out, this woman is a member of the Chippewa Tribe living here in the South. She and I drift to the breakfast table. Our conversation turns to the four colors of the sacred circle and how the colors used here are not necessarily the same colors used by Western or Plains Indians when representing the four directions of the compass. She talks more of the divergences and convergences in Native practices.

The topic of the use of tobacco had come up in the smudge ceremony. Its use is fairly complicated. Smoke, whether tobacco or wood, acts in a symbolic way to take over our transgressions, our bad feelings. Smoke is also used as a vehicle to transport our prayers to heaven.

Later on Saturday morning I have a brief, recorded, conversation with Phil Hewitt, who is a non-Indian, a student of American Indian culture, and a helper for Mr. Earl. Yet I get no impression that he is trying to pass himself off as an Indian. He was born and reared in New Jersey and his father was a minister. Phil came to Robeson County and attended the University of North Carolina at Pembroke, majoring in American Indian Studies. He lives in North Carolina.

Q: What is the purpose of the prayer ties?

Phil: On the last day of the ceremonies at sunset they are burned in the fire to send back energy to the Creator. Tobacco is the herb of unity . . . tobacco in pipes [is] used in ceremonies to bring people together . . . the other herbs are cleaning agents . . . each has its own role and all work together to make the "whole" . . . it's the order of the universe.

Q: Are the ingredients universal amongst American Indians?

Phil: No, because the herbs are chosen locally . . . Now fire . . . fire is at the core of Native American ceremonies . . . the idea of sending prayers to heaven by way of fire is fairly universal . . . not only in the Americas but around the world.

Q: It seems to me that there is some resistance to Native religion by those who are fundamentalist Christians.

Phil: "I am the way" was an interpretation of Christ's words, which were applied by the missionaries; for them "I am the way" became "that is the only way"!

Q: But the members of the Gathering don't seem to have any conflict between Christianity and their ceremonies?

Phil: No, and I don't either . . . you see . . . the form of the early [Christian] church was not significantly different from Native society . . . no hierarchical system . . . no certified priest . . . then they got a clergy. The earliest church was close to what is the structure of Alcoholics Anonymous—no governing body, no president, yet it is a living entity that grows and lives and breathes and it obviously continues. Actually, this is the way the early church was . . . everyone is a peer . . . everyone is equal. For example, Earl considers himself as a trusted servant . . . does not consider himself the head . . . does not issue edicts . . . will give strong suggestions . . . but doesn't dictate . . . all much like the original Christian church.

Q: Have you been adopted into the Lumbees?

Phil: Well, no . . . but I have been a part of the Gathering for fifteen years now . . . being a part is not something like opening a bag of chips and saying "have some." You know, we get some Looky Lucys . . .

Q: "Looky Lucys," what do you mean by that?

Phil: Oh, people who come to watch a little . . . to gawk . . . for them it remains a game . . . it's dilettantism.

Q: Is the Gathering widely known?

Phil: Well, no, but people know [about it] . . . you see, traditional religions demonize Native practices . . . it goes back to Europe and the Roman Empire . . . whenever they would conquer lands they would eliminate indigenous practices and substitute Roman ways . . . so when the Europeans came here they had adopted Roman values . . . [the most important] being the search for personal wealth and power. [long pause] . . . You know, this year we lost one of our great elders, Spotted Turtle—Raymond Clark. He was important for our Gathering!

Q: Why was that?

Phil: He was trusted by all Lumbees and he was also a member of the Gathering . . . sort of a link [between the Gathering regulars and other Lumbees].

Phil concludes that he has spent most of his life studying Native practices and the history of Christianity. So ends my interview with him.

The topic of prayer ties came up in my conversation with Phil because, prior to our interview, others around the social fire had been working on putting together the prayer ties. As I was watching these activities Melanie grabbed some fabric, a bag of herbs, and then commanded, "Make yourself useful!" As I made myself useful, the topic of the spiritual use of tobacco arose.[8]

When the prayer ties were made and strung they were taken to the sacred fire and tied at the appropriate part of the circle in preparation for their role on the final evening of the Gathering.

Now it is late Saturday morning. I suddenly remember that I have an appointment in Dillon County, South Carolina. From there I plan to head over to Horry County, where Chief Buster Hatcher and the Waccamaws of South Carolina are having their spring equinox ceremonies. Unfortunately, my car breaks down again, this time in rural Dillon County. After stopping there I try to start the car, but it keeps blowing an important fuse. After getting help I am able to go and buy a handful of fuses; then I decide to head north on I-95.

Therefore, I miss talking with Chief Hatcher and observing his tribe's ceremonies. I had wanted to talk with him about his interpretation of the term "the Red Road." Instead, on March 21 I e-mailed him concerning this topic. His response follows:

> As to the Red Road, it means different things to different people. To me it means that I know and understand that every living thing on God's earth has a right to exist here without my interference. We are all a part of each other and we have to live to a standard that reflects our respect for all of the earth and all of its inhabitants, including those that walk, crawl, fly, swim, and grow from her face. If one truly walks the Red Road, you can believe what (s)he says and (s)he can be trusted at your back. The term is used all over, and sometimes only as a badge.
>
> I believe that the primary difference in the Red Road and the ways of Christianity is that they (Christians) act from fear of a vengeful God who would punish them eternally for minor infractions (but he loves them). I (we) do not fear our creator, we cannot be separated from him. It is as if a marble is placed on an anvil and smashed with a hammer. No matter how small a piece flies away, no matter how far it flies it will always be a part of the marble. We (all of God's creation) will likewise always be a part of God. We act from respect and not fear.
>
> I hope that helps.

Via e-mail I asked him if he knew anything about a Native American church near the Catawba reservation, a church Earl Carter made reference to over the past weekend. On March 22, 2006, Buster answered: "The church you are referring to is a Christian church but attended primarily by Native people, I am fairly sure . . . we had a Native church on the old Dimery Settlement. It was called El Bethel Missionary Baptist Church. It burned down in 1986 and again in 1987, and was never rebuilt the second time. We have photos of it and one of its pastors is still alive. Strange that it burned twice with no electricity or plumbing, but it did."

After this exchange I decided to contact a Catawba Indian who has insight into the spiritual paths of members of her tribe as well as a number of American Indians in the Carolinas. She is Beckee Garris, about whom I have written previously. I asked her, via e-mail, about the church just referred to and her description of the Red Road. Herewith is her April 12, 2006, response:

> Tanake Kane' (uncle) Gene,
>
> I am glad you had a great experience with attending the sacred fire ceremony. Just make sure you don't make any direct mention of what

you saw or heard there as it is sacred and thus not open to being written about. The church Mr. Earl was talking about is called Red Path Baptist church on Passmore Rd, just off the Rez. It is Baptist to the truest sense of the faith based church, they just have Native drumming instead of the normal piano or organ music. The preacher who used to serve this church is of Cherokee descent. There is a Methodist church in Neeses, S.C. that Cathy Nelson is the lay minister of and their whole service is Native American. I have been there once as well. I think you know Cathy.

As for the Red Road, that term has a wide range in its use. It is the Red Road to Sobriety based on the 12 steps of AA but from the Native American view point. And that is what we base our Talking/Healing Circle on also.

Ms. Cathy Nelson is of Ojibwa heritage. As I recall her background, she was born and reared in the upper Midwest, but then she moved with her parents to South Carolina near Ridgeville. Her stepfather, now deceased, was very helpful for the Edisto Indians in a number of ways including, with the help of Cathy, the starting of a dancing/drumming group for young Edistos.

Now also involved as a lay minister, Cathy answered my e-mail inquiry with this statement on June 19, 2006:

Hello Gene. The name of our church is Rocky Swamp American Indian Ministries. The church building was built in 1808 by Creek Indians and white settlers as a Methodist Episcopal meeting house. The original structure is sound and used weekly. Six years ago at a Native American Family Conference which is sponsored by the United Methodists, a woman from S.C. commented that this was the first time she could worship as Indian and Christian. She asked if we would worship that way in South Carolina. I said, "yes" and the rest is history.

Every Sunday we hold a sharing circle in Bible Study and a worship service which incorporates Native Christian hymns with drums, flutes, and rattles. Some are in a Native language which was given for our use by a Lakota holy man who carries one of the 12 sacred pipes of the Lakota people . . . The Unity Pipe. Other hymns are in Creek or English. We've written several of our own. The service is more ceremonial than Anglo-Christian. We also have a Sweat Lodge on the grounds. We hold a Sweat Ceremony at least once a month. This is completely traditional. We also have a Medicine Circle for ceremony and worship outdoors in the round. We have also held traditional healing ceremonies and conducted Vision Quests.

For many of us . . . we were taught secretly to honor our spirituality while the well-meaning institutional church openly taught us that if we did anything Indian we would "burn in hell forever." For the first time, we are able to grow spiritually and worship.

We have about 44 members from all over SC: York, North Augusta, Aiken, Summerville, Cottageville, Moncks Corner, Blythewood, Denmark, Bamberg, Columbia. We are from many nations: Pee Dee (Creek), Cherokee, Edisto, Wassamasaw, Monican, Lakota, Ojibwa, Cree, Catawba. When we do ceremony, we explain the culture of origin and honor those traditions.

The Red Road is walking a Sacred Path in a good way. We not only talk of the Red Road, we wrote a hymn about it. It is part of an ancient Medicine Circle teaching which survives in spite of the best efforts of the U.S. government and its armies and the Euro-Christians to wipe it out.

O life is like a sacred circle when you walk the good red road: we dance to pray, we pray to heal, we heal to live, and we live to dance. Life is like a sacred circle when we walk the good red road.

Blessings and peace,
Cathy

Clearly, the evolving interest and practice of contemporary Native spirituality has found ways to coexist with various Christian churches: some Methodist, Baptist, nondenominational, and others. In this regard I understand the United Methodist Church has recently passed a national resolution to encourage the teaching and practice of American Indian spirituality in their local churches.

Beckee Garris helped in organizing South Carolina's first Native American Prison Program (NAPP). The primary purpose of NAPP was to provide a means for the practice of Indian spirituality in correctional settings in a manner consistent with traditional culture, thereby promoting the healing of mind, body, and spirit.

As with African Americans, "the significant number of Native Americans in prison is highly disproportionate to the composition of Native Americans in the general population." Additionally, according to the United States Public Health Service, American Indians in comparison to the rest of Americans have 321-percent greater problems with alcoholism.

In response to these negatives, the NAPP was created. The program in South Carolina offered counseling for inmates, a Native reading program, and traditional practices such as the sacred pipe ceremony, the talking circle, smudging, and the medicine wheel. In this last practice, seen as a powerful healing journey, the sacred seven directions are studied in depth along with the detailed symbolism of each: "This wheel speaks of the self-dignity of all Beings and teaches Native values while one walks the Red Road."[9]

The South Carolina division of NAPP was led first by John George, a Catawba traditional medicine advisor. Then it was led by John Abrams, a Christian minister. Despite the potential for conflict of interest, Mr. Abrams told me in a 2006 e-mail communication that NAPP was not a religious program. Instead, the focus was on the brotherhood of Native people and on the Native culture that binds American Indians together. However, his opinion that NAPP was not a religious program appears to contradict the fact that the South Carolina prison system allowed NAPP into the prisons because it was specifically positioned as a Native religion—otherwise it probably would not have been approved by the state prison system.

Unfortunately, the South Carolina NAPP program has been dissolved as of 2008. However, there are other forces at work that reflect the increasing interest by American Indians in the Carolinas in establishing the legitimacy of their religious and identity needs. On June 13 of 2008 the governor of South Carolina signed into law Bill #H-3798, the "Marriage Bill," as it is called by Indians. This bill allows chiefs and spiritual leaders of state-recognized tribes to conduct marriage ceremonies and sign appropriate documents. Prior to this law only "ministers of the Gospel, Jewish rabbis, officers authorized to administer oaths in the state" were permitted such authority.[10]

This bill was initiated by leaders of the South Carolina Indian Affairs Commission (SCIAC), the nongovernmental organization made up of a number of tribes and defined in Chapter 6, but it is safe to say that all of the state-recognized tribes and groups actively supported this bill. The SCIAC also initiated the passage of another bill that allows for Native artists to use wild turkey feathers in their crafts, a right previously denied, I am told.[11]

From the preceding, it seems plausible that there is a small but intense renaissance of Native spirituality going on in the Carolinas. Further, it seems that the assertion of Indian identity, which has been very active in the past thirty years, is tied to Pan-Indian spiritual traditions. One of these traditions is the power of having a vision.

In September of 2005, I received an e-mail from Beckee Garris telling of a vision she had experienced a few days before:

I want to share an experience I had last week. For a couple of days I was unable to sleep because I did not know the meaning of what I had seen . . . I was driving to work along Reservation Road and the road curved. When I drove into the fullest part of the curve I saw what looked like major heat waves coming up from the road, but it only went the width of the highway. But it also took on the look of a carnival mirror. I saw a shadow of a small bird which turned into the shape of someone wearing a cape. The only way I can describe it is like Batman or Dracula flying down to the ground. But it was transparent. I could see the highway and other things on the other side of this mirror/window/heat waves. It startled me a great deal as this went on for about 30 seconds. I never saw a face as it was as if I was following this. It was not coming towards me.

Since there seems to be a cultural link for all tribes to have one or more tribal members who have visions I decided to tell of my vision to a Catawba I am at peace with and someone I respect from another tribe. Both told me I have a great mission ahead of me that will affect my people in a positive way. One of the two told me that it might be a calling to be the medicine woman for my people. If I have this gift then he told me that I would need to totally embrace myself into learning the ways. I have toyed [in the past] with this idea . . . but I have lacked the dedication to do anything other than talk.

Nearly a month went by, then she sent me another e-mail:

I thought I would tell you about another event that happened to me. I was working at the Cultural Center two Saturdays ago. About 30 minutes before it was time for me to close a woman with three children came into the center. She said she did not know why she was there but she was just drawn to the place when she saw our sign along the interstate. I said, before I knew what was coming out of my mouth, that she came there to see me because I had a message for her. She looked like she was not surprised by that at all. It sure surprised me! . . . She looked around the craft-store and said she had dreamed she was dancing around a fire and talking in a strange language. I told her she has Native American in her lineage (she was African American). She began to cry.

I then asked her where she was from. Her response was that she didn't live anywhere. She had been led by God to just keep moving around for the last 5 years seeking something . . . I told her she still had to keep seeking but she was close to finding her answer. I also told her that she would find it in S.C., . . . here (meaning Rock Hill) . . . She asked if she could pray with me. When she took my hands and started praying I could feel her pulling my energy out of me. It was so strong of a feeling that I wanted to snatch my hands away . . . Then she told me she was healed . . . I talked to a spiritual healer about it. He told me what to do to get my energy restored.

Then in late October of 2005 came a big surprise. Beckee Garris, granddaughter of Chief Samuel Blue, while filing materials at the Cultural Center in the director's office, came across a videotape copy of a film. She wrote to me:

I discovered a tape [that came] from the University of Pennsylvania. It is a copy of a silent, black and white tape made in 1927. It has Chief Sam Blue, his sister Sally Brown and several Catawba Indian children playing in the snow. There are more people on there that I recognize as well. Grandpa Blue and another man were doing a bear dance and a wild goose chase dance. It is not done the same way we have been doing our wild goose dance. This one was being done by both men and women. They linked arms and they altered the direction each person was facing. They danced weaving in and out like we do the snake dance. Great to know now we can teach the kids two new dances.

It also has some very sacred material showing the Cherokee doing a ghost dance. I am not sure how we obtained a copy, but we have it.

It made me proud and so overwhelmingly sad at the same time. Oh how I wish there was sound to this tape as I could tell Grandpa Blue (from grandmother's side) and Granny Sally (from my granddad's) were conversing in their Native tongue.

Beckee Garris, born in 1948, I believe, keeps busy all the time. Not only does she work at numerous tasks for her tribe, but she is also a mother and grandmother. But can she reduce her workload and study "the way"? Will she become the tribe's medicine woman, a traditional medicine advisor? What exactly will be the path taken for her Red Road?[12] These are the questions entering my mind as I conclude this chapter, this book.

In conclusion, the Cofitachequi—that expanded Catawba domain—used the river system of what is now southern North Carolina and a large part of South Carolina to help unite its chiefdom. Five hundred years after the dissolution of the domain, I have attempted to follow this precolonial "footprint" as a road map. On my contemporary road trip, I have in fact traveled interstate highways, hard tops, and back-country dirt roads following the approximate stamp of the original domain.

In a span of twenty-five years these physically real trips (as well as others on the electronic highway) have revealed that against considerable odds American Indian identity has persisted and strengthened as more and more American Indians are seeking the Red Road. I hope that this book brings to light those who remain.

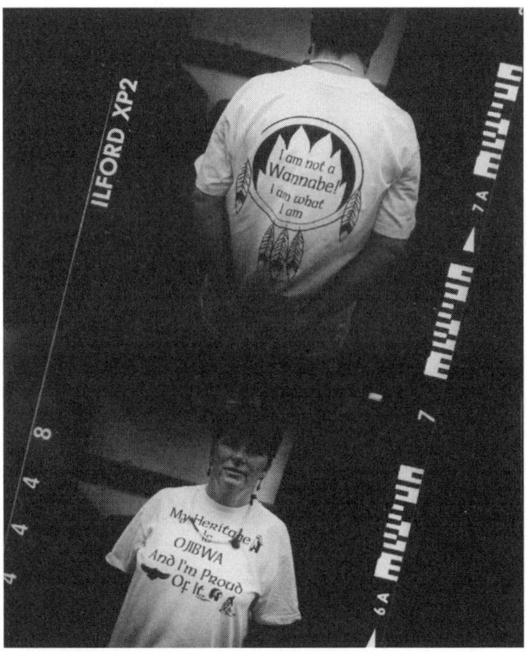

21. Cathy Nelson, Ojibwa living in South Carolina, 1994

22. Hands of Nola H. Campbell, Catawba potter, 1984

23. Wenonah George Haire, DMD, Catawba, 1990

24. Powwow scene, Columbia, South Carolina, 2001

25. Lorraine Locklear, Pee Dee (born in Robeson County), 1985

26. Tanya Howell, Pee Dee (now living in North Carolina), 1985

27. Lurleen Muckenfuss, Edisto, 1984

28. Anthony Davidson, Edisto, in 1992; elected chief in 2007

Appendix: On Tribal Recognition

This section includes basic guidelines for federal tribal recognition, for North Carolina tribal and group recognition, and for South Carolina tribal and group recognition. In addition, this appendix contains a section that is a sample of membership requirements from a few tribes in North and South Carolina. Some of these enrollment statutes are quite simple and direct while others are long and complex. In the interest of brevity this appendix will keep to the core of each.

I. Federal Recognition

In regard to the highly prized federal recognition, it is worth noting that the most current standards were not set by federal statute but by complex decisions of the Department of the Interior, Bureau of Indian Affairs in 1994. At present there are 562 tribes with this "federal" recognition. The current standards are contained in twenty pages of the federal register with the crucial criteria contained in two pages.

A. Mandatory Criteria

Herewith are the seven core requirements, all of which are mandatory criteria for federal recognition:

1. The petitioner has been identified as an American Indian entity on a substantially continuous basis since 1900.
2. A predominant portion of the petitioning group comprises a distinct community and has existed as a community from historical times until the present.
3. The petitioner has maintained political influence or authority over its members as an autonomous entity from historical times until the present.

4. The group has a current governing document including its membership criteria. In the absence of a written document, the petitioner must provide a statement describing in full its membership criteria and current governing procedures.
5. The petitioner's membership consists of individuals who descend from a historical Indian tribe or from historical Indian tribes, which combined and functioned as a single autonomous political entity.
6. The membership of the petitioning group is composed principally of persons who are not members of any acknowledged North American Indian tribe.
7. Neither the petitioner nor its members are the subject of congressional legislation that has expressly terminated or forbidden the federal relationship.

B. Arts and Crafts Act of 1990

All those tribes and groups who have achieved either federal or state formal recognition can benefit from the Arts and Crafts Act of 1990. This federal legislation states that only Indians belonging to recognized tribes and groups are allowed to market their handicrafts as "Indian made" and to sell them at Indian craft fairs. This legislation halts the economic loss to Indians due to questionable, even fraudulent, claims by non-Indians estimated at between four hundred and eight hundred million dollars a year.

II. North Carolina Recognition

In 1976, the North Carolina Commission of Indian Affairs was authorized to establish procedures for legal (state) recognition of American Indian tribes and groups.

A. Native American Indian Tribe

The commission defines a "tribe" as a population of Indian people all related to one another by blood, tracing their heritage to Indian tribes indigenous to North Carolina within the past two hundred years.

Five of the following criteria must be satisfactorily met to achieve state tribal recognition:

1. Traditional North Carolina Indian names.
2. Kinship relationships with other recognized Indian tribes.
3. Official records (birth, church, school, or other) recognizing the people as Indian.

4. Letters or statements from state or federal authorities recognizing the people as Indian.
5. Anthropological or historical accounts tied to the group's Indian ancestry.
6. Letters or statements from presently recognized tribes or groups or their representatives attesting to the Indian heritage of the group.
7. Any other documented traditions, customs, legends, and so on that signify the group's Indian heritage.
8. Participation in or grants from sources or programs designated as being for Indian only.

B. Native American Indian Group

For recognition as an Indian "group," the commission states that only groups with descent traceable to Indian tribes indigenous to North Carolina at least for the past two hundred years shall be considered for recognition.

III. South Carolina Recognition

In 2004, the South Carolina Commission for Minority Affairs established procedures for recognition of American Indian tribes and groups.

A. Definitions

1. "Tribe" means an assembly of Indian people comprising numerous families, clans, or generations together with their descendants who have a common character, interest, and behavior denoting a separate ethnic and cultural heritage, and who have existed as a separate community, on a substantially continuous basis throughout the past one hundred years. In general, core members of the tribe are related to each other by blood. A tribal council and governmental authority unique to Native American Indians govern them.
2. "Group" means a number of individuals assembled together, who have different characteristics, interests, and behaviors that do not denote a separate ethnic and cultural heritage today, as they once did. The group is composed of both Native American Indians and other ethnic races. They are not all related to one another by blood. A tribal council and governmental authority unique to Native American Indians govern them.

B. Native American Indian Tribe

The commission lists criteria for state tribal recognition. Requirements 1 through 9 must be satisfactorily met:

1. The tribe is headquartered in the state of South Carolina and indigenous to this state.
2. Historical presence in the state for the past one hundred years and the entity meets all of the characteristics of a "tribe" as previously defined.
3. Organized for the purpose of preserving, documenting, and promoting the Native American Indian culture and history, and has such reflected in its bylaws.
4. Exists to meet one or more of the spiritual, social, economic, or cultural needs of Native American Indian people through a continuous series of educational programs and activities that preserve, document, and promote the Native American Indian culture and history.
5. Claims supported by official records including birth certificates, church records, school records, U.S. Bureau of the Census records, and other pertinent documents.
6. Documented kinship relationships with other Indian tribes in and outside the state.
7. Anthropological or historical accounts tied to the group's Indian ancestry.
8. A minimum of one hundred living descendants who are eighteen years of age or older, whose Indian lineage can be documented by a lineal genealogy chart, and whose names and current addresses appear on the tribal roll.
9. Documented traditions, customs, legends, and so on that signify the specific group's Indian heritage.

C. Native American Indian Group

Requirements 1 through 5 of the Native American Indian Tribe category and an additional sixth requirement must be satisfactorily met to achieve state recognition:

6. Letters, statements, and documents from state or federal authorities that document a history of tribe-related business and activities that specifically address Native American Indian culture, preservation, and affairs.

D. Limitations

The commission establishes the following limitations for any form of state recognition:

1. All American Indian "entities" are subject to the same laws as all other citizens.
2. No rights to establish gambling.
3. No rights to any land claims.

IV. Tribal Roll Requirements

This last section reports on tribal roll requirements (abbreviated) for a few of the tribes mentioned in the text.

A. Catawba Indian Nation

Every living member of the Catawba Indian Nation whose name is listed on either the 1943 or 1961 base membership roll. Also, every living descendant of anyone who is listed on the base membership rolls. There is, also, an appeals process.

B. Eastern Band of Cherokee Indians

Enrollment is governed by tribal ordinance No. 284, June 24, 1996, which restricts enrollment to those with a direct lineal ancestor who appears on the 1924 Baker Roll, which is the base membership roll and contains the name, birth date, "blood quantum," and roll number of enrollees. Note: A person must possess at least one-sixteenth degree of Eastern Cherokee blood.

C. Waccamaw of South Carolina

This tribe divides its membership into two categories. There are the "core members," each of whom must be a lineal descendant of one (or more) of the Indian members of the community now known as the Dimery Settlement (see Chapter 6). This core membership is never to fall below 51 percent of the total tribal roll. The second category comprises "members" who must present documentation attesting to Indian ancestry regardless of tribal affiliation (such documentation is listed in their bylaws).

D. Pee Dee Indian Tribe of South Carolina

The membership of this state-recognized tribe is of people living near the Little Pee Dee River in Dillon County. The chief tells me that the tribe does not use any blood percentage for proof of Indianness but that one's genealogy "says you are Indian." This evidence comes from birth certificates, census records, family genealogy charts (going back "at least to one set of great-grandparents"), and other such sources.

Notes

Introduction

1. Charles M. Hudson, ed., *Four Centuries of Southern Indians* (Athens: University of Georgia Press, 1975), 1.

2. Gene Waddell, "Cofitachequi: A Distinctive Culture" (*Catalogue of South Carolina Historical Society* [Autumn 2000]), 8. *Cofitachequi,* I am told, is pronounced "co-fit-ah-check-ee."

3. Blair A. Rudes, Thomas J. Blumer, and J. Alan May, "Catawba and Neighboring Groups," in *Southeast,* ed. R. D. Fogelson (*Handbook of North American Indians,* vol. 14, William Sturtevant, general editor, Washington, DC: Smithsonian Institution Press, 2004), 301–7.

4. Ibid.

5. Ibid.

6. Charles Mann states that European diseases caused a death rate of anywhere from 75 percent to 95 percent of the population of the Natives of the Americas. How did this happen? Many of the Europeans who came to the "new world" carried livestock diseases to the Native Americans, who not only had no immunities to these diseases but also had little social concept of creating quarantines as a means of disease control. See Charles C. Mann, *1491: New Revelations of the Americas Before Columbus* (New York: Knopf, 2005), 92–101. See also *The Invasion of America: Indians, Colonialism, and the Cant of Conquest* (New York: W. W. Norton, 1976), by Francis Jennings, who contends that European diseases, especially smallpox, killed off 90 percent of eastern-coast Natives. Mann also reports that the Native Americans had a much greater precontact population than earlier estimates, especially along the Atlantic coastline and in Mexico. This information corresponds to Claudio Saunt's estimate that the population in the Southeast was from 1.3 to 4 million. Claudio Saunt, "History until 1776," in *Southeast,* ed. Fogelson, 128.

7. There are 464 Cherokee full-bloods, according to a December 6, 2006, article in the weekly newspaper *Cherokee One Feather* (Cherokee, NC) (tribal enrollment office data).

8. On June 2, 1924, Congress passed the Citizenship Act of 1924, which states that "all non-citizen Indians born within the territorial limits of the United States be, and they are hereby, declared to be citizens of the United States: provided, that the granting of such citizenship shall not in any manner impair or otherwise affect the right of any Indian to tribal or other property" (U.S. Code, Title 8, sec. 1401[a][2]). In this context a non-citizen Indian means, as I understand it, a person who is a member of a federally recognized tribe; in other words "citizen Indians" were at the mercy of state laws in that era. Native Americans, in actuality, were accorded rights of citizenship as "persons within the meaning of the law" in 1879 by Judge Elmer Dundy in a U.S. District Court in Omaha, Nebraska (*Standing Bear v. Crook*). See "United States, ex rel. Standing Bear v. George Crook, a Brigadier-General of the Army of the United States," The Avalon Project at Yale Law School, http://www.yale.edu/lawweb/avalon/ntreaty/ncase001.htm. An affidavit of Indian descent is reproduced in Wesley DuRant Taukchiray, Alice Bee Kasakoff, and Gene Crediford, "Contemporary Native Americans in South Carolina," in *Indians of the Southeastern United States in the Late Twentieth Century,* ed. J. Anthony Paredes (Tuscaloosa: University of Alabama Press, 1992), 79.

9. Several Native people have asked me versions of the question of why "Indians are the only ethnic group in America that is not allowed to evolve"; the second statement is from Arthur Clark, Wassamasaw Indian Group, interview with author, May 16, 2004.

10. Joanna C. Scherer, "You Can't Believe Your Eyes: Inaccuracies in Photographs of North American Indians," *Exposure* 16, no. 4 (1978), 10–12.

11. Ibid.

12. James C. Farris, "Photography and the Navajo," *Exposure* 29, no. 1 (1993), 32.

13. Dorothea Lange's famous "migrant mother" Madonna image—made during the Great Depression—revealed a distressed, depressed look. This "look" seemed to encapsulate the anxiety of that stressful era and became a look that numerous photographers, filmmakers, and even advertisers sought to imitate in imagery for their varied agendas.

14. Hulleah Tsinhnahjinnie, "Compensating Imbalances," *Exposure* 29, no. 1 (1993), 30.

Chapter 1

1. Thomas John Blumer, *Catawba Indian Pottery: The Survival of a Folk Tradition* (Tuscaloosa: University of Alabama Press, 2004), 60.

2. Ibid., 119.

3. It is my understanding that for the early part of the past century, African Americans were not allowed on the reservation. This attitude reflects, back in time, upon the colonists who "tried to play one dark race against the other on the southern frontier . . . Slaves rose in rebellion at Stono, South Carolina. Terrified whites turned to Catawba Indians, noted for their slave hunting skills, to recapture or slay all rebels" William Loren Katz, *Black Indians: A Hidden Heritage* (New York: Atheneum, 1986), 106. See also James H. Merrell, "The Racial Education of the Catawba Indians," *The Journal of Southern History* 50, no. 3 (August 1984): 363–84; Charles Crowe, "Indians and Blacks in White America," in Hudson, *Four Centuries of Southern Indians,* 148–65.

In 1990 in Washington, D.C., I had an exhibit of portraits of American Indians and a woman who appeared to be African American came up to me and told me, without any trace of bitterness, that she can trace her Catawba ancestry. She was a "Black Catawba." Today at the annual festival African Americans attend without any apparent problems.

4. See the citizenship discussion in Note 8 of the Introduction.

5. As a Catawba informant told me: "The system just didn't care . . . they believed that a good Indian was a dead Indian."

6. Jesse Burt and Robert B. Ferguson, *Indians of the Southeast: Then and Now* (Nashville, TN: Abingdon Press, 1973), 119–21.

7. Charles M. Hudson, *The Catawba Nation* (Athens: University of Georgia Press, 1970), 59, 75–76.

8. In 1959, the federal government encouraged tribal members to assimilate and renounce their tribal land and their federal recognition. The Catawba Nation petitioned Congress for termination of its federally recognized tribal status, and members were given money for the purchase of land, thus shrinking the reservation size. See "Catawba History," at http://www.dickshovel.com/Catawba.

9. This was Rosie Harris Wheelock; see Blumer, *Catawba Indian Pottery,* 91.

10. The Carlisle Indian School in Carlisle, Pennsylvania, was created in the late nineteenth century by the federal government in an early effort to enforce an assimilation policy. The government desired to take—often by force—young Native Americans from their tribes to this training school. For more information on United States assimilation policies including those applied to Indian education and religion, as well as tribal status, see Dr. C. Blue Clark, "Assimilation Era," *From Warrior to Saint: The Life of David Pendelton Oakerhater,* http://digital.library.okstate.edu/Oakerhater/essay.html; American Indian Heritage Support Center, "Education," http://home.aihsc.info/education.htm.

11. The 1840 Treaty of Nations Ford negotiated a treaty between an Indian tribe and a state authority, thus violating the famous 1790 Indian Non-Intercourse Act, which reserved to the U.S. Congress the right to acquire Indian

land (Act of July 22, 1790, 1 Stat. 137). See Douglas Roger Nash, "Indian Lands," http://library.findlaw.com/1999/Jan/1/241490.html.

12. "Excerpts from the Catawba Land Claims Settlement Act of 1993," http://www.catawba-people.com/cat_settlement_act.htm.

13. Tim Carrier, producer/director, *Those Who Remain* (South Carolina Educational Television, 1993). Note that I worked with Tim Carrier, a former student, as a consultant on this work. We both agreed that the title was a good one for his documentary.

14. "Pact with Catawbas Broken Already," *The State* (Columbia, SC), June 21, 1993.

15. *Sayonara,* released in 1957 and featuring Marlon Brando, is a moving tale of race relations between an American man and a Japanese woman who must face prejudice from both sides.

16. "The Lottery at Five Years: Tribe Says Lottery Killed Its Business," *The State* (Columbia, SC), December 17, 2007.

17. Beckee Garris, e-mail message to author, December 24, 2007.

18. Ibid.

19. "Catawba Tribal Chief Steps Down," *The Herald* (Rock Hill, SC), March 18, 2007.

20. Garris, e-mail, December 24, 2007.

21. In 2004, Beckee translated her poem into the Catawba language with the help of Claudia Priest, a linguist and volunteer with the Cultural Center. In November of 2004 she recited her poem to a large audience at the annual festival in the Catawba tongue.

Chapter 2

1. *US News and World Report,* college editions for 1994, 2000, and 2004, and University of South Carolina data (http://www.sc.edu/aboutusc/). Minority enrollment, by way of a comparison to that of the University of South Carolina, at the University of North Carolina at Pembroke in 2004 was 23 percent Indian, 22 percent black, and 2 percent Hispanic.

2. James H. Merrell, *The Indians' New World: Catawbas and Their Neighbors from European Contact through the Era of Removal* (Chapel Hill: University of North Carolina Press, 1989), 55.

3. Ibid., 81, 97.

4. Raymond D. Fogelson, "Cherokee in the East," in *Southeast,* ed. Fogelson, 337–40.

5. Will Moreau Goins, ed., *South Carolina Indians Today: An Educational Resources Guide* (Columbia, SC: Phoenix, 1998), 25–26.

6. Will Moreau Goins, written communications to author, 2005 and 2008. For the complete, detailed criteria please refer to "South Carolina Cherokees and Native American Tribal Enrollment," cherokeesofsouthcarolina.com/tribalenrollment. ECSIUT (Eastern Cherokee, Southern Iroquois and United Tribes) is a 501(c) not-for-profit organization.

7. "Indigenous Chic: American Indian Numbers Grow with Changes," *The State* (Columbia, SC), January 26, 1992.

8. There has been also a long history between the Catawbas and Cherokees in regard to the making of pottery (and its designs) and the selling of this pottery.

9. In recent times, Cherokee children have been learning the language through immersion classes in which they speak only in Cherokee. *Cherokee One Feather* (Cherokee, NC), June 7, 2007.

10. Sharlotte Nealy, *Snowbird Cherokees: People of Persistence* (Athens: University of Georgia Press, 1991), 17, 45.

11. Rose Hooper, "Harrah's Cherokee Casino Celebrates Its Fifth Year," *The Sylva Herald* (Sylva, NC), November 28, 2002.

12. Amanda Presley, "Native Concerns: Original Americans Balance Dueling Identities in the Face of One Struggle," *Free Times* (Columbia, SC), 2004.

13. Will Moreau Goins, e-mail message to author, December 27, 1999.

14. The ECSIUT mission statement is found at "The Eastern Cherokee, Southern Iroquois and United Tribes of South Carolina, Inc.," http://www.cherokeesofsouthcarolina.com/ecsiut.

15. Maria Jackson, *The Holly Hill Observer* (Holly Hill, SC), 2000.

16. Joey Holleman, "Native Americans Claim Birthright," *The State* (Columbia, SC), February 18, 2005.

17. Will Moreau Goins, e-mail message to author, June 25, 2008. In this e-mail he cites an article written by Jim DuPlessis, "Native American Business Expo: Charting Heritage, Trade Paths," *The State,* May 29, 2008.

18. From personal and written communications with Wes Taukchiray. As with many Americans, Taukchiray has an Indian heritage through a grandparent. However, his grandmother was not born or raised in an Indian community nor can he trace any distinct tribal roots. Thus, according to him, he cannot claim that he is an American Indian based on his own criteria.

19. Paul Tosto, "Passing the Heritage," *The State* (Columbia, SC), November 17, 1996.

20. Charlotte Heth, ed., *Native American Dance: Ceremonies and Social Traditions* (Washington, DC: Smithsonian Institution Press, 1992), 1.

21. It doesn't seem too much of a stretch to assert that the heart/drum beat is a way of celebrating the pre-Christian worship of the Earth Mother. In Bud-

dhism, as I understand it, the first manifestation from the world of spirit to the physical world is sound, specifically the primordial, sacred sound of Om.

22. Heth, *Native American Dance,* and typical handouts found upon entering powwows.

23. She may have been referring to an Indian association called the Wassamasaw Indians of Varnertown and Cross, South Carolina. Their root community has been recognized for one hundred years, and in my experience with them, they have been through too much to be considered, now, as wannabees. See Chapter 5.

24. Holleman, "Native Americans Claim Birthright."

25. Ibid.

26. Chris McCarter, "Long Time Coming: Native Americans Receive Official Recognition from South Carolina," *Greenville News* (Greenville, SC), February 23, 1995.

Chapter 3

1. This information comes from interviews with Bruce Rippeteau, director (now retired) of the South Carolina Institute for Archaeology and Anthropology (SCIAA), and Chris Judge, also of SCIAA. Those who built this mound, being from the Mississippian period, spoke a Muskogean language. Later, in the pre–de Soto and early de Soto eras, those Native Americans who lived in this region were the Santee Indians and spoke, probably, a Siouan language.

2. Leland Ferguson and Gene Crediford, *Contemporary Native Americans in South Carolina* (Columbia: South Carolina Committee for the Humanities, 1986), 5.

3. Unpublished papers of Wes Taukchiray.

4. Ibid.

5. The surname of Swett has the contemporary spelling of Sweat (sometimes Sweet).

6. Associated Press, "286 Indians Live at White Oak," *The State* (Columbia, SC), September 5, 1982.

7. Kay Gordon, "The Santees," *The Columbia Record* (SC), January 6, 1983. T. L. Scott owns a grocery/gas station in this community.

8. Mrs. Helen Amerson, a white person, worked on behalf of the Santees for over twenty years. She was secretary, grant writer, and program manager.

9. *The Holly Hill Observer* (Holly Hill, SC), July 1978 (twenty persons enrolled in program).

10. Chief Crummie said that he was sure there was another community of

Indians hidden away near the Commbee River. I have tried over the years to locate such a community as he described it but have been unsuccessful.

11. Stanley Crummie, in 1985, appeared to be in his late teens. He appears to be unable to work, as he was born handicapped.

12. Fire Tower Road gets its name from the tall fire tower located midway on that road between the White Oak Church/Community Center and T. L. Scott's grocery store. Directly across from the tower is Utson Platt's compound consisting of a few acres with four houses and a trailer.

13. In 1983 a man came to the Council of Native Americans office in Columbia and offered to donate a tract of land to the Santees so they could form a reservation. However, according to my informant, the then-director turned down this offer without any explanation. This information came to my attention some twenty years after the event. Who this man, a white man, was remains a mystery. Apparently no one at White Oak knew of the offer.

14. The direct quote "we just want to be what we is" comes from Tim Carrier's video documentary entitled *Those Who Remain.*

15. In a 2005 telephone conversation with Ruby Pratt, she told me that Oscar has lost his foreman's job, even though he was close to a possible retirement at age sixty-five.

16. Associated Press, "Santee Tribe Among Three More Recognized Within the State," *The Times and Democrat* (Orangeburg, SC), January 28, 2006.

Chapter 4

1. Taukchiray et al., *Indians of the Southeastern United States,* 91.

2. Carrier, *Those Who Remain.*

3. Alvin M. Josephy Jr., *500 Nations: An Illustrated History of North American Indians* (New York: Knopf, 1994), 226.

4. Taukchiray et al., *Indians of the Southeastern United States,* 92–93.

5. Ibid., 94.

6. It is important to bring the reader up to date on changes in the politics of the Edistos and on their efforts to gain formal recognition. For nearly thirty years the tribe has been working on federal recognition that is still a work in progress (in 1979 they filed a "letter of intent to petition"). In late 2007, the tribe elected a new chief, Anthony Davidson, grandson of Georgia Muckelvaney Davidson. An insider tells me that, unlike the retiring chief, Anthony considers formal state recognition to be an important and realizable short-term goal for the tribe. Hence, the Edistos are planning in 2008 to petition the Minority Affairs Commission for recognition as an Indian tribe.

7. A few weeks after my interview with Theresa I received a letter from her. In this letter—well written with a direct, clear prose—she stated the sources of her sadness and made me promise not to reveal the contents. I wrote back to thank her for her candid letter, promised never to reveal the contents, and then tried to encourage her to continue to write, to keep a diary, to go to school so as to write more, to write about her life, perhaps in fiction form. Her writing is that good, I believe. To this date I have not heard from her. The reader is advised to examine closely the series of portraits of Theresa Creel taken over a span of nearly twenty years, a number of which are on the photo CD of this book.

Chapter 5

1. At this time, the photographer's name was Marion Post, as she did not marry until a few years later. Paul Hendrickson, *Looking for the Light: The Hidden Life and Art of Marion Post Wolcott* (New York: Knoff, 1992), 5.

2. See this book's CD for reproductions; see also the Library of Congress archives of the Farm Security Administration's photographs in the "American Memory" section of www.loc.gov.

3. U.S. Census Bureau data for Dorchester County, South Carolina, 1900, as listed on www.HeritageQuestonline.com.

4. Wesley Taukchiray, "Records Identifying the Varner Family near Carnes Crossroad, SC, as American Indians, 1930–1938" (unpublished paper).

5. Wes Taukchiray, "History of Pine View Indian School," *North Charleston News* (SC), April 3, 1996.

6. Ibid.

7. From the unpublished research of Wes Taukchiray with a working title of "Possible connections between the Catawba Nation and Indian families in the South Carolina low country, in the light of Catawba business trips to the city of Charleston after the Revolutionary War." A number of years ago, Taukchiray informed Ethel and Robbie Clark of this very possible Indian connection to the Catawbas. In consequence, Ethel and Robbie filed for a new marriage license listing their race as "Catawba Indian."

8. McDonald Furman, "Old Issues or Redbones," *The State* (Columbia, SC), July 19, 1896. "Old issue," which Furman does not define, meant free blacks prior to the Civil War and was a well-known term at one time, Wes Taukchiray tells me.

9. Bo Peterson, "Local Tribe Reclaims Its Roots," *Charleston Post and Courier* (SC), April 17, 2005.

10. Brewton Berry, *Almost White: A Study of Certain Racial Hybrids in the Eastern United States* (New York: MacMillan, 1963).

11. Peterson, "Local Tribe Reclaims Its Roots." I am very puzzled as to why the Wassamasaw did not apply for recognition as a tribe rather than a group, since they have met all the requirements, in particular the requirement for having at least one hundred years of existence as an Indian community.

12. This information comes from the Appalachian Society of American Foresters, South Carolina Division, "SC Natural Areas: Wassamassaw Natural Area," http://www.apsaf.org/sc/na/wassamas.htm.

13. Gene Waddell, "Cusabo," in *Southeast,* ed. Fogelson, 254–58. This and other writings state that the term *Cusabo* was imposed as a collective, tribal name by the Europeans. Further, according to other historical sources the Sampas were a part of the Cofitachequi chiefdom. See Gene Waddell, *Indians of the South Carolina Low Country 1562–1751* (Columbia: University of South Carolina Press, Southern Studies Program, 1980), 284.

Chapter 6

1. Holleman, "Native Americans Claim Birthright."

2. Merrell, *The Indians' New World,* 95–98. His figure probably includes Waccamaws on both sides of the Carolina border.

3. South Carolina Information Highway, "South Carolina—Indians, Native Americans—Waccamaw," http://www.sciway.net/hist/indians/waccamaw.html.

4. Chief Buster Hatcher and the Council of the Waccamaw Indian People, *The Waccamaw Indian People: The Twelfth Annual Indian Arts Festival and Powwow* (pamphlet), 2004, 6.

5. Forest Hazel, "The Dimery Settlement: Indian Descendants in the South Carolina Low Country," *The Independent Republic Quarterly* 29, no. 4 (Fall 1995): 32–36. A 1725 map by a person named Herbert covers parts of the Southeast and all of South Carolina. It shows the Waccamaw and Pee Dee rivers (spelled "Peede") and places the name "Waccamaw" (Indians?) on or very near the Dimery Settlement. It is the belief of Chief Hatcher that the last-known Waccamaw village was located there, at the Dimery area.

6. Hatcher and the Council of the Waccamaw Indian People, *The Waccamaw Indian People,* 7.

7. *School Directory of South Carolina,* Horry County, South Carolina, 1930–1960.

8. Hatcher and the Council of the Waccamaw Indian People, *The Waccamaw Indian People,* 7.

9. *Horry Herald* (Conway, SC), February 16, 1905, 3.

10. In a 2005 e-mail I asked Buster Hatcher what he did in response to this man's challenge. He replied: "I was sore because I had had the surgery from my

injuries in Vietnam and I could hardly move but I chased him to the counter and into the kitchen . . . but my g-friend was crying and screaming and they were calling the law and I knew I had better leave. I didn't figure the law would be much help to me."

11. Hatcher and the Council of the Waccamaw Indian People, *The Waccamaw Indian People,* 7.

12. Chief Buster Hatcher, e-mail to author, 2005.

13. Ibid. Chief Hatcher's sparrow story came to the author via this cited e-mail that was sent subsequent to the 1994 interview.

14. See the appendix, where South Carolina recognition procedures are shown to prevent gambling and land claims.

15. In a 2008 e-mail, Chief Hatcher informed me that a potato bank is a hole in the ground about three feet in diameter and about eighteen inches deep with pine straw in layers with potatoes, turnip roots, and yams, and covered with dirt.

16. In 2004, the tribe received a donation from Shawn and Shirley Perkins of twenty acres of land on the old Dimery Settlement.

17. At the beginning of 2008 Chief Hatcher told me via e-mail that the federal petition is about 80 percent complete: "I have to attach the tribe to the tribe of 1851. I hope to make my case on the records of churches and so forth in and around the Dimery Settlement."

18. For more information, see Patricia Barker Lerch, "State-Recognized Indians of North Carolina, Including a History of the Waccamaw Sioux," in *Indians of the Southeastern United States in the Late Twentieth Century,* ed. J. Anthony Paredes, 44–71.

Chapter 7

1. U.S. Census Bureau, *The American Indian and Alaska Native Population: 2000* (Washington, DC: Government Printing Office), 2002. With an unemployment rate of 11 percent, McColl's population is made up, in terms of race, of 1,668 whites, 480 blacks, and 350 Indians.

2. U.S. Census Bureau, *American Indian Population: 1990* (see www.census.gov/main/cen1990.html); U.S. Census Bureau, *American Indian and Alaska Native Population: 2000.* In the 2000 census, Marlboro County is listed as having a total population of 38,818, of whom 947 are American Indian; Dillon County has 30,722, of whom 679 are listed as American Indian; Marion County has the greatest population of the three, with 35,466, of whom only 90 are American Indian.

3. City-Data.com, "Marlboro County, South Carolina (SC)," www.city-data.

com/county/Marlboro_County-SC.html; City-Data.com, "Dillon County, South Carolina (SC)," www.city-data.com/county/Dillon_County-SC.html.

4. Taukchiray et al., *Indians of the Southeastern United States,* 80.

5. Saunt, "History until 1776," 132.

6. Ibid.

7. Wes Taukchiray, letter to Leland Ferguson (Department of Anthropology, University of South Carolina), June 10, 1985.

8. Ibid.

9. Ibid.

10. Carrier, *Those Who Remain.*

11. Ibid.

12. Ibid. Please note that the flag song is a specially composed song with a text honoring flag and country. Many tribes have their own flag song. This information comes from Heth, *Native American Dance,* 133. However, I can find no reference to a "hover song" in this book or any other source.

13. Native Americans used a very strong tobacco with the Latin name of *Nicotiana rustica* in religious practice with emetic teas to help invoke spirit beings. Also, tobacco was used by warriors prior to going into battle and as an aid in prayer as well as other in ceremonies. But all accounts indicate that indigenous people used it sparingly. Cultivated tobacco, much weaker, is called *Nicotiana tabacum.* See R. D. Fogelson, ed., *Southeast* (*Handbook of North American Indians,* vol. 14, William Sturtevant, general editor; Washington, DC: Smithsonian Institution Press, 2004), 224, 387, 487, 489, 625, and especially 685. I discuss the use of tobacco in present-day spiritual ceremonies in the concluding chapter.

14. Holleman, "Native Americans Claim Birthright."

15. "Santee Tribe Among Three More Recognized Within the State," *The Times and Democrat* (Orangeburg, SC), January 28, 2006.

16. *South Carolina Indian Voice,* newsletter, February 8, 2006, http://southcarolinaindianaffairs.com/newsletter.html.

Chapter 8

1. U.S. Census Bureau, *American Indian Population: 2000,* 10, Figure 5. It should be stated that these figures are based upon the Census Bureau's category of "American Indian tribal grouping alone." The census has a second category, "American Indian tribal group alone or in any combination," for counting those people who marked American Indian and another race. Using the second category there would be 730,000 Cherokees in the United States!

2. Lumbee Regional Development Association, "Lumbee History," http://www.lumbee.org/history2.html. This site was created by the Lumbee Regional

Development Association of Pembroke and does not claim to be the official web site of the Lumbee Nation.

3. These are the Cherokees with 7,700 members, who were accorded state recognition four years after the Lumbee; then the Coharie with 1,880 (state recognition in 1917); the Haliwa-Saponi with 1,800 (state recognition in 1965); the Indians of Person County with 220 (state recognition in 1983); the Meherrin at 270 (state recognition in 1986); the Waccamaw Siouan with 2,365 (state recognition in 1971 of a tribe different from the Waccamaws of South Carolina found in Chapter 6). U.S. Census Bureau, *North Carolina American Indian Population: 2000,* www.census.gov/main/cen2000.html, and information provided by Wes Taukchiray.

4. U.S. Census Bureau, *American Indian Population: 2000.* This figure is based upon category 1. Using category 2, North Carolina's Indian population increases to 132,000. Likewise, using category 2, South Carolina's Indian population increases from 13,700 to 27,460.

5. The sociologist Gerald M. Sider wrote extensively on contemporary topics concerning the Lumbee. In particular, there is his 1993 book, *Living Indian Histories: Lumbee and Tuscarora People in North Carolina* (Chapel Hill: University of North Carolina Press, 1993). Also, there is a book by Karen Blu, an anthropologist, titled *The Lumbee Problem: The Making of an American Indian People* (New York: Cambridge University Press, 1980).

6. Linda E. Oxendine, "Lumbee," in *Encyclopedia of North American Indians,* ed. Frederick E. Hoxie (New York: Houghton Mifflin, 1996).

7. Lumbee Regional Development Association, "Chronological and Legislative History of the Lumbee," on the "Lumbee History" page at www.Lumbee.org/history2.html.

8. Theda Perdue, *The Cherokee* (New York: Chelsea House, 1988), 13–25. Dr. Perdue lectured at the University of South Carolina in 1989 on this topic.

9. The colonists also encouraged Native Americans to hunt for other Natives for the purpose of selling the captured ones into slavery. On a separate note, there is often a belief that prior to colonization Native Americans lived an ideal life, a life often sentimentalized into the stereotype of the "noble savage." In fact, according to a recent South Carolina Educational Television program, life for Native Americans was difficult.

10. North Carolina Rural Economic Development Center, "Rural Resource Guide: Legal Services Programs," www.ncruralcenter.org/guidebook.

11. Cynthia Hunt, "Looking Back While Walking Forward," *Carolina Indian Voice,* May 25, 2000, 2.

12. Ibid, 5. See *Maynor v. Morton,* 510 F.2d 1255 (D.C. Cir. 1975).

13. Elmer M. Savilla, "A View from the East: Who Should Cast Stones at the Lumbee Nation?" *Indian Country Today (Lakota Times),* September 6, 1988, 5.

14. Fergus M. Bordewich, *Killing the White Man's Indian: Reinventing Native Americans at the End of the Twentieth Century* (New York: Doubleday, 1996), 63.

15. Ibid, 79.

16. "America's Best Colleges," *US News and World Report,* 2003.

17. University of North Carolina at Pembroke, "American Indian Studies," 2005–2006 catalog via www.uncp.edu/catalog.

18. Mary Margaret Steedly, "The Evidence of Things Not Seen: Faith and Tradition in a Lumbee Healing Practice" (Master's thesis, University of North Carolina, Chapel Hill, 1979), 28.

19. Ibid, 46.

20. Arvis Locklear Boughman and Loretta O. Oxendine, *Herbal Remedies of the Lumbee Indians* (Jefferson, NC: McFarlan, 2004), 3.

21. Steve Wall and Harvey Arden, *Wisdom Keepers: Meetings with Native American Spiritual Elders* (Hillsboro, OR: Beyond Words, 1990), 58.

22. In the book *Herbal Remedies of the Lumbee Indians,* Daystar Dial discusses how Vernon Cooper "was a master practitioner of 'pulse diagnosis,' a technique he learned from his grandmother. Pulse diagnosis is primarily practiced in eastern medical schools of thought, along with acupuncture." Boughman and Oxendine, *Herbal Remedies,* 125.

23. City-Data.com, "Waxhaw, North Carolina," www.city-data.com/city/Waxhaw-North-Carolina.html; City-Data.com, "Maxton, North Carolina," www.city-data.com/city/Maxton-North-Carolina.html.

24. City-Data.com, "Waxhaw, North Carolina," www.city-data.com/city/Waxhaw-North-Carolina.html.

25. It must be noted here that the spiritual use of tobacco—and other related ceremonies—in modern-day eastern Indian practices are believed by scholars to be a Pan-Indian incorporation of similar, traditional practices from the Plains Indians, especially the Lakota. This issue of adopting western rituals into southeastern Indian ones is explored in greater detail in the concluding chapter.

Chapter 9

1. Jennings, *Invasion of America,* 239.

2. Frank G. Speck, "Catawba Herbals and Curative Practices," *The Journal of American Folklore* 57, no. 223 (January–March 1944), 37–50.

3. American Cancer Society, "Native American Healing," March 26, 2007, http://www.cancer.org/docroot/ETO/content/ETO_5_3X_Native_American_Healing.asp?sitearea=ETO.

4. Arlene Hirschfelder and Paulette Molin, *Encyclopedia of Native American Religions* (New York: Facts On File, 2000), 253.

5. Examples are White Bison, Inc., "Firestarter Trainings," whitebison.org/

firestarter/index.htm; Native American Information Service, "A Short History of Pan-Indianism" (July 30, 1997), www.hartford-hwp.com/archives/41/119.html; B. A. Robinson, "Native American Spirituality" (January 13, 2008), www.religioustolerance.org/nataspir.htm; Minnesota Department of Corrections, "American Indian Use of Tobacco" (May 31, 2004), info.doc.state.mn.us/DocPolicy2/FormsWorking/NSI/302.310WRML.htm.

6. Beckee Garris, e-mail message to author, January 6, 2008.

7. Big Thunder (Algonquin) and Red Jacket (Seneca), "The Ripoff of Native American Spirituality," at geocities.com/capitolhill/congress/9134/spirit.

8. Tobacco played an important role in past times and also does so in the present. Often Native people mixed tobacco with other substances such as the bark of certain trees, leaves, herbs, or oil to form a milder substance called *chan sha'sha* in the Siouan language. Aboriginal tobacco was in small supply and was sacred. It was used in agricultural rites such as in the blessing of the harvest. The rising tobacco smoke was (and is) regarded as a means of communicating with the spirit world, of making contact with the supernatural world (the Iroquois believed the ascending smoke carried their petitions to the creator). Additionally, tobacco was and is used medicinally. As Hirschfelder and Molin write, "Today traditional native people use tobacco as a sign of respect and as an offering when praying to the creator" (*Encyclopedia of Native American Religions,* 305).

9. The quoted statements and other information in this section concerning the Native American Prison Program were taken from the NAPP web site, www.nappofsc.org, which has been taken down.

10. *South Carolina Indian Voice,* newsletter, June 5, 2008, http://southcarolinaindianaffairs.com/newsletter.html, and e-mail message to author from Chief Hatcher, June 19, 2008. It is worth noting that the state of South Carolina does not give such authority to an Islamic imam.

11. *South Carolina Indian Voice,* newsletter, June 5, 2008, http://southcarolinaindianaffairs.com/newsletter.html, and e-mail message to author from Chief Hatcher, June 19, 2008. Information on the passage of the "Turkey Bill" can be found in Katrina Goggins, "SC American Indians: New Laws Step to Autonomy," *The State* (Columbia, SC), July 15, 2008 (this newspaper article was sent to me by Will Goins, PhD, and leader of the ECSIUT Indian group).

12. Beckee Garris informed me in January of 2007 that she has begun her college career at the University of South Carolina Lancaster, majoring in American Indian Studies and history.

Bibliography

Barton, Bruce, Cynthia L. Hunt, and Linda Oxendine. *Pembroke: A Centennial Retrospective 1895–1995*. Pembroke, NC: Pembroke Centennial Commission, 1995.

Blu, Karen. *The Lumbee Problem: The Making of an American Indian People.* New York: Cambridge University Press, 1980.

Blumer, Thomas John. *Catawba Indian Pottery: The Survival of a Folk Tradition.* Tuscaloosa: University of Alabama Press, 2004.

Bordewich, Fergus M. *Killing the White Man's Indian: Reinventing Native Americans at the End of the Twentieth Century.* New York: Doubleday, 1996.

Boughman, Arvis Locklear, and Loretta O. Oxendine. *Herbal Remedies of the Lumbee Indians.* Jefferson, NC: McFarlan, 2004.

Burt, Jesse, and Robert B. Ferguson. *Indians of the Southeast: Then and Now.* Nashville, TN: Abingdon Press, 1973.

Carrier, Tim, producer/director. *Those Who Remain,* South Carolina Educational Television, 1993.

Crowe, Charles. "Indians and Blacks in White America." In *Four Centuries of Southern Indians,* ed. Charles M. Hudson, 148–65. Athens: University of Georgia Press, 1975.

Curtis, Edward S. *The North American Indian.* 20 vols. Cambridge: The University Press, 1907–1930.

Dial, Adolph L., and David K. Eliades. *The Only Land I Know: A History of the Lumbee Indians.* San Francisco: Indian Historian Press, 1975.

Farris, James C. "Photography and the Navajo." *Exposure* 29, no. 1 (1993):31–40.

Ferguson, Leland, and Gene Crediford. *Contemporary Native Americans in South Carolina.* Columbia: South Carolina Committee for the Humanities, 1986.

Fogelson, Raymond D. "Cherokee in the East." In *Southeast,* ed. R. D. Fogelson, 337–53. *Handbook of North American Indians,* vol. 14, William Sturtevant, general editor. Washington, DC: Smithsonian Institution Press, 2004.

Gilpin, Laura. *The Enduring Navajo.* Austin: University of Texas, 1968.

Goins, Will Moreau, ed. *The People Speak: A Collection of Writings by South Carolina Native Americans in Poetry, Prose, Essays and Interviews.* Columbia, SC: Phoenix, 2002.

———. *South Carolina Indians Today: An Educational Resources Guide.* Columbia, SC: Phoenix, 1998.

Hazel, Forest. "The Dimery Settlement: Indian Descendants in the South Carolina Low Country." *The Independent Republic Quarterly* 29, no. 4 (Fall 1995): 32–36.

Hendrickson, Paul. *Looking for the Light: The Hidden Life and Art of Marion Post Wolcott.* New York: Knoff, 1992.

Heth, Charlotte, ed. *Native American Dance: Ceremonies and Social Traditions.* Washington, DC: Smithsonian Institution Press, 1992.

Hirschfelder, Arlene, and Paulette Molin. *Encyclopedia of Native American Religions.* New York: Facts On File, 2000.

Holleman, Joey. "Native Americans Claim Birthright." *The State* (Columbia, SC), February 18, 2005.

Hudson, Charles M. *The Catawba Nation.* Athens: University of Georgia Press, 1970.

———, ed. *Four Centuries of Southern Indians.* Athens: University of Georgia Press, 1975.

Jennings, Francis. *The Invasion of America: Indians, Colonialism, and the Cant of Conquest.* New York: W. W. Norton, 1976.

Josephy, Alvin M., Jr. *500 Nations: An Illustrated History of North American Indians.* New York: Knopf, 1994.

Katz, William Loren. *Black Indians: A Hidden Heritage.* New York: Atheneum, 1986.

Lerch, Patricia Barker. "State-Recognized Indians of North Carolina, Including a History of the Waccamaw Sioux." In *Indians of the Southeastern United States in the Late Twentieth Century,* ed. J. Anthony Paredes, 44–71. Tuscaloosa: University of Alabama Press, 1992.

Mann, Charles C. *1491: New Revelations of the Americas Before Columbus.* New York: Knopf, 2005.

Merrell, James H. *The Indians' New World: Catawbas and Their Neighbors from European Contact through the Era of Removal.* Chapel Hill: University of North Carolina Press, 1989.

———. "The Racial Education of the Catawba Indians." *The Journal of Southern History* 50, no. 3 (August 1984): 363–84.

Nealy, Sharlotte. *Snowbird Cherokees: People of Persistence.* Athens: University of Georgia Press, 1991.

Oxendine, Linda E. "Lumbee." In *Encyclopedia of North American Indians,* ed. Frederick E. Hoxie. New York: Houghton Mifflin, 1996.

Perdue, Theda. *The Cherokee.* New York: Chelsea House, 1988.

Rudes, Blair A., Thomas J. Blumer, and J. Alan May. "Catawba and Neighboring Groups." In *Southeast,* ed. R. D. Fogelson, 301–18. *Handbook of North American Indians,* vol. 14, William Sturtevant, general editor. Washington, DC: Smithsonian Institution Press, 2004.

Saunt, Claudio. "History until 1776." In *Southeast,* ed. R. D. Fogelson, 128–38. *Handbook of North American Indians,* vol. 14, William Sturtevant, general editor. Washington, DC: Smithsonian Institution Press, 2004.

Scherer, Joanna C. "You Can't Believe Your Eyes: Inaccuracies in Photographs of North American Indians." *Exposure* 16, no. 4 (1978):6–19.

Sider, Gerald M. *Living Indian Histories: Lumbee and Tuscarora People in North Carolina.* Chapel Hill: University of North Carolina Press, 1993.

Speck, Frank G. "Catawba Herbals and Curative Practices." *The Journal of American Folklore* 57, no. 223 (January–March 1944):37–49.

Steedly, Mary Margaret. "The Evidence of Things Not Seen: Faith and Tradition in a Lumbee Healing Practice." Master's thesis, University of North Carolina, Chapel Hill, 1979.

Taukchiray, Wesley. "Records Identifying the Varner Family near Carnes Crossroad, SC, as American Indians, 1930–1938" (unpublished paper).

Taukchiray, Wesley DuRant, Alice Bee Kasakoff, and Gene Crediford. "Contemporary Native Americans in South Carolina." In *Indians of the Southeastern United States in the Late Twentieth Century,* ed. J. Anthony Paredes, 72–101. Tuscaloosa: University of Alabama Press, 1992.

Tsinhnahjinnie, Hulleah. "Compensating Imbalances." *Exposure* 29, no. 1 (1993): 29–30.

Waddell, Gene. "Cofitachequi: A Distinctive Culture." *Catalogue of South Carolina Historical Society* (Autumn 2000):8–15.

——. "Cusabo." In *Southeast,* ed. R. D. Fogelson, 254–64. *Handbook of North American Indians,* vol. 14, William Sturtevant, general editor. Washington, DC: Smithsonian Institution Press, 2004.

——. *Indians of the South Carolina Low Country 1562–1751.* Columbia: University of South Carolina Press, Southern Studies Program, 1980.

Wall, Steve, and Harvey Arden. *Wisdom Keepers: Meetings with Native American Spiritual Elders.* Hillsboro, OR: Beyond Words, 1990.

U.S. Census Bureau. *The American Indian and Alaska Native Population: 2000.* Washington, DC: Government Printing Office, 2002.

Index

Numbers in italics refer to illustrations in the text or on the CD.